THE 720° SNAPSHOT:

An Innovative Approach to Leadership
Decision Making to Help You to See Beyond
What Is Seen

Dr. Charles A. Moody, Jr.

DEDICATED TO...

MY WIFE, FELICIA

who has been by my side through life's ups and downs and been my bedrock. Thanks for the time, the prayers and the support.
Oh yeah... and also the *editing*! Love you.

MY MOTHER, DOROTHY BROWN

who instilled a very strong work ethic and love and passion for academics in me as a child. Mom, thank you for taking me with you, even as a baby, as you worked on your master's degree. I can still remember those days driving with you and Dad down to Prairie View A&M. I hope now you see that your sacrifice was all worth it!

ACKNOWLEDGEMENTS

I would like to acknowledge some very special people in my life who have contributed in some way to the completion of this work. First of all, I would like to acknowledge my father in the ministry, Apostle Dr. Dana Carson, for all that you have shown me in life and ministry and for being the example that you are to me.

Next, I would like to express my thanks to Dr. Bramwell Osula. Thank you for being my academic mentor, pushing me to think broadly and deeply, and challenging me to go beyond the scope of normal academics to bring my doctoral skills and training to a level where people can truly understand them.

To my staff, Elder Shauntice Rutley, Belinda Clark, and Mia Talley for all of their support, hard work, and belief in me. Thank all of you for your sacrifices. You all make me better, and without you, I could not do what I do. I really appreciate you!

To Pastor Marq Curl for preaching for me all those times I had to turn work in, thank you!

Lastly, to my group of readers (Vickie, Antoine, Tammy and Gail), for sitting up day and night reading through every page and giving great recommendations on how to make this a success. I appreciate you!

QUICK FACTS ABOUT 720° LEADERSHIP

WHAT IS THE DEFINITION OF 720° LEADERSHIP?

720° Leadership is a strategic approach designed to increase the effectiveness of leadership decision making by equipping leaders with a tool that will help them to examine all of the critical factors that should be considered when making organizational decisions.

HOW DOES 720° LEADERSHIP WORK?

The 720° Leadership approach guides leaders through making an assessment of their internal motivations and fears, their organization, their followers, and their external environment from multiple perspectives in order to produce the best possible decisions.

WHY IS 720° LEADERSHIP NECESSARY?

A 720° Leadership approach is necessary because a 360° assessment approach is no longer sufficient in today's rapidly-changing, volatile market. While 360° leadership equipped leaders to view the circumference of their leadership influence in their organizations, 720° leadership doubles the viewpoints for leaders, giving them a clearer and more accurate perspective of the contributing factors that should be considered when making decisions.

WHAT IS 720° LEADERSHIP COMPRISED OF?

The 720° Leadership paradigm is represented by four connecting triangles, or triads, each representing a different variable influencing leadership decision-making. Standing alone, each triad geometrically represents 180°. However, when the four triads are combined into one comprehensive tetra-triad, the sum total of the triads is 720°.

TABLE OF CONTENTS

PART 2: THE TASK TRIAD

Building an Awareness of Choices, Capabilities, and
Commodities Available to Address the Task at Hand

PART 3: THE ISSUE TRIAD

Building an Awareness of the Internal and External
Threats You Stand to Face when Tackling the Task

PART 4: THE LEADER TRIAD

Building an Awareness of Who You Are, What You Have to Offer, and How It All Affects the Way You Approach a Task

PART 5: THE FOLLOWER TRIAD

Building an Awareness of Who Might Work with You and How Far They Might Be Willing to Go to Successfully Execute a Task

PART 6: THIS IS PERSONAL
How YOU Impact Your Leadership Decisions and Actions

PART 7: TAKING A CLEAR SNAPSHOT OF THE SITUATION
How to Practically Engage Moody's 720° Decision-Making
Model to Achieve More Effective Leadership Results

FRUSTRATED LEADER?
YOU'RE NOT ALONE!

Have you ever been driving or riding in to work in the morning, and the closer you came to your workplace, the more you were tempted to simply bypass your job and keep on going, because you thought, "I can't DO this anymore!"? Did the thought of walking into your office and facing yet another day of ineffectiveness, excuses from workers, and lots of activity but no real productivity make you cringe? Did the mental image of looking around a conference table at a team of blank-faced people who, though their expertise and aptitudes look *great* on paper, specialize only in failing your expectations and puzzle you with their inability to execute the simplest of assignments as a team? What's worse, did the stress of having to give an account for the lack of progress associated with your assigned leadership tasks make your chest begin to hurt, your head begin to pound, or your body break out in a cold sweat? If so, the bad news is that you perfectly fit the description of a frustrated leader. The good news, however, is that you are not alone, and there is help for you!

Forbes Magazine reports that more than 2 million Americans quit their jobs every single *month*, even in a depressed economy in which their odds of quickly securing another job and source of income to maintain their livelihood are uncertain. Although the company within these groups of workers who jump ship is mixed, consisting of leaders, mid-level managers, and even worker-bee type employees, the motivation behind their move seems to be consistent. Those employees simply can no longer bear the thought of existing in their workplaces as they are in their current state, and they cannot see anything in the immediate forecast that promises to transform the environment or atmosphere in which they work into a bearable one. Many times, when leaders choose to say their goodbyes, their motivation behind walking away from what others might deem enviable positions or very respectable salaries is not a lack of love for their companies or organizations; it is that the mental toll that working there takes on them is so unbearable that they feel like they must make a career change for their own well-being.

Leadership frustration is one of the prime reasons that leaders tend to walk away from career opportunities that they once considered to be positions of great privilege, growth, and potential, both in the corporate and non-profit world. Psychologists characterize frustration as an emotion that individuals experience when they feel blocked from reaching a desired goal or outcome, and they emphasize that an individual's level of frustration is directly proportionate to the goal's level of importance that he or she is trying to accomplish.[1] Leaders are tasked with accomplishing big goals on behalf of their organizations; consequently, their levels of frustration when it comes to accomplishing such lofty goals stand to be higher than non-leaders within the same organization.

Many people have little empathy for the frustrations and other stresses that leaders must face when organizing and managing others in the corporate world. After all, these same leaders who are asked to accomplish big goals are also provided with access to bigger offices, bigger perks, bigger benefits packages, and bigger salaries. Even in the non-profit world, leaders, if not compensated with bigger salaries, are often compensated with other large perks that their non-leader counterparts are not afforded. However, to whom much is given, much is required. Leaders face tremendous pressure to be productive and effective in their leadership roles, and when they fail to meet these expectations, a sense of frustration can easily set in, causing them to re-evaluate whether all of the perks are worth the pressures of having to perform in such a capacity.

While some leaders might consider frustration a simple and inescapable part of any job in which they are faced with overseeing a team of people assembled to accomplish a certain task, the effect that these high levels of frustration, experienced over prolonged and extended periods of time, can have on a leader's health can be quite debilitating. When leaders consistently do not meet their goals, their frustration can adversely affect every area of their lives, including their mental health, their physical health, their marital and parental relationships, their friendships, and even their spiritual lives.

Every day, countless frustrated corporate and non-profit leaders abandon their posts, not because they do not love their organizations or are no longer committed to their cause, but because, despite their best efforts, they feel completely ineffective at bringing their organization's vision to pass. With each new leadership conference and management seminar they attend, their hopes are elevated for returning to their workplace as a leader who has been empowered to turn things around and increase productivity; however, the zeal soon wears off when their new knowledge fails them and they find themselves behind the closed doors of their office, once again holding their head in their hands and wondering what went wrong. After so many tries, finding oneself impotent, ineffective, and unproductive day after day becomes an exercise in maintaining a sense of dignity in the face of circumstances that yell, "You're losing!" and "You're just not a good leader!" Before long, in order to maintain their mental well-being, many leaders in such a position join the ranks of the millions of Americans who feel they have no other choice but to jump ship and seek greener pastures. If this sounds like something that you are considering, I have a newsflash for you: it's *too soon* to throw in the towel! You've endured too much for too long to give up now, and as much as you think your organization would be better off without you, it actually *needs* you – your vision, passion, knowledge, expertise, experiences, and all of the gifts and talents that you have to offer! If your organization has not put you on notice, fired you, or canceled your contract, don't you quit! Hang in there, and keep reading, because change is coming!

Despite the bad news surrounding the state of many frustrated leaders today, the reality is that just because you are a leader does not mean that you must, invariably, be a frustrated one! As a strategic leadership expert and consultant, I have analyzed many case studies, interviewed a myriad of leaders across the nation, and conducted my own research on how to transition leaders from frustration into fruitful producers. As difficult as it is to believe after being frustrated and ineffective for so long, believe me when I say that you *can* position yourself to enjoy being the leader of your company or organization! It is more possible than you think!

Before we begin, I must warn you that the process that I have developed to drive this leadership transition is neither a passive nor a painless one. It calls for your participation in taking a bold, daring, and insightful look at your organization, a brave and honest introspective look at yourself, and a courageous look at your followers that must be coupled with the guts to confront the issues that are hindering your ability to move those under your leadership. However, coupled with this caution is an assurance: if you are willing to put in the work and invest the time and energy necessary to take a multi-dimensional view of your organization, yourself, and your followers, you can, without a shadow of a doubt, take your leadership productivity and effectiveness to the next level, AND you can once again enjoy being a leader!

Can you imagine looking forward to getting to work in the mornings and leaving work every day with a smile on your face because you accomplished the majority of your goals? It can happen! I know this to be true based upon the countless leaders with whom I have consulted, helping them to transition out of frustration and into fruitful productivity. Just as I have assisted other leaders with this process over the years, I can also assist you!

Through the upcoming chapters of this book, you will find valuable resources to help you examine every possible contributor to leadership effectiveness. As you read, you might find that you are sorely deficient in one or two areas more than other areas. In such cases, utilizing the book as a reference manual and reading only those chapters of the book that apply to your deficiencies is perfectly acceptable. This book is written in a format such that each chapter can stand alone, providing you the specific learning and tools that you need to address that particular area of leadership.

The 720° Snapshot

PART 1:
DEVELOPING AWARENESS

How *Frustrated* Leaders Can Become More *Fruitful*

Help! I'm *Completely* Frustrated!

An Introduction to "The Moody 6"
Change Components for Leadership Transformation

Are You *Really* Aware of What's Going on Around You?

Opening Your Eyes to See What Most Others Cannot!

360° Assessments Are No Longer Enough!

Your Leadership Awareness Must Span a Full 720°

The 720° Snapshot

CHAPTER 1

HELP! I'M COMPLETELY FRUSTRATED!

An Introduction to "The Moody 6" Change Components for Leadership Transformation

The Starting Point: Who's to Blame for Where You Are?

When you first realized that you were growing frustrated with your organization because you felt like you had hit a brick wall and were at a standstill, to what or to whom did you attribute your leadership ineffectiveness? Who was to blame for your inability to pull what was necessary out of your followers to get things done? Who was to blame for the lack of results, the unmet goals, and the disappointed expectations? Did you begin to beat your workers up for their consistent failures, or did you beat yourself up for the outcomes you were experiencing? The answers to these questions matter more than you think!

When leaders realize that they have become ineffective and unproductive in advancing their goals and organizational mission and vision, it is easy for them to look around at their organization and its systems, culture, employees, or any wide range of individuals or reasons in order to attribute the blame for their lack of effectiveness. Leaders who have operated in such a state for a prolonged period of time might even be prone to angrily lash out at their followers for not listening, not critically thinking, not performing up to par, and being lackluster in their energy when it comes to executing the leader's demands, ultimately producing results that reflect poorly on the leader's abilities to lead. However, the wise leader does not allow the stresses and frustrations that he might encounter to divert his focus; instead of attributing blame for his results externally and focusing upon how others should change to help him achieve greater levels of effectiveness, he focuses on what he himself can do to increase his level of effectiveness.

Our *locus of control* refers to the extent to which we believe we can control the events that affect us. According to this well-researched concept developed by personality psychologist Julian Rotter, if a person possesses an external locus of control, he believes that fate, luck, or outside forces are responsible for what happens to him. Those operating out of this paradigm tend to be ready to blame others for who they are, how they are, and what they are experiencing in life, feeling that the fate of their outcomes are beyond their ability to control. Further, those with an external locus of control are said to experience "learned helplessness," a belief that they are at the mercy of certain external forces – including bad luck and misfortune – and unable to affect change in their own lives. What's more, people who operate out of an external locus of control are fatalistic; they believe that no matter what they do, things will always be this way – forever.

In contrast, if a person possesses an internal locus of control, he believes that one's own ability, effort, or actions determine what happens. Those operating out of this paradigm tend to take responsibility for both their actions and their outcomes. Rather than believing in luck, they believe in mere cause and effect, and as a result, they feel empowered to change their outcomes for the better. Having an internal locus of control puts the power in the hand of the individual to change his outcome at will, because he understands that things are only the way they are because of something he has done. If he wants to see different results, he merely needs to undertake different actions, and a change is on the way!

In order to begin your process of transitioning from frustrated leader to fruitful and productive leader, it is important that you first understand where your locus of leadership control lay. This is an essential starting point! If you operate out of an external locus of control, you will look around your company or organization and say, "Something in the environment is causing me to be an ineffective leader. There's really nothing that I can do." In doing so, you will not approach the change process with the optimism and energy you need in order to be successful; your feelings of impotence, inefficacy, hopelessness, pessimism, and skepticism about whether this process can actually work will permeate every lesson and exercise that you engage in throughout the process. However, if you operate out of an internal locus of control, you will look around the same company or organization and say, "Something about me is causing me to be an ineffective leader. Since I can control me, there is definitely something I can do to become a more effective leader!" When you start out on your journey of transformation with this mindset, it engenders feelings of hope, encouragement, optimism, and empowerment!

If you will be an effective leader, you must be committed to learning the following:

1. What you can and cannot control
2. How you can influence things that are outside of your locus of control
3. How you can utilize the momentum of things that are outside of your control to strategically position you and your organization for advantage

The research of cognitive therapists has supported time and time again that our thoughts and expectations directly influence our feelings and behavior. Thus, in order to achieve maximum results as you embark upon this change process, we need you as a leader to believe that there are things that you can change about yourself and the way that you process and operate that can lead to drastic and measurable changes in abilities to lead!

What Does It Take for Leaders to Go from Being Frustrated to Fruitful?

Leaders who are ready to move forward with the leadership transformation process must accept the fact that there are multiple layers to their leadership ineffectiveness; it is multi-dimensional and not as simplistic as they might think. Understanding this, because their problem is multi-dimensional, so must their solution be multi-faceted in order to address every aspect of their leadership problems.

There are certain dimensions that any leader must be able to successfully navigate in order to become a truly effective leader. After much scientific research and investigation, I have systematically isolated the six components, identifying how each one impacts a leader's effectiveness when isolated as an individual component as well as how each of the parts works synergistically with the others to contribute to the whole of the leader's performance.

THE "MOODY 6":

CHANGE COMPONENTS FOR LEADERSHIP TRANSFORMATION

AWARENESS

ATMOSPHERE

ACTION

AUTHENTICITY

ATTITUDE

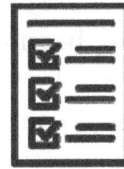

ACCOUNTABILITY

THE "MOODY 6"
AWARENESS

SELF-ASSESSMENT QUESTION:

Am I consciously aware and sensitive to the various elements that are either contributing to or impeding my abilities to lead successfully?

HOW AWARENESS AFFECTS LEADERSHIP SUCCESS:

When we become cognizant – or aware – of which issues are contributing to our leadership success, we can maximize and build upon them. In the same fashion, when we are aware of which issues are impeding our leadership success, this knowledge helps us to understand what mindsets and behaviors we might need to modify, drastically change, or outright abandon. When such changes are guided by principles and tenets that are proven to result in greater leadership effectiveness, the leader will inevitably begin to experience more successful outcomes.

THE "MOODY 6"
ATMOSPHERE

SELF-ASSESSMENT QUESTION:

What changes have recently taken place in my constantly-changing environment that are currently facilitating or hindering my abilities to lead successfully?

HOW ATMOSPHERE AFFECTS LEADERSHIP SUCCESS:

The rapid evolution, development, and transmission of information that occur within our world affect us more than we recognize. Because times are ever changing, people are ever changing, and because people make up our organizational atmospheres, our atmospheres are also ever changing. In light of this, what might have worked for us as leaders in one climate might not work as effectively the following year, because the atmosphere has changed. Leaders who understand that atmospheres are constantly changing become more flexible in their leadership approaches, opting for what will work to produce results in the current climate rather than being staunchly committed to those mentalities and behaviors that have worked in the past.

THE "MOODY 6"
ATTITUDE

SELF-ASSESSMENT QUESTION:

Is my mental posture one of being totally prepared to abandon whatever mentalities and behaviors are hindering my success as a leader in order to adopt new and unfamiliar mentalities and behaviors that will result in real leadership success?

HOW ATTITUDE AFFECTS LEADERSHIP SUCCESS:

Engaging in the process of change as a leader is not for the timid or the faint of heart. In order to consistently experience real change, leaders must approach the change process with a bold, aggressive "Whatever it takes" mentality that says that no matter how uncomfortable or challenging the change process becomes, their commitment will be to engendering their success rather than to maintaining their comfort. Along with this mentality comes an internal commitment to operate out of principles that have been proven to work rather than out of behaviors and practices that are comfortable to them. When leaders develop such an aggressive attitude towards the accomplishment of their leadership goals, leadership success will be the inevitable result.

THE "MOODY 6"
AUTHENTICITY

SELF-ASSESSMENT QUESTION:

Am I self-aware enough to embrace the truth surrounding the innermost beliefs, values, emotions, strengths, weaknesses, and motives that define who I truly am? Am I prepared to allow this "authentic me" to engage in sincere, open, and honest relationships with those whom I lead?

HOW AUTHENTICITY AFFECTS LEADERSHIP SUCCESS:

Leadership is less about tyrannical dictatorship than about building open, honest relationships with followers. However, to build such relationships, leaders must lead out of their most self-aware, genuine, and positive selves. This level of openness fosters reciprocal relationships with followers, empowering them with a sense of organizational significance and ownership. Authentic leaders are sensitive to the needs of followers, including what is necessary for them to do their jobs effectively, while followers openly communicate what will make them more successful in accomplishing their goals. The inevitable result of this open and honest collaboration: greater levels of organizational productivity and leadership success.

THE "MOODY 6"
ACTION

SELF-ASSESSMENT QUESTION:

Am I prepared to push past the mere desire to change and take action to engage whatever mental and physical energy, time and resources are necessary to become an effective leader? Am I willing to continue making such sacrifices until I see a prolonged manifestation of greater levels of leadership success?

HOW ACTION AFFECTS LEADERSHIP SUCCESS:

When we finally reach the internal conclusion that change is necessary in our lives, mental assent is not enough; we must take action and engage our physical faculties in the process! No matter how desperately we desire change in our mind, we must understand that there will be no manifestation of change without our intentional effort. Leaders must step out and participate fully in their own change process, sacrificing their time, energy, and focus to manifest real change in their lives. Then, as a result their mental commitment coupled with their physical participation in the process, they will put themselves in a position to produce results as successful leaders.

THE "MOODY 6"
ACCOUNTABILITY

SELF-ASSESSMENT QUESTION:

Which like-minded individuals are holding me closely and consistently accountable to my self-initiated process of becoming a successful leader?

HOW ACCOUNTABILITY AFFECTS LEADERSHIP SUCCESS:

In order to be effective in any area of life, we must operate under some form of accountability by answering to someone for our actions. Knowing that we will be required to provide an account to someone else regarding our progress towards a particular goal tends to motivate us to perform at a greater level. After all, none of us likes to be in a position of having to openly admit that we have failed at something! Building accountability into our change process makes us strive harder towards our goals, even if only to save face with our accountability partner! Decisions that are made in private often fail in private. Only leaders who are committed to the process of change will dare to allow another person to hold them accountable. Because of this, they place themselves in optimal position to attain their goal of becoming a successful leader.

The 720° Snapshot

CHAPTER 2

ARE YOU REALLY AWARE OF WHAT'S GOING ON AROUND YOU?

Opening Your Eyes to See What Most Others Cannot

Madonna & Walmart Execs: MASTERS of Awareness!

Have you ever wondered what the most successful icons in our society have in common? What is it about some people that makes them phenomenally successful at their craft? After all, others who seem to invest just as much preparation, energy, and effort into the same craft often end up trapped under a glass ceiling, realizing only average returns from the same level of investment. Economic strategy academician Robert M. Grant examined this particular phenomenon in an effort to determine what commonalities wildly successful people tended to have in common. Grant carefully researched subjects from various contexts ranging from Hollywood to Wall Street, including notably iconic and successful subjects like pop sensation Madonna.

Madonna, born Madonna Louise Ciccone in 1958, burst onto the pop music scene in 1983 with her first global hit *"Holiday."* With her counter-cultural, edgy style of dress, provocative dance moves, and her unique musical sound, the 25 year-old would go on to record an amazing thirteen studio albums, sell more than 300 million records worldwide, embark on several world tours for which she became the top touring female artist of all time, win more MTV Video Awards than any other artist in history, be inducted into the Rock and Roll Hall of Fame, become a major-feature actress and director, form a television and movie production company, birth a music and media entertainment company, launch her international "Material Girl" clothing line as well as a lifestyle brand, open a series of fitness centers, and become a recognized humanitarian and human rights activist.

In addition to setting several Guinness World Records as the best-selling female recording artist and the fourth best-selling act of all time, this "Queen of Pop" is touted as a world changer and international influence of unparalleled proportions. In the words of The Daily Telegraph, "Madonna has changed the world's social history and has done more things as more different people than anyone else is ever likely to."[2] However, if you have ever heard Madonna sing, you might notice that she is not the best singer in the world; her vocal skills are merely adequate at best, and there are legions of immensely talented artists in the music industry that could easily sing circles around her. Considering this, how has this average, outspoken singer, who is fastly approaching the ripe "old age" of 60 – a time when most wind down and look forward to retirement – managed to stay SO relevant and SO influential in popular culture to the extent that her brand power increases in direct proportion with her age?

While you ponder this enigma, let's take another example into consideration. When Sam Walton, businessman and former J.C. Penney employee, opened Walmart Discount City store in 1961, little did he know that this "Store #1" would become the first of thousands of stores and "supercenters" to blanket the American landscape, known for selling quality products in high volumes for low prices. Soon after, he opened his first home office and distribution center in 1970, and in the same year, became publicly traded on the New York Stock Exchange. Immediately, the brand experienced growth unprecedented by any other store in history, grossing billions of dollars and experiencing rapid expansion around the U.S. as it invaded the sales markets traditionally cornered by small mom and pop retail stores on the Main Street of small towns. When Sam Walton stepped down as CEO in 1988, he had just helped the company celebrate its 25th anniversary the year before, marked by 1,198 stores with sales of $15.9 billion and 200,000 associates. From there, Walmart executives drove the brand full steam ahead, using its supercenter concepts to surpass the sales of Toys "R" Us in toy sales, opening stores in South America and Europe, and slaughtering its biggest rival competitors Kmart and Sears in profitability. By the mid 1990's, the brand expanded into offering wholesale goods at its Sam's Club and opened smaller "Neighborhood Market" stores throughout communities across the U.S. Today, these same corporate executives have led Walmart into the position of being the most powerful retailer in the United States, noted as America's largest corporation on the Fortune 500 list, reporting revenues of nearly $200 billion, and controlling nearly a quarter of the retail grocery and consumables business. Between the brand's food and drug stores, supercenters, neighborhood stores, general merchandise stores, membership warehouse clubs, soft discount stores, restaurants, online sales, multi-million dollar satellite network linking all of its operating units with unprecedented logistical efficiency, international holdings of more than 6,300 stores, the creation of its own electric company in Texas to supply their stores with cheap power at wholesale prices, e-commerce division, online video streaming company, mail subscription service, financing program, and its never-ending development of private-label brand products and customer-friendly services, Walmart is poised to maintain a fixed position as the world's largest public corporation when ranked by revenue.

If you have ever been to a Walmart, you know that it is quite a wonderland of products, from groceries, to electronics, to apparel, home goods, and more. However, despite the great variety of products that it has to offer, these are often not the best or highest quality products out there. In fact, if we want the highest quality products, Walmart would not be the first choice for many of us; quality is not synonymous with Walmart. Some might say that people frequent Walmart just for the low prices it offers. However, there are plenty of other stores with lower prices on various goods as well. Considering these things, how have Walmart executives managed to all but corner the U.S. and global markets with its stores, including the apparel, groceries, electronics, toys, home goods, etc. that they sell? How have these executives ensured that Walmart enjoyed such staying power and continued to consistently build its influence, brand power, and revenue despite economic recessions, high rates of joblessness, and the constant competition that arises in the retail market? After all, a myriad of new department stores have tried to break into the market over the past several decades, and despite their best efforts, most have failed. The vacant buildings and big box spaces of real estate that lay empty in strip malls across America are testament to those who dared to establish a retail store that could enjoy even a small percentage of the growth and sustainability of a store like Walmart, but they were unsuccessful at their attempts. What is it about the executives who drive a brand as unspectacular as Walmart that have positioned it for such resistance to cultural changes, such stamina over the decades, and such fortitude to weather any economic climate? How in the world have Walmart executives managed to keep the brand relevant when other retail executives crashed and burned in their efforts?

When Robert Grant studied phenomena like Madonna and Walmart executives, the goal of his research was to answer questions like yours. After all, if we are able to isolate what makes iconic players like these tick, maybe we could pick up a few lessons on how to follow in their footsteps and realize our own successes, right? People tend to regard icons like Madonna and business geniuses like the Walmart executives as those who are able to maintain an uncanny ability to influence culture at levels that are unparalleled, not just over a few years, but over decades. Not only do they maintain their relevance, but despite changes in the world beyond their control, they manage to stay on top, growing exponentially in brand power every step of the way! In every sense of the definition, they are our cultural leaders! Not surprisingly, Grant's research yielded some interesting results surrounding one particular key element that these leadership successes shared: Awareness!

If you will ever become the successful leader that you desire to be – one whose success transcends that of being short-term and local and becomes one whose brand and success are relevant over the long-term, ever-evolving, influential, and global – you must increase your level of awareness! You see, Madonna, Sam Walton and the Walmart executives that succeeded him, and others whose global brands are on such a high level of success that we would call them "iconic" are keenly aware of themselves and the world that surrounds them. Many would like to attribute their successes to being "chosen ones," "having a special gift," or even possessing some deep, enigmatic ability to influence people. However, the truth is that there is no "secret" to their success. Research has supported that they have simply become masterful about being intentionally, deliberately, and determinedly aware. In other words, they operate with their eyes wide open!

So, what do you believe? There are opponents to taking such a position on leadership; as a strategic leadership expert, through years of research, I have become intimately aware of all of them. For example, there is the camp that will always promote the notion that "Successful people like that are born that way." In subscribing to the belief that certain people are born as superstar leaders, they position themselves among the "Leaders are born, not made" crowd. However, I happen to passionately believe that great leaders are made, and I suspect that you do, too. Think about it: would you be reading this book if you thought that great leaders could not be made? The mere fact that you are taking the time to invest time and energy into becoming a better leader means that you believe that a great leader can be made!

One of the most glaring examples that I refer to in order to support my assertion that great leaders can be made is through the study of the most successful leader to ever walk the face of the earth, Jesus Christ. I say that He is the most successful leader for good reason: He started His grassroots movement with scarce resources and just a few good men more than 2,000 years ago, and since that time, billions of people have become a part of His movement, the publication that tells His story is the best-selling book of all time, and His name is known in every nation, in every language, and in practically every home in the world. Further, rather than losing momentum, despite being more than 2,000 years old, His movement is gaining momentum! If *this* is not the most iconic and successful leader of all time, I don't know who is! I mention the leadership of Jesus Christ because His style is a prime example that great leaders can indeed be made. When Jesus called His disciples, He said to them, "Follow Me, and I will make you fishers of men." These men were not leaders by occupation; there were several fishermen and a tax collector among them. However, Jesus made them into leaders, investing His time, energy, and training in order to transform them. They were born as mere simple men, but Jesus helped them to become something that they were not: great leaders whose faith-filled works would continue to impact the world thousands of years after their lives ended! Still have doubts that leaders can be made?

If you are able to buy in to the idea that great leaders can be made, you might also be dealing with another reason to find examples like Madonna and Walmart executives relevant to the possibilities of what you yourself can attain as a leader. You might be thinking, *Well, people like that are in a different league. I'm just little old, insignificant me trying to lead my organization and survive another year. They're one – or two – in a million, and no matter what we do, successes like that don't happen for the average people like me.* Well, you could not be more wrong! It's not just people like Madonna and Walmart executives that experience such success in their leadership; there is a very long list of individuals and organizations that have been aware enough to be able to elevate their levels of success to iconic levels. Are you familiar with Dr. Dre, Ice-T, Ice Cube, or Jay Z? These guys started out as rappers and evolved into billionaire headphone maker, mainstream lead actor in the top-rated Law and Order television franchise, lead Hollywood actor and producer, and sports franchise owner / businessman, respectively. Sure, other rappers try to follow in their footsteps, but they consistently fall short, because they have not tapped into the missing success factor of awareness, so they do not experience the same long-term, ever-evolving success.

Perhaps rap music is not your thing, and you are not "aware" of the personalities within this genre that have become household names around the world. Well, have you ever heard of Michael Jordan, Magic Johnson or LeBron James? These guys started out as average basketball players, burst into the NBA as exceptional basketball players and team leaders, and evolved into multi-million dollar fashion brands, business moguls and endorsement machines. What's more, they have occupied these positions of high-level success for years. Basketball not your thing? Try golf and Tiger Woods. Golf not your thing? Try superstar chef personalities like Gordon Ramsay, Wolfgang Puck, and Rachel Ray; perhaps you have seen their television shows, visited their restaurants, and even have their pots, pans and cooking utensils in your kitchen. Cooking not your thing? Consider the successes of non-profits like Habitat for Humanity, Big Brothers and Big Sisters, and the Make a Wish Foundation. These all started as small operations who were determined to fulfill a particular mission designed to enhance the lives of others, and now they are multi-million dollar organizations with global brands that sustain their momentum even when their active marketing campaigns are silent.

The point is clear: regardless of what industry you research, there are those within the industry that have made themselves emerge from the ranks, stand out from the average, and succeed beyond their competitors' wildest dreams. These are individuals and groups that are able to leverage one particular gift, talent, skill set, dream, or mission, build it, and make it evolve into a multiplicity of things that qualifies them in our eyes as high level successes. Even after their competitors research how they did what they did, no matter how much they follow their successful counterpart's footsteps to the letter, they most often fail to achieve the same success. But why?

The reason that you and other leaders can research how these iconic leaders did things, retrace the steps that they took to get to where they are, and even study interviews with them that might give you insight into how they think, and yet continue to produce lackluster results, is because you lack awareness. When you do not engage this key element of success, you can conceptually take every single action that iconic successes have taken in the same order that they took them, and you will still fail to attain their level of success. Awareness matters!

In order to become a successful leader, you must possess a keen awareness of things about yourself as well as various elements in the leadership atmosphere and be willing to take actions – based upon your high level of intentional awareness – that will position you and your business or organization to have a competitive advantage in society. When you are able to effectively engage in this process on a continual basis, you will be well on your way to stand-out success!

CHAPTER 3

360° ASSESSMENTS ARE NO LONGER ENOUGH:

Your Leadership Awareness Must Span a Full 720°!

The Era of the 360° Assessment Is Swiftly Passing Away!

If you worked in corporate America at any time during the 1990's, you might be familiar with the concept of 360° feedback assessments. Companies large and small utilized this assessment method which was systematically designed to collect opinions about individual workers from those within their work context in order to allow the individual to clearly see how others perceived him or her. The 360° feedback assessment was a breakthrough in the assessment world for good reason. Previously, assessment tools would only allow for the individual to assess himself or for the boss to assess the individual, usually at the time of year during which annual performance appraisals were conducted. However, 360° feedback, also known as *multi-source assessment, multi-rater feedback*, or *multi-source feedback*, was a way of providing a more complete picture of the individual's performance that went beyond that of the individual's self-perception; it gathered data that included perceptions about the individual from the boss or supervisors, peers and colleagues, and subordinates, and sometimes even included the perceptions of customers, clients, and key stakeholders. Once collected, this feedback was analyzed and compiled into one comprehensive feedback report about the individual's performance.

This new approach was revolutionary! It was clear to see how multi-dimensional feedback results gathered from everyone within an individual's immediate work context could paint a better picture of the worker than one-dimensional feedback results. Organizational development experts the world over embraced the tool with excitement about the untapped insights that such feedback could provide. With the feedback that individuals received from their 360° assessments, individuals could select areas that their co-workers deemed to be problems, weaknesses, or hindrances to effective productivity in the workplace and develop improvement plans that would result in better workability and increased performance output. Results were also widely used as a means for employers to review the progress of their workers for the sake of granting promotions and/or increases in pay.

As complete a perspective as the 360° feedback approach was considered to provide by human resource departments around the world, I submit to you that while it is complete, it is not complete enough! Leaders all over the world have undergone 360° assessments, and yet, they have remained average in their leadership at best. As passionate and committed as they are to change, and as willing as they are to uncover and address their weaknesses and areas that are problematic to their productivity, most are no further now than where they were when they took the assessment – they are just more informed about where they fall short as leaders now than they were before. Could it be that they are missing something huge that stands between their willingness to become a successful leader and the manifestation of actually becoming one? The answer is a resounding yes!

After years of observation, research, and study, I developed an original concept which I titled *Moody's 720° Leadership Decision-Making Model* – the key to heightening your awareness, which is the key element that most people miss in their efforts towards becoming a high-level, successful leader. This feedback model is one that goes beyond the 360° assessment, as it provides a 720° perspective of the various factors that influence one's leadership effectiveness within an organization. In it, I have utilized the elements of the most proven key success factors in the world of strategic leadership development and combined all of the layers of leadership into one comprehensive model that can be easily understood by the average person.

You might ask, *Why is the model considered to be a 720° perspective rather than a 360° perspective? Doesn't 360° represent a complete loop, or a comprehensive review that considers everything that people have to say?* While 360° does represent a complete loop in assessing feedback, it only allows leaders to consider the feedback from the circle of *human* resources that surrounds them in the workplace as they attempt to make the adjustments that will result in becoming better leaders. However, feedback from human resources is not the only intelligence that should be used to become a better leader; there is other feedback that speaks just as loudly as the feedback from people within the work circle that should be taken into consideration. The leader should be aware and in-tune with each of these voices. For example, when a leader is making a decision:

- What do the organization's tangible and intangible resources have to say about the matter?
- What does an appraisal of the organization's strengths and weaknesses speak to the leader?
- How do the external environment and organizational culture weigh in on the matter?

- What is it about the leader's personal and professional life and leadership style that stands to impact the decision?
- How do the perspectives and viewpoints of the followers factor into all of this?

Each of these is a consideration whose feedback speaks as loudly as that of the people who provide feedback in one's work circle through 360°, and when a leader takes such things into consideration, the individual is sure to be a better leader. Thus, when an individual is trying to become a better leader, he must not only be aware of what the voices of the people surrounding him in the organization are saying, but he must be aware of what the organization itself is saying! It is for this reason that I consider my approach to go beyond that of being 360° feedback; it is a 720° approach because it makes leaders aware of feedback from other dimensions that weigh in just as heavily on their ability to be better leaders as the feedback of the people around them. Simply put, this model provides a more comprehensive, more realistic, and more accurate awareness of feedback than that which 360° assessments can offer. As a result, *Moody's 720° Leadership Decision-Making Model* can help to heighten leaders' awareness, thus helping them to be more strategic in their approaches, more comprehensive in their understanding of how various factors impact their leadership effectiveness, and more prone to leadership success!

> *A 720° approach makes leaders aware of feedback from other dimensions that weigh in just as heavily on their ability to be better leaders as the feedback of the people around them.*

There are four key elements that comprise *Moody's 720° Leadership Decision-Making Model* and each of these elements is represented by one of four distinct triangles within the Tetra-triad (*tetra* meaning "four"): the Task Triad, the Issues Triad, the Leaders Triad, and the Followers Triad.

THE LEADERSHIP TETRA-TRIAD

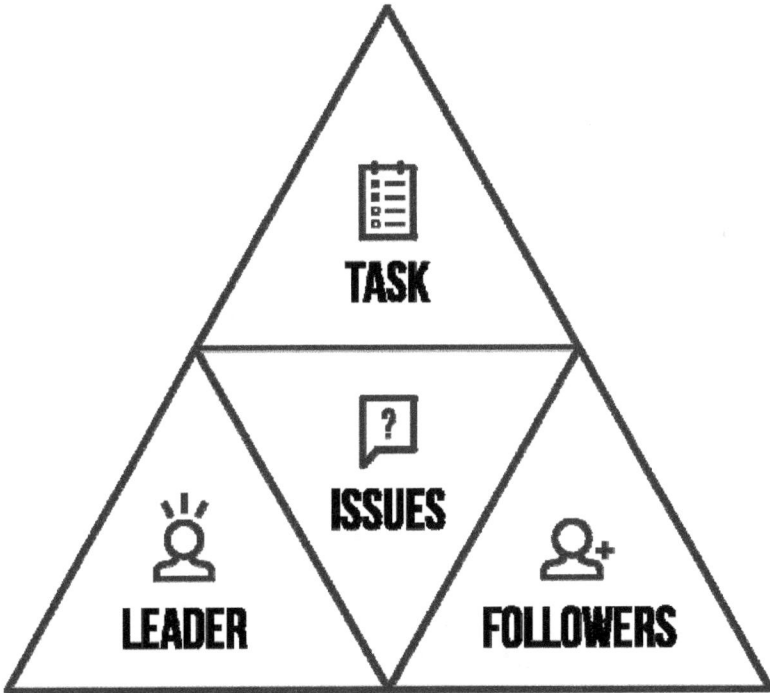

Although *Moody's 720° Leadership Decision-Making Model* is comprised of four distinct triads, or triangles, none of the triads operates as a stand-alone element of awareness; each is simultaneously active and interactive in every leadership moment and leadership decision, which allows the leader to be aware of the feedback that each one contributes to the conversation at the same time. For example, when a leader is about to make a critical decision about the business or organization, he or she does not think first about the Tasks, then about Issues, then about Leaders, and then about Followers. Instead, each of these component parts comprises a whole filter of awareness through which the leader sifts his thought process when making a decision.

PART 2:
THE TASK TRIAD

Building an Awareness of Choices, Capabilities, and Commodities Available to Address the Task at Hand

Task Triad Side 1:
Organizational Resources

What do I have to work with to execute my task?

Task Triad Side 2:
Appraisal

Do we have the capacity to execute the task?

Task Triad Side 3:
Strategic Choices

How can I gain an advantage over my competitors in the market or create a new market altogether?

THE TASK TRIAD

RESOURCES

Tangible
Intangible
Human

APPRAISAL

Key Factors
Strengths
Weaknesses
Level of Need

TASK

STRATEGIC CHOICE

Differentiation
Blue Oceans

TASK:

The smallest identifiable and essential piece of a job that serves as a unit of work, and as a means of differentiating between the various components of a project.[3]

The first triad of *Moody's 720° Leadership Decision-Making Model* is the Task Triad. It is comprised of three sides, elements, or sets of considerations about which the leader should be aware when making decisions regarding a given task: Resources, Appraisal, and Strategic Choices.

Leaders who do not approach tasks with the awareness that comes from carefully considering their organizational resources, making appraisals of their organization, and assessing what strategic choices should be made in light of the task at hand risk making poor leadership decisions. They will tend to approach or assign organizational tasks based upon passion, emotion, or some perceived, immediate organizational need rather than based upon an accurate assessment of whether the task can and should actually be performed. When leaders operate with a lack of awareness of such elements when approaching a task, the result is a set of frustrated workers and a frustrated leader, all of whom are frustrated because the leader has once again positioned the organization for a lose-lose outcome.

CHAPTER 4

TASK TRIAD SIDE 1: ORGANIZATIONAL RESOURCES

ASSESSMENT QUESTION:

What do I have to work with to execute my task?

When you are approaching a particular task, goal, or assignment as a leader, you must know what you have to work with in order to execute it successfully. Simply put, organizational resources are the people, places, and things that you have available and at your disposal to execute a particular task.

As a leader, making an accurate assessment of your organization's resources will equip you with a better understanding of what your organization is capable of executing in its current state. Being able to complete any type of goal or task effectively first requires the evaluation of the finances, materials, connections, people, time restraints, and other elements that you have to work with in order to get the job done. This is an important first step, because the level of resources available to the leader directly affects the strategy that he or she will execute in order to accomplish the task.

In order to appraise the resources necessary for the tasks that are before them, leaders must be able to readily determine whether their available resources possess the ability to get the job done. For example, if someone is in the business of growing grass and selling it as sod to residential builders, the two most vital resources necessary to accomplish this task are water and sun. Going to the Las Vegas desert to start this business is a bad strategic choice, because he or she will not have access to water to irrigate the grass fields – a necessary resource for executing the task. In the same regard, trying to start this business in a place like Michigan, where land is cheap, might also not work. There are a lot fewer hours of sunlight in the north than in the southwest, and added to this is the fact that Michigan freezes like the tundra in the winter! Leaders must be able to assess whether they can reasonably fulfill the tasks before them with the resources that are available to them.

Additionally, when a leader is making an assessment of which resources are available to get the job done, there must be a match between what the task requires and what resources are available to execute the task. For example, a good leader would never use a Lamborghini to haul hay from one place to another. This would be a clear mismatch between task and resources. A good leader would not use a person with a strong, hard, and dry personality to engender good feelings and a sense of care and concern with customers or clients. Again, this would be a mismatch between task and resources.

Leaders must also take into account considerations of how their access to resources will affect the choice they make concerning when and how to execute the task. For instance, if a leader has access to lots of financial resources and has a full year to complete a particular project, there is much more flexibility in which methodology to choose surrounding which approach will be used to perform the task and more latitude to make mistakes along the way throughout the strategic execution of the task. However, the fewer the resources available to a leader, whether finances, time, people energy, etc., the more refined the strategy must be; in this case, the approach must provide more "bang for the buck" and more yield for the investment. There is less wiggle room for making mistakes, so the leader must make decisions in a way such that *everything* is maximized!

Oftentimes, non-profit leaders who are asked about their organizational resources will reply that they have none, because they feel that they have few to no resources to work with in order to execute their organizational tasks. However, every organization has *some* level of resources at its disposal. These resources need only to be identified and maximized. A prime example of this concept is often seen in the non-profit arena, where in the average non-profit organization, people will only give a certain amount of their time and energy. For instance, if a leader has five volunteers coming to the organization's new facility to do some painting for two hours each, the leader must ask him or herself, "How can I best maximize the time and energy that these five volunteers are willing to give me?" The leader must determine whether the volunteers' hours would be best spent at the local home improvement store purchasing paint and supplies (one staff person could do this in advance rather than everyone else waiting around), whether their hours should be used to prepare the room for painting (one or two guys could do this in advance in half an hour), or whether their hours should be spent applying the paint (seemingly the best use of their time and energy). Leaders must become masterful at making choices that lead to the maximization of resources!

The 720° Snapshot

Various types of organizational resources might be at a leader's disposal for use when carrying out a task, and these resources tend to fall into one of three categories:

1) Tangible Resources
2) Intangible Resources
3) Human Resources

Task Triad Side 1 | Organizational Resources
CATEGORY 1:

TANGIBLE RESOURCES

Tangible resources include the finances, equipment, and facilities that are available for the organization's use to execute a given task. While it is believed that the more tangible resources an organization has, the better the leader can lead, this belief is a myth. Having access to lots of tangible resources at one's disposal – lots of bells and whistles – can foster a false sense of confidence in a leader, leading him to believe that he automatically has a huge advantage over his competitors; however, this might only be a perceived advantage. The reality is that having the most money and resources does not automatically mean that a leader and an organization can realize success. It's not about what you have; it's about what you do with it! Businesses and organizations that started out with bank accounts well into the black and the finest late-model equipment available in their industry close their doors every day. Success boils down to maximizing the resources that are available to your organization – as limited as they might be – not to the mere acquisition and accumulation of resources and equipment.

> *Success is not about the resources you have; it's about what you do with them!*

Leaders that are able to effectively maximize their organization's resources, particularly if these resources are abundant, can often choose from a host of methodologies that can be utilized to acquire a strategic advantage over their competitors. Organizations with limited resources are forced into being more selective about how they spread their resources around, because they need to get more done with smaller facilities, often older equipment, and less money. For example, if a large business or organization is attempting to market a new product or service, it might spend $20,000, knowing that this investment might only yield 300 new clients or customers. The return on their investment might seem small to others, but it is acceptable to them; they have many more financial resources at their disposal, so they can afford it. However, a small business or organization might attempt to market a new product or service with a budget of $100. With this $100, they set a must-have goal of acquiring 20 new customers or clients, because these are the last of their resources; if they do not generate more customers or clients with this campaign, they might be forced to close their doors soon. Unlike a large company with lots of financial resources, a smaller company or organization might live or die off of one campaign, so every penny of their financial resources counts. Every dollar that is spent must be maximized to produce a desired end 100% of the time!

Task Triad Side 1 | Organizational Resources
CATEGORY 2:

INTANGIBLE RESOURCES

Intangible resources include elements like brand strength, intellectual property, technology, and corporate relationships that are available for the organization's use to execute a given task. If you ask average business owners what they would prefer to have in terms of resources, most would not even think twice; they would inevitably say that they would rather have access to the tangible resource of money over anything else. However, a great amount can be accomplished by an organization through a leader's maximization of its intangible resources, so these should not be ignored.

Consider the intangible resource of brand strength, which is a measure of the strength that a particular brand has over its competitors; when a brand has a well-known name, it is considered to have good brand strength. Though many leaders do not leverage their organization's brand strength, it is a valuable intangible resource, nonetheless. If a business or organization effectively develops its brand strength, this intangible resource can go a long way in helping the organization attain its objectives, accomplishing things that other organizations must spend their valuable dollars in order to achieve. Oftentimes, the name of a brand in and of itself has enough power to drive an initiative towards success. Take the Apple logo, for example. If Apple places its logo on something – *anything* – the recognition of that logo alone will drive the customer base to consume it through the purchase of a product. The Apple logo has powerful brand strength because it possesses the ability to demand customer resources (i.e., it gets them to spend their money on Apple products, regardless of the above-market price point)! Businesses and organizations should be intentional about developing and strengthening their brands, because this intangible resource can result in great value for the organization!

Consider another intangible resource that leaders would do well to leverage: corporate relationships. Corporate relationships are some of the most underestimated intangible resources by leaders, largely because they involve our interaction with people. Today's society seems to value such personalized interaction less and less every day. However, when leaders are able to effectively leverage corporate relationships, they can often gain access to additional resources available through their corporate connections

Corporate relationships are some of the most underestimated intangible resources that leaders possess!

that they might not possess within their own organizations. In many cases, when leaders are able to negotiate partnerships with other corporate entities, the partnering organization might even use its brand strength to enhance the strength of the leader's brand. Access to these additional resources and leveraging points helps the leader to accomplish the task more effectively and efficiently than trying to accomplish it using his organization's tangible and intangible resources alone. Good leaders never underestimate the power of relationships. Even further, good leaders do all they can to build and maintain these relationships, because they recognize the value of these intangible resources.

HUMAN RESOURCES

Human resources include the people, or human capital, available for the organization's use to execute a given task. In order to execute a task with effectiveness and efficiency, you must maintain an awareness of (1) the number of people allocated to a given task, (2) the individual and collective skill sets available from this group, and (3) the amount of time that has been slotted for the individuals to complete the task. An assessment of these factors will ensure that the leader makes the proper decisions concerning which people to place in which roles to carry out particular functions according to their capacities and will also ensure that the leader carries reasonable expectations surrounding what they can produce within a certain amount of time.

Human resources are really the power that gets the wheels turning in the organization!

Human resources are really the power that gets the wheels turning in the organization! While systems give birth to products, and products give birth to revenue, people are the resources that actually make the system work! In fact, systems without people are simply policies in a book or words on a piece of paper. Good leaders understand that the people who do the work and execute the systems and policies of an organization are the *real* value of an organization. An organization can possess an abundance of financial resources, the newest equipment, and the most cutting-edge technology, but without quality human resources in place to work with them, these other resources are futile. People matter!

Systems without people are simply policies in a book or words on a piece of paper.

When financial resources become tight within a business or organization, the reflex to downsize the number of employees can be an almost immediate response. However, good leaders recognize that downsizing does not necessarily turn into profit. Instead, when there is a need to downsize, they find other resources within the organization that they can do without for a season. When leaders downsize their human resources due to a scarcity of financial resources, they tend to put significantly greater pressure on the workers who remain, as these individuals are forced to also complete the work of those who are no longer with the organization. This can engender a sense of fear, distrust, stress, strain, and anxiety on the remaining workers. Consequently, their levels of execution, effectiveness, and productivity suffer; they are no longer able to yield the same results in executing tasks because of the increased demands for their time, energy, focus, and attention. Thus, smart leaders always look for alternatives to cutting their resources, reserving the trimming down of their human resources as a last possible option.

Leaders at the helm of non-profit organizations, particularly churches, should be keenly aware of not only building their human resources, which are their congregations, but also ensuring that these individuals have good feelings. In order to lead their people effectively, pastors must constantly assess how the people feel about them as the leader, how they feel about the worship service, and how they feel about the church. For leaders not to consider the emotional state of their human resources is to set themselves up for failure. How people within the congregation feel directly impacts their church attendance, their giving, their willingness to invite others to attend church, and consequently, the sustainability of the organization.

For leaders not to consider the emotional state of their human resources is to set themselves up for failure.

Because non-profit organizations and churches tend to have many more people resources than tangible resources, leaders of these types of organizations must develop the ability to leverage the energy and the efforts of the large numbers of human resources available to them. If executed skillfully, they have the ability to use these resources to make a huge impact in certain environments. People resources can be very powerful in the non-profit setting, because they can equate to the money, power, energy, information capital, and impact that the organization needs but lacks access to in and of itself. For example, if a church or non-profit organization can move 1,000 people to volunteer for several hours for a particular program or function, the productivity of the work that they produce might equate to upwards of $50,000! Thus, good non-profit and other organizational leaders maintain a high level of awareness about the human resources that are available to them to execute the tasks ahead of them, and they do all they can to ensure that their members maintain good feelings about them as leaders and about the organization.

As the leader of a church organization, I can bear first-hand witness to the benefits of maximizing the human resources of a non-profit organization. Like most churches, I have the arduous task of leading my church with limited financial resources. However, rather than resigning myself to a small vision and concluding that my church and I could never do anything significant because our lack of financial resources, as a good leader, I got smart. I had to figure out how to work around the fact that I did not have money for staffing, marketing, and all of the other necessities that help to make organizations successful. The route I took is one that has paid off in priceless ways! I learned to develop individuals, using my time and energy to build up their strengths, foster their levels of buy-in, leading them in developing a sense of ownership, and training them on how to be successful leaders. As a result of the human resources that I have personally developed, I now have a sharp, leadership savvy, dedicated

If you develop your human resources, they will consistently go above and beyond to bring a task or goal to pass, because they no longer consider it to belong to the organization but to them. They own it, and the success of it reflects them.

group of individuals that are eagerly willing to give what most would consider extra-ordinary amounts of their time, talent and treasure to advance my church's mission. My members are priceless! There is no way that I could have ever paid the types of salaries to bring people of this caliber aboard; however, today, because of my recognition of the value of my human resources and my investment in them, all that they do for the ministry, they do for free. As a result, I am able to accomplish with my limited numbers of members and little to no money what many churches several times my size cannot accomplish – and I can do them more effectively!

If you can develop your human capital, give ownership to it, value it, and appreciate these resources for what they have to offer, these individuals will perform tasks on an unheard-of, remarkable level, giving you access to discretionary effort that is lacking in most other organizations. In fact, they will consistently go above and beyond to bring a task or goal to pass, because they no longer consider the task or goal to belong to the organization but to them. They own it, and the success of it reflects them. Of course, it goes without saying that when the effort that these resources contribute is lacking, the organization often has to scramble to make up for it through the outlay of finances that are already scarce in the ministry. Thus, it is especially important for non-profit and other organizational leaders to invest their time and energy into the development of their human resources.

Task Triad Side 1 | Organizational Resources
SUMMARY & CONCLUSIONS

In summary, leaders must become skillful in answering the question posed by the Resources side of the Task Pyramid, "What do I have to work with to execute my task?" Without answering this critical question, leaders oftentimes set themselves up to have unfounded, baseless, and inappropriate expectations of those within their organizations as they seek to accomplish given tasks. This leads to leaders feeling a sense of hurt, disappointment, and frustration. They have engaged in the exercise of mental masturbation, gaining pleasure at the thought of something happening that is only a groundless fantasy.

They have engaged in the exercise of mental masturbation, gaining pleasure at the thought of something happening that is only a groundless fantasy.

Know What's In Your Hand, and Put It To Work!

Rather than misappropriating their expectations, good leaders make a comprehensive assessment of their resources and approach the execution of their organizational tasks with realistic, sound, and practical expectations. Therefore, I urge you to increase your awareness by always asking, "What do I have to work with to execute my task?" and then be brave and insightful enough to deal with it and act according to your reality!

CHAPTER 5

TASK TRIAD SIDE 2: APPRAISAL

ASSESSMENT QUESTION:

Do we have the capacity to execute the task?

It is the work of leaders to actively appraise specific aspect of their organizations each time they approach a task. To appraise something simply means to assess the value or quality of something, or to estimate or evaluate the worth or significance of a thing. In light of this, when leaders are preparing to carry out tasks, they must be able to first determine what values and qualities their organizations possess that will make carrying out the desired task feasible. Additionally, they must evaluate which characteristics of the organization are more likely to facilitate the task being completed as well as what characteristics of the organization are likely to hinder the task being completed in the most efficient and effective manner possible.

Every organization has certain capabilities that are unique to them within an industry and that give them value and significance. As a result of the great diversity that exists in the personalities, training, education, exposure, and individual talents of the people in the organization, as well as the varying environments in which they operate, access to resources, etc. no two organizations' characteristics will ever be exactly the same in terms of what they have to offer in value and significance. Each organization is distinctive, containing its own unique set of characteristics that make it special and define its worth; one organization might be special because it possesses power and potential in a certain area, so it maximizes the use of this area at every opportunity when approaching a task. However, another organization might be completely lacking in power and potential in that same area, so it will minimize the involvement and impact that it has on any task that it undertakes. It is the work of leaders to appraise how, why, and what features make their organization special and unique so that they can maximize the use of their valuable and advantageous characteristics, thus minimizing the effects of the damaging and detrimental characteristics when attempting to carry out a task.

Various areas of appraisal are necessary for the leader to examine when carrying out a task, and these areas of appraisal tend to fall into one of four categories:

1) Key Success Factors
2) Strengths
3) Weaknesses
4) Level of Need

KEY SUCCESS FACTORS

Appraisal begins with identifying key success factors – the most important traits or characteristics that contribute to the success of an organization's ability to accomplish what it has set out to accomplish. Business dictionaries would define them as the combination of important facts that is required in order to accomplish one or more desirable business goals[4]. Key success factors are the main things that work together to make the business pop, expand, and develop. They are the critical elements that must be present in order for the organization to be able to effectively accomplish its goals of growth and productivity! Every organization has key success factors, some more than others. However, in order to be able to maximize their use for the organization's benefit, they must first be appraised and identified by the leader.

Take, for example, John and the CCC's first big community project: the health screening event at a local apartment complex. Before assigning the event to his team, John had undoubtedly identified several key success factors needed to be present: the effective engagement of community partners to provide health services, the effective engagement of volunteers to work at the event, and sufficient financial resources to advertise and execute the mission of the event. Unfortunately, even though John identified these key success factors – the factors that must be present in order for the event to be executed successfully – prior to assigning the event to his team, his failure to follow up on his team and hold them accountable for ensuring that these key success factors were present is a primary reason that the event met its demise. Appraisal and identification of key success factors is only one side of the coin; the leader must also ensure that the key success factors are actually present when it is time to execute the plan!

STRENGTHS & WEAKNESSES

Although strengths and weaknesses define two distinct sets of characteristics within an organization, I discuss them together because they are two sides of the same coin. The effects of one have a direct impact on the other, and neither can be discussed exclusively without a consideration of the other.

> *Awareness of the organization's flaws empowers the leader to assess every step of the strategic execution plan and ask, "Are there any areas in this plan that might be impacted by our organization's weaknesses?"*

Strengths are proficiencies that come very easily for an organization. When properly appraised, identified, and leveraged, an organization's strengths can make all the difference in propelling the organization to success. A strength denotes an organization's capacity to resist force or pressure and represents some type of capital, knowledge, skill, or other advantage that the organization possesses over other similar organizations [5]. Simply stated, it is whatever gives an organization the upper hand, facilitating its ability to take the lead in doing something over and above its competitors' ability to do so. A strength is what helps the organization to succeed and win!

When leaders become aware of their strengths through the appraisal process, this knowledge serves a major benefit to them and their organization when they are approaching the execution of a task. Because strengths represent something favorable that they have but others do not, they need only ask themselves, "Are we making full use of our strengths in the approach that we are taking towards this task?"

On the other hand, weaknesses are deficiencies that can be considerably difficult for an organization to engage in to produce an output. In many cases, in order for an organization to function in the area of its weaknesses, it must invest substantial energy into the effort, and even this extra energy is no guarantee that it will yield its desired results in the area. Simply stated, weaknesses are flaws that increase an organization's risk of a failure[6].

It is the work of a leader to appraise, identify, and maintain an awareness of the organization's flaws when approaching a task. If weaknesses are present anywhere in the leader's strategy to accomplish the task, they can easily sabotage the success that the leader is pursuing. Awareness of the organization's flaws empowers the leader to assess every step of the strategic execution plan and ask, "Are there any areas in this plan that might be impacted by our organization's weaknesses?" If such areas are identified, the leader can then take action to either remove the threat of the weakness' impact or at least strive to minimize it. Thus, being empowered with an awareness of an organization's strengths and weaknesses places the leader in a great position to be able to maximize the impact of the organization's strengths and minimize the impact of the organization's weaknesses in order to produce the most successful output possible.

> *It is the work of a leader to appraise, identify, and maintain an awareness of the organization's flaws when approaching a task.*

For some leaders, especially those who do not consider their organizations to be doing very well, making an appraisal of their weaknesses is the last thing in the world that they want to do. They ask, "I know that my organization is full of weaknesses. Do I *really* want to make myself feel worse as a leader by pinpointing the areas where my organization is failing?" In response to such a question, I would answer that the ostrich approach – the one in which leaders bury their heads in the sand so that they cannot see the danger that is approaching – does not

eliminate vulnerability. The mole approach – the one in which leaders live totally underground in the darkness with no exposure to light (which moles do not need to move around) – does not work either.

Rather than walk around in the dark, leaders must be enlightened about everything in the world around them that can impact their organization, including their strengths and weaknesses. No organization can function effectively if it is isolated from the rest of the world and led by a leader who chooses to walk around in the dark, ignorant of his organization's flaws!

You will never be the effective leader that you can be without a keen awareness of your organization's weaknesses! Do you remember Achilles? He was one of the most popular heroes of Greek mythology because he was a successful warrior who met a surprisingly tragic end. You see, Achilles led a great army and fought heroically as a mighty warrior during the Trojan War, killing many men, including Hector, the greatest fighter for Troy in the Trojan War. Achilles seemed invincible! However, as invincible of a warrior leader as he appeared to be, Greek mythology tells us that he was killed towards the end of the Trojan War when he was shot in the heel with an arrow. Every other part of his body was invulnerable except his heel; his heel was his weakness – his most vulnerable point! Thus, as a result of the smallest of wounds, to his heel of all places, the great and mighty warrior met his death!

> *Like Achilles, not appraising and having an awareness of your organization's weaknesses could be your fatal flaw!*

Like Achilles, not appraising and having an awareness of your organization's weaknesses could be your fatal flaw! As long as he was operating in his strength, Achilles was a great warrior and noble leader who could do anything! However, with as many strengths as he had, no amount of them could compensate for him not knowing where his weak point was. So it is with you as a leader! Knowing your strengths are great, but this knowledge means nothing without also having knowledge of your weaknesses. Remember: they are two sides of the same coin!

Operating in a state of ignorance about your weaknesses makes you as a leader vulnerable to repeatedly engaging in tasks that will negatively impact your organization. As a result, everything that you undertake will either fail or at least have disappointing outcomes. Much of the time, resources, and energy that you invest into completing tasks will be wasted. Most of all, you as a leader, will grow more and more frustrated each time you confidently approach a task and fail at it. Therefore, do not be afraid to appraise and increase your awareness of the shortcomings that threaten everything that you attempt to do in your organization! The bottom line: your weaknesses will inevitably sabotage your ability to achieve your desired outcomes if you do not proactively identify and deal with them!

My organization is a wonderful example of how strengths and weaknesses must be appraised, identified, and mitigated in order to successfully execute a strategic task. One of the things that come very easy for my church organization is that of creativity; our levels of creativity are off the charts, and everyone around us knows that it is a clear organizational strength! As a result of this unique characteristic, using our creativity to change things within the organization can be done on the turn of a dime; everyone understands the plan, everyone is on board, everyone contributes, the elements of the plan easily fall into place, and before you know it, the change is made, and the end product is amazing!

> *The bottom line: your weaknesses will inevitably sabotage your ability to achieve your desired outcomes if you do not proactively identify and deal with them!*

However, while creativity is undoubtedly a major strength of ours, systems are not. A system is a set of processes, methods, and procedures that are designed to ensure that certain outcomes are met. In our case, the outcome that needs to be met is that of ensuring that the changes that we have made using all of our creativity are actually anchored in place and sustained. The unfortunate reality, though, is that the ability to execute systems is a weakness of ours. As a result, we are not very good at maintaining the changes that we have invested countless time, creative energy, and resources into making. Not long after we have implemented one of our creative new plans, we find ourselves trying to figure out why it no longer looks like what we'd originally planned for it to be or function how we originally intended for it to function.

For example, my team and I can totally transform the décor of a facility. Give us three days, and we will change the entire look and feel of the place, giving it a total makeover from top to bottom with lots of new and innovative features! Give us three months after this, however, and things might look a little different! The maintenance schedule, volunteer resources, financial resources, security procedures, etc. that should have been used to maintain the look and function of the facility are absent because there are no systems to ensure that they are present. Why? Because systems are our weakness! As a result, in the past, the appeal of the new look and new features would crumble, lessening more and more with every passing day. Eventually, the changes would no longer reflect the original vision that we had for them.

Understanding how the strengths and weaknesses of my organization work together and taking strategic approaches towards my tasks as a leader means being aware that my people will always be enthusiastic and engaged in change but quite unenthusiastic and prone to disappearing when the time comes to maintain these changes. Consequently, in order to operate as a wise leader, I take these factors into consideration at the onset of the plan, ensuring that I build in a means of making my highly-creative team accountable in some way for systematically helping to maintain the creative changes that we have made. In this way, "After all," I tell my staff, "change that is not sustained by systems is not true change at all!" Leaders must be able to find ways to capitalize on their strengths while mitigating the impact that their weaknesses might have on their progress and productivity.

Task Triad Side 2 | Appraisal
CATEGORY 4:

LEVEL OF NEED

Individuals who lead organizations are masterful jugglers. The demands on their time and attention are high, and there are always more tasks to do than time to do them. For this reason, in order to make the most efficient use of their time and energy, leaders must assess the level of need of the assignment at hand prior to approaching the task. Thus, leaders must ask questions like:

- *Is it really necessary to complete the task right now in light of all of the other things that are demanding my attention?*
- *How imperative is this task as it relates to its impact on one of the key success factors for this event?*
- *Is there a hard, fast timeline directly attached to this task or assignment getting done?*
- *If I do not complete this task right now, how will it affect the progress of the other members of my team?*

High level-need tasks are those that directly impact one or more key success factors within the organization and should be prioritized. *Anything* that might compromise the organization's ability to win deserves priority attention! Additionally, high level-need tasks should be given higher allocations of resources (time, energy, manpower, focus, etc.) than non-priority projects in order to ensure that they are fully completed. On the other hand, low level-need tasks are those that do not make a real impact on any of the key success factors within the organization. Whether or not the task is done at the moment will not affect the progress or

> *Anything that might compromise the organization's ability to win deserves priority attention!*

productivity of anyone else in the organization, because the task does not have a lot of other pieces attached to it. Low level needs will get done; they will just not get done *right now*!

I recommend that you start your day off by making a list of all of the tasks that are demanding your immediate attention. If you are like most leaders, there will inevitably be many. Then, go down your list and assign a level of need to each one. For example, put an "A" next to the tasks that are high-level needs, and put a "B" beside the tasks that are low-level needs. Then, go back through all of your high level needs for the day and number them in order of importance. For example, "A-1" will be your highest priority of the day. "A-2" will be your next highest level priority. Continue with this appraisal process until you have gone through your entire list. With each task you make a priority, ensure that you also assign the right amount of resources towards being able to accomplish it. For example, if your highest priority of the day is to deliver a completed radio commercial to the radio station for an upcoming event, you might need to ensure that several key individuals are present for a script meeting (human resources), that the technology is available to record the voiceover (technology resources), that a check is ready to deliver with the completed commercial (financial resources), and that someone is available to make the delivery of the final commercial and payment. If any of the resources that are needed to accomplish your high priority task are missing, you will not be able to fully execute your high level-need tasks!

If you are a Type A Personality, one who is driven, aggressive, ambitious, and determined to "do it all," truly appraising a task's level of need might prove to be difficult for you. Why? Because Type A leaders tend to make every task an A-1 level of priority! In their minds, everything is urgent, and everything must be completed immediately! While this approach might seem like a good idea, the reality is that when everything is a priority, nothing is a priority. In their efforts to get everything done, leaders like this end up investing their emotional, intellectual, and energy resources into a lot of low-level need tasks, and when it comes time to addressing tasks that really are critical and high-level need, they have neither the time nor the energy left to do so!

I must admit that I have been guilty of doing just this! One year, I worked tirelessly on making a grand production of a New Year's Eve worship service for the church that I pastor. I personally had my hand in each and every aspect of the planning, from making videos to be shown throughout the evening, to arranging music, working with the singing and dancing, and every other possible aspect of the production so that it would be just what I'd imagined. However, after doing all of that, once the time came for me to prepare my sermon, I was exhausted; I had no more energy to pour into planning into the most important element of the worship service! As a result, the sermon, which was the most crucial part of the service, was terrible that day. Let my mistake be a learning opportunity for you: don't just appraise and assign tasks to higher and lower levels; invest your valuable resources into high-level need tasks *first*, because the last thing you want to do is run out of steam – and resources – before you get down to them on your list!

Task Triad Side 2 | Appraisal
SUMMARY & CONCLUSIONS

It's a Really Good Idea, but
Can You Actually Get It Done?

In summary, it is essential for every leader to ask the ultimate question posed by the Appraisal side of the Task Pyramid: "Do we have the capacity to execute the task?" Goals are good, but:

- Does your organization have the capacity to attain the goal?
- What key factors are necessary to attain the goal, and is your organization able to ensure that these key factors are present?
- Are you strong enough in the areas that you need to be strong, and are you able to mitigate your weaknesses enough to keep them from sabotaging the attainment of your goal?
- Is the task even worth your time, energy, and focus right now?

These are the appraisals that good leaders make in order to increase their awareness of what they have to work with so that they can determine from the onset whether or not they have what it takes to execute the task.

The reality is that oftentimes, your big dreams and your organizational reality will not be synonymous; there are things that you would love to accomplish with your organization that are simply beyond your reach and capabilities in your current state. For example, you might say that you want to increase your marketing presence in the region, so you set out to secure the city's largest billboard, which is located in a prime spot along the main highway. After you complete your due diligence and collect the information you need, you conduct an appraisal of whether the task can be executed or not – key factors, strengths, weaknesses and level of need. The level of need part is easy: you have a need for some high-profile marketing in order to drive people to your organization. However, the results of your appraisal go on to reveal that the company requires you to submit your own art design, but you neither have a designer, nor can you afford one. Then, the cost for the billboard is about 15 times what your budget will allow, so you cannot afford the spot either. In this case, the task does not match your organizational capacity to execute it. Does this mean that your marketing efforts are dead in the water? No! It simply means that, for the time being, you will need to scale down your marketing to a level that can be directly met with your organization's current capacity – a level more reachable and attainable!

God is into Making Appraisals, and So Should You Be, Too!

Those who are familiar with the Bible might recall the story of Moses and the twelve spies who went into Canaan. I refer to it because it is one of my favorite examples of the necessity of appraisal. It also shows us that God is an appraiser! God had promised His people that He was going to give them the land called Canaan, which was a rich, abundant land that flowed with milk and honey. However, before the people could go in to inhabit the land, they would have to go to war with its inhabitants first. God had promised them the land, but He wanted them to invest some effort into inhabiting it before He would ultimately give them the victory and allow them to dwell there. In light of this battle that loomed between them and the possession of their promised land, God inspired Moses, the leader, to send spies into Canaan. Why? To make an appraisal of the task that was before them! As Moses sent 12 spies to spy out the land, he instructed them:

> Go up this way into the South, and go up to the mountains, and see what the land is like: whether the people who dwell in it are strong or weak, few or many; whether the land they dwell in is good or bad; whether the cities they inhabit are like camps or strongholds; whether the land is rich or poor; and whether there are forests there or not. Be of good courage. And bring some of the fruit of the land.[7]

It is clear to see that Moses really knew how to conduct an appraisal! In addition to the careful instructions of the appraisal, he even instructed the spies to bring some of the fruit of the land back so that he and the rest of the camp could see how abundant it was with their own eyes. Moses realized something that every leader must realize in order to be effective at executing tasks: careful assessments are necessary in order to develop effective strategies.

Careful assessments are necessary in order to develop effective strategies.

If we do not strategize properly, even though we might be filled with energy and passion, we will fail at our task because we lack an adequate plan to succeed. If you are wondering about the outcome of the story, I am happy to inform you that it is a happy one! After the spies went in to conduct the appraisal, ten of them came back with a conclusion that the task was beyond their capacity to execute because the inhabitants of the land were stronger than they were. However, the remaining two spies came back with a favorable report, saying that if the Lord delighted in them – and He did – they would be victorious, because the protection of the current inhabitants had departed from them. Eventually, under the leadership of Joshua, Moses' successor (and one of the two spies who had returned with a positive report after the appraisal) God's people conquered the inhabitants of the land and took possession of Canaan, the land that God had promised them.

Not Making Proper Appraisals Can Result in a Monster of a Mess!

Let's say you want to increase your customer base by 500 new customers this year. Next, you conduct an appraisal of whether your organization has the capacity to actually handle 500 new customers. Do you have the infrastructure to contain 500 new customers? Are your facilities and physical space large enough? Is your web space able to handle the additional traffic? Do you have the human resources to effectively service 500 new customers, or would there be a big bottleneck? Would your receptionist be able to handle the phone calls and online inquiries of 500 new customers? The point is clear: before you launch into a new task as a leader, take the time to think things through. If you embark upon a task without making the proper appraisals of your organization's capacity to handle the task itself or the outcomes of it, you will be creating a monster of a mess for yourself as a leader and for your organization!

Just imagine: you would set your customers up to have a frustrating experience with you, there would be negative reports flying around about your organization because you were not prepared to service such large numbers, and your business would be in worse condition than if you had never initiated the influx of new people! Internally, your staff would be frustrated and de-motivated, and you would be frustrated with yourself for not adequately scanning through and making the proper assessments to determine whether or not your organization could handle both the task and its outcomes. Do yourself a favor: if you cannot service the task and its outcomes, don't try to be a superhero, let it go! If it is clear that your organization does not have what it takes to make the venture successful, walk away from it!

Do you have the capacity?

I recall one incident in which I had to appraise my reality and let go of something because I did not have the capacity for the task. I had created a product for pets and was interested in selling it at the local big box pet retailer, so I called the store's corporate office. One of the very first questions he asked me stopped me in my tracks: "Do you have the capacity to provide ten thousand of your products to us for our stores nationwide?" Well, since I was just one person making the products, and I was making them one at a time, the answer was clearly a "No"! That appraisal was a fast process; it was so fast, in fact, that it ended my pet store retail product quest before it ever got started.

SWOTS and Surveys:
Two Effective Means of Appraisal

Looking for effective ways to conduct an appraisal of your organization? The appraisal process does not have to be a lengthy or complicated one. Most leaders appraise their organizations through a process called a "SWOT Analysis," with SWOT being an acronym for Strengths, Weaknesses, Opportunities, and Threats. Typically, this structured planning process calls for the appraisal of internal strengths and weaknesses and external opportunities and threats and involves the input of a team of leaders and stakeholders. For a less-complex method of appraisal, leaders might simply develop and disseminate some surveys to the organization's personnel and key stakeholders with a few questions to be answered. In any case, whichever route you choose to take, ensure that an appraisal is made. Careful appraisals mark the difference between leaders who make organizational messes and those who make their organizations successes!

CHAPTER 6

TASK TRIAD SIDE 3: STRATEGIC CHOICES

ASSESSMENT QUESTION:

How can I gain an advantage over my competitors in the market or create a new market altogether?

Every choice that an effective leader makes must be a strategic one; there is no room for trivial and unplanned choices when approaching a set of tasks. Regardless of the size of the tasks under consideration, a strategic choice – one that is designed to deliberately and intentionally increase the organization's competitive advantage – must be made concerning how to approach them. "What is a competitive advantage?" you might ask. While business dictionaries would define it as a superiority gained by an organization when it can provide the same value as its competitors but at a lower price, or can charge higher prices by providing greater value through differentiation[8], it basically boils down to an organization's ability to have the upper hand.

You are undoubtedly familiar with other organizations and companies that have a strategic advantage in the market. Perhaps one of the most popular ones is the Apple brand. Many people think that Apple has always had the upper hand in the market because it is simply Apple. However, the primary reason that Apple has been able to acquire and maintain a competitive advantage in the market is because it was the first to innovate. It is no secret that the execs at Apple are innovation geniuses, always pushing themselves to be edgy and to produce the "next big thing"! For example, Apple revolutionized the music industry with iTunes; they were first to market with mp3 downloads and music streaming, and they ensured that each and every one of their subsequent "next big things" automatically carried their music streaming technology, including iPhones, iMacs, iPods, and iPads. Others have followed their suit, like Google Music, but these imitators will always lag behind the original innovators. Why? Because Apple was first in matching its organizational strengths to the changing trends in the environment, and being first matters a lot in the ability to gain a competitive advantage!

In order to make strategic choices that will be most effective in helping their organizations to gain a competitive advantage when undertaking a set of tasks, leaders must first be fully informed about the internal and external environments in which they operate. First, they must possess a keen awareness of what their organizational strengths and capacities are. Then, they must always remain current with the trends that are occurring in the world around them. As they are able to consistently match what their organizations can offer internally to meet the ever-changing trends in the external environment, they will secure and maintain a competitive advantage!

Various categories of strategic choices are available to the leader when approaching a set of tasks. However, the primary choices that are able to result in acquiring a competitive advantage fall into two categories:

1) Differentiation
2) Blue Oceans

DIFFERENTIATION

Differentiation is the unique qualities and characteristics that make your organization unique – what makes you stand out to the external environment as being special and appealing. Because possessing the ability to stand out and be appealing to customers is especially necessary in order to gain a competitive edge and be a successful organization, leaders must approach tasks by asking, "How can I approach these tasks in such a way that it helps our organization to stand out and be selected by the largest share of consumers possible?" Being able to answer this question takes an intimate understanding of what the customer desires, what quality products and services the organization can offer, and the changing trends and demographic shifts of the customer base.

Strategies of differentiation will vary from organization to organization, because each organization is different in what it has the strength and capacity to offer to a particular market. Some organizations will choose to be differentiated based upon cost; they will provide the lowest cost option for a particular product or service in the market, and this makes them stand out to price-conscious consumers. Other organizations will choose to be differentiated based upon quality; they will provide a higher quality product or service at a higher cost than others who offer the same product or service, and this will make them stand out to quality-conscious consumers who value making high-quality purchases without close scrutiny of the cost. Different customers have different needs, and it is up to each organization to research and understand the needs of its

> *It is the work of the leader to ensure that there is always a consistent match between the organization's strategy and the customers' needs.*

customer base in order to ensure that it is able to meet these needs. When an organization's differentiation strategy meets the needs of the customers, this relationship generally results in a sale, a client, a referral, a reference, etc. It is the work of the leader to ensure that there is always a consistent match between the organization's strategy and the customers' needs and to maintain these relationships once they are established so that they can grow and develop.

It should be said that the work of identifying customers' needs is not a one-shot deal for leaders. The needs of customers are forever changing, so leaders must be intentional about being aware of trends that are occurring in the external environment. Awareness of these trends will provide indicators about where leaders currently need to be, where they will need to be in the future, how the needs of their customer base are evolving, and at what rate their customers' needs will outgrow the products and services that the organization currently has to offer. What works for an organization as a differentiation strategy today will not work for that same organization tomorrow, because people – and what they need – are changing! Possessing the key attribute of awareness, particularly of demographic shifts of consumer needs, keeps leaders on their toes, because it ensures that the organization is continually making strategically differentiating changes internally that match the external rate of change!

You might be thinking, "This all sounds good, but I really don't have time to stay current and keep up with all of the changes going on in society around me. Why can't I just pick something that makes my organization stand out in the crowd and stick to it? After all, it's been working for us all of these years, so why change?" There's a good explanation for this, and it is taught to us by the Tyrannosaurus Rex.

In ancient pre-historic times, the Tyrannosaurus Rex, or T. rex, was the king of the dinosaurs. Because of its size and strength, it was such a looming adversary and a vicious, formidable foe that all regarded to be the master of all pre-historic animals. However, after some time, the prey upon which the T. rex fed changed and evolved; it got faster and savvier, which increased its ability to survive the great predator. However, though his prey adapted and changed, the T. rex did not. As a result, the T. rexes no longer had the ability to hunt, catch prey, and eat.

Since the T. rexes were also unable to change their diet, they eventually all died off and became extinct. What does your organization have to do with the story of the T. rex? If you resist the process of adapting your organization's strategic differentiating approach to the needs of your customer base, you will eventually no longer have any customers upon which to "feed" in order to sustain your organization, and you too will become extinct!

> *If you resist the process of adapting... you will eventually no longer have any customers upon which to "feed" in order to sustain your organization, and you too will become extinct!*

As a good leader, you must always be in touch with what is happening around you. The world is changing and advancing so quickly, right before our very eyes! For example, the World Wide Web was first officially introduced to the public in 1991 [9]. Though the Internet has only been around for only 25 years or so, it has completely revolutionized the way that we communicate, the way we gather information, the ways in which we buy, sell, and do business, the way we entertain – the way we do just about everything in our lives! With the advent of the Internet and the level of global connection that it affords us, our society has been able to do more in 20 years than it has been able to do in the past 200 years. The rate of change that it has facilitated is exponential, and organizations that have not maintained pace with the Internet or either extinct or are breathing their last breaths. In order to survive and thrive, you as a leader must ensure that your organization remains current! How do you stay current? By ensuring that your differentiating strategy is dynamic, not static, and periodically adapting your strategy to meet the needs of people living in a society that continues to change faster than the speed of light. You must be able to lead your organization in adjusting to the trends so that you can always maintain your competitive advantage by standing out!

One of the key mistakes that I see leaders making is that of waiting too long to engage in change. When you question them about their outdated approaches and strategies, they will reply with things like, "Yeah, we've been looking into doing things differently for some time. At some point, we'll just shut things down for a little while, figure out how to catch up, and then start operating out of a newer system." They might also offer responses saying, "I know we need to change. We're going to completely overhaul things later this year and start completely fresh." While these might sound like good ideas to you, in my professional opinion, they are quite the opposite. If you paid attention during your high school physics class, you might be familiar with Newton's first law of motion: every object in a state of uniform motion tends to remain in that state of motion unless an external force is applied to it. This law is often more commonly referred to as the "Law of Inertia." In any case, the premise is that if something is moving, because of inertia, it tends to stay in motion until something stops it from moving. Once you stop the object, though, it takes more energy to start it moving again than it does to keep it in motion or even change its direction. Am I trying to sneak in a physics lesson just for the heck of it here? No! My point is that it takes much less energy to introduce gradual changes into your organization than it does to stop all of your processes, do an about face, and change direction. It takes more energy to stop your old activity and start a new activity than to simply keep things moving and make changes along the way.

Most organizations try to get to the top of the bell curve, and when they finally reach their peak performance one day, they pledge that they will make any necessary changes to the organization, because at this point, they have the latitude to use some of their energy to focus on such changes. However, such an approach is problematic, because at this point, they are on their way down the other side of the bell curve. The wise thing to do would be to make changes in the organization along the way as they are climbing towards their peak. If they choose to wait and make changes later on as their ball begins its rolling descent, they will have to completely stop the ball's downward momentum – which takes a lot of energy – and then exert up to six times more energy to push it back up the mountain!

Your adaptation to the world around you does not need to be a long, drawn-out, or complex process. Instead, stay aware of the external trends, and find a way to adapt what you are already doing to what is necessary to keep you current, differentiated, and appealing to consumers whose needs are constantly changing. Make subtle changes in your organization as you go along by capitalizing on energy, people, and trends around you. Be like the pro surfer who has mastered the art of riding waves. When he first jumps into the water with his board, he paddles out into the distance to the point where the waves begin to build. While the wave is still small, he stays with it, patiently watching and waiting for his big opportunity. Then when he sees the wave begin to grow into a massive swell, he stands up on his surf board and uses his skill and technique to ride it out! Good surfers, and good leaders, identify waves of change out in the distance, watch them carefully, and when the time comes, seize the opportunity to ride them in to glorious victory!

No one – with good sense, that is – stands at the break of a wave and waits for the water to crash down on him. This would be the equivalent of a leader, rather than keeping an eye out for coming changes and capitalizing on them, sitting at the helm of his organization and waiting for the new trend to crash down and destroy his organization! Tasks must be executed according to a strategy of differentiation that leads to a competitive advantage, and a strategy of differentiation must be developed based on the changes that are rapidly taking place in the external environment!

BLUE OCEANS

"Blue Ocean Strategy"[10] is a method of strategic thinking that, rather than battling for resources with other competitors in your market, seeks new, untapped markets that are wide open for growth. When leaders make strategic choices about a set of tasks utilizing this strategy, they do so by asking themselves the question, "How can we offer customers features and elements that have never been available before at an affordable price?"[11] Thus, while a differentiation strategy assesses what the organization can do to make itself stand out and be chosen from amongst the other competitors in the market, Blue Ocean strategy assesses what new market it can enter that has no competition so that it can be the first and only choice available providing a particular product or service.

New market spaces, or blue oceans, are not necessarily geographic locations; they are market spaces, niches or opportunities. Take churches and technology, for example. The vast majority of churches have websites that are, for all intents and purposes, billboards to merely advertise their worship services and programs. As such, they remain static, and rarely change their content unless an update is made to the calendar and an advertisement for a new event is added to the website. However, in today's mobile society characterized by increased access to the Internet through mobile phones, people are growing more and more accustomed to engaging websites for greater purposes than that of merely viewing advertisements and collecting information. They desire to actively engage, interact with, and connect with organizations through their websites. Understanding this, businesses are increasingly making their websites more dynamic so that they can be a place of relational connection, as they know that the development of such connections will eventually lead to customers, clients, and sales. Although businesses are seeing this trend and adapting to it, the church has been a slow responder. Thus, for the business world, engaging consumers through their websites is a competitive market in which each must find a way to differentiate itself. In contrast, for the church "industry," dynamic, engaging websites that serve as a place of relational connection are a Blue Ocean opportunity.

There is a clear explanation for why church leaders tend to shy away from engaging people through technology, and it is steeped in nothing more than outdated thinking and tradition. You see, many church leaders believe that if they begin to effectively engage people in cyberspace, those same people will see no reason to attend their worship services in person – and isn't the only indicator of a church's success that matters the number of people that actually attend the worship service on a Sunday morning? Traditionally speaking, yes. Strategically thinking, no.

Smart church leaders will see and take advantage of the wide open, Blue Ocean opportunity before them by re-thinking their definition of what a church assembly is. Why can't a church assembly be comprised of people sitting in the actual church facility as well as those who are viewing and actively participating in the worship service online through a dynamic website? Why can't a person join the church, receive prayer, donate to the church, attend worship services, grow in a relationship with God, and even volunteer to do things for the church virtually through the church's website? What's more, why can't a person connect with the church through wearable and virtual technology? These are Blue Ocean opportunities, but only those church leaders who are bold enough to re-examine their dated mentalities and traditional practices will ever actually step out to embrace them.

Of course, the church world is not the only context where Blue Oceans exist; they exist everywhere and are plenteous for those who are seeking these clear waters. For example, consider the health industry. Someone approaching a set of tasks with Blue Ocean strategy would ask questions like, "Can we use technology to deliver health services to people?" "Is it possible for us to help a doctor not only assess, but regularly interact with and monitor a patient's health status?" "Can we use 3D printers to practice surgery on individuals?" These, my friend are Blue Oceans. They examine possibilities and opportunities to do things that are not being done based upon current trends, so the competition in these markets is a non-factor. This is, by far, the greatest competitive advantage that an organization can have!

Then, for the sake of helping you to gain an even better understanding, consider the food services industry. In my city, there is a company that launched a new app called "Instacart." Through the Instacart app, you can order groceries and have them delivered to your home in just one hour. The developers probably figured, "Hey! People can order hot food and get it delivered from restaurants, but what about busy people who do not have the time or energy to go buy groceries from the grocery store? No one else is delivering groceries, so we will!" Instacart has linked its app to products available in grocery stores and other retailers around the area, and all the consumer has to do is select what is needed, order, pay, and wait for the speedy delivery. Even better, the consumer is not obligated to purchase all of your goods from one store; someone can order meat from the grocery store and a pack of t-shirts from Target! The convenience of the service is unmatched. Indeed, by being aware of the society's needs in their area and meeting these needs through easy, convenient ordering and fast delivery, they have tapped into a vast Blue Ocean!

Task Triad Side 3 | Strategic Choices
SUMMARY & CONCLUSIONS

New Technologies Mean Changes that Affect Your Choices!

In summary, every leader must ask the ultimate question posed by the Strategic Choices side of the Task Pyramid: "How can I gain an advantage over my competitors in the market or create a new market altogether?" In order to gain a competitive advantage, good leaders must be aware of what is happening in the external environment in order to ensure that their organizations are keeping pace internally. New and evolving technologies and other advancements in our society are resulting in changes occurring at a rapid rate around us, and these changes predictably result in changes in customers' needs. In order to effectively match the changes in your customers' needs with the products and services that you have to offer, you must stay informed of what is happening in the world; you must become comfortable riding on the cutting-edge of technology! Not to do so will inevitably lead to your organization becoming extinct... and I doubt that this is a part of your exit strategy!

Not matching changes in your customers' needs with what you have to offer will inevitably lead to your organization becoming extinct... and I doubt that this is a part of your exit strategy!

Once you are aware of your customers' changing needs, you must make strategic choices to approach tasks that are designed to ensure that your organization is able to stand out among the competition. Once needs are identified, you have two choices: 1) choose a strategy of differentiation that makes you stand out or 2) seek out a completely new and untapped market, or Blue Ocean. The truth of the matter is that unless you are able to identify and meet customers' needs in your own unique and individual way, you will never be able to generate enough financial resources necessary to sustain your organization. Thus, making strategic choices is not just a recommendation; it is a necessity for your organization's survival!

Filter Your Tasks through Strategic Choices or All Will Be Futile!

Without approaching a set of tasks with the **Strategic Choices** of the **Task Triad** in mind, leaders are bound to engage in exercises of futility – exercises that, though they seem to be good ideas, do nothing to help the organization to gain a competitive advantage. Leaders are rarely short of having lots of good ideas, but strategic choices must be made when selecting which ideas and tasks will result in the most advantageous outcomes for the organization. If an idea is not going to contribute towards helping the organization to gain a competitive advantage in some way, executing it will rob the organization of valuable time, money, and energy and will result in the leader feeling like he is running in place – spinning his wheels – because despite his hard work, the organization is not getting ahead. Making strategic choices when approaching a set of tasks helps to ensure that the leader selects the right tasks, utilizing the right amount of resources, and that the end result is targeted towards the right outcome. Taken together, this process generally equals success!

The 720° Snapshot

Building an Awareness of the Internal and External Threats You Stand to Face when Tackling the Task

Issue Triad Side 1:
Organizational Environment

Are we internally positioned and prepared as an organization to do what we are seeking to do?

Issue Triad Side 2:
External Environment

What forces or considerations outside of my organization affect my cost and ability to do what I do inside of my organization – and my ability to continue doing it in the future?

Issue Triad Side 3:
Organizational Culture

What are the structure and style of this organization's culture, and am I working with it or against it as I implement change?

The 720° Snapshot

THE ISSUE TRIAD

EXTERNAL ENVIRONMENT

Market Trends

Technology

Demographics

Porter's 5 Forces

- ▶ Competitors
- ▶ Suppliers
- ▶ Potential Entrants
- ▶ Substitutes
- ▶ Buyers

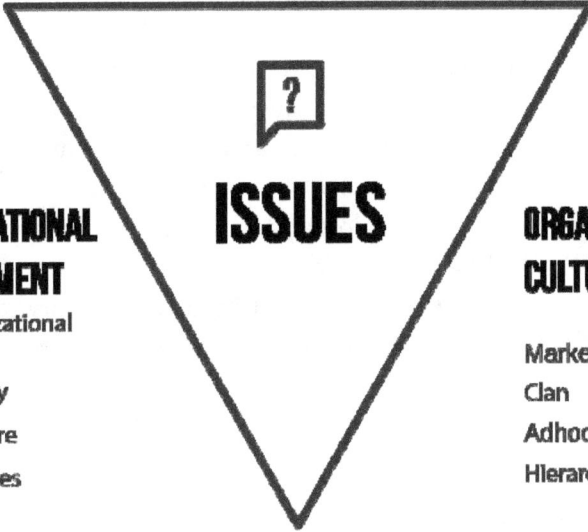

ISSUES

ORGANIZATIONAL ENVIRONMENT

- ▶ Organizational Design
- ▶ Strategy
- ▶ Structure
- ▶ Processes
- ▶ People
- ▶ Rewards

ORGANIZATIONAL CULTURE

Market

Clan

Adhocracy

Hierarchy

ISSUE:

A point of discussion or dispute.[12]

The second triad of *Moody's 720° Leadership Decision-Making Model* is the Issue Triad. It is comprised of three sides, which the leader should be aware of when making decisions about governing the organization: Organizational Environment, Organizational Culture, and External Environment.

The Issue Triad helps leaders to understand all of the forces that contribute to the success in a specific environment or organization. Each of the three areas of issues, including Organizational Environment, Organizational Culture, and External Environment, is always working in and on an organization at the same time, regardless of whether their effects are detected by leaders or organizational personnel. The Organizational Environment side explains "What we do," the External Environment side explains "Why we do what we do," and the Organizational Culture side explains "How we do what we do in a great way"! Leaders must be cognizant of these internal and external issues, because they will undoubtedly have a direct impact on the productivity and progress of the organization.

If leaders are not aware of the issues within their organizations, they do not have a genuine understanding of how their organizations really work at all!

When leaders operate with an awareness of the issues that impact the inner workings of their organization, they are able to regulate the effects of them, ensuring that the issues that can benefit the organization are exploited and the issues that can serve as a detriment to the organization's progress are eliminated – or at the very least, minimized. I would even dare to go so far as to say that if leaders are not aware of the issues within their organizations, they do not have a genuine understanding of how their organizations really work at all! Thus, in order to work an organization effectively, it is vital that leaders understand how each set of issues influences the inner workings of the organization, both individually and collectively.

Organizations are organisms, and organisms are not self-contained, autonomous entities. No organization operates on an island disconnected from the rest of the world. Instead, organizations are dependent upon many other external resources, units, and people with which they must interact and to whose influence they must adapt in order to survive. With this understanding, leaders can adjust their strategies and rates of change inside of the environment to keep pace and to be consistent with the influences and rates of change in the external environment. Simply stated, when changes occur outside of the organization, this marks the need for adjustments to occur on the inside of the organization. As a result, the organization is dynamic and ever-changing and adapting for survival, not static. Without this understanding, the organization is destined for failure.

The Issue Triad helps leaders to be aware of various elements that are in play when leaders are making decisions regarding a certain issue in the organization. We no longer live in a linear society in which one plus one will always equal two. Instead, there are many considerations to be made that make the outcomes that one might traditionally expect obsolete! The reason that this is true is clear: there are many competing factors, changing trends, and societal shifts in the external world that cause change in

> *When changes occur outside of the organization, this marks the need for adjustments to occur on the inside of the organization.*

our internal world. As a result, strategy is no longer linear, but dynamic, and even when a leader makes strategic choices that are designed to realize a particular, desired outcome, several different outcomes are possible.

Therefore, good leaders not only wait to see what societal shifts will occur and how they will impact the internal workings of their organizations; they pull out their binoculars and intently study the horizon, looking for any potential changes on the way that might serve to disrupt their inner workings. They look for outliers that can impact the effectiveness of the strategic plans that they have set into motion. By having such foresight, effective leaders are never blindsided by the impact of changes in the external environment; they foresee their arrival and are waiting for them when they come. Then, they make the necessary adjustments to their internal environment, which are often only slight changes, rather than having to make radical readjustments or throw out their strategic plans altogether.

Ultimately, the Issue Triad supplies the leader with insights into the multiple layers of forces that can make or break an organization's ability to be successful, equipping the leader with a more accurate decision-making model which he can use to critically think through his processes, and adjust his specific strategies. This, in turn, positions the leader to experience greater probabilities of success when leading an organization, as he is now empowered to operate out of a comprehensive and informed position rather than out of a passionate and emotional one.

CHAPTER 7

ISSUE TRIAD SIDE 1: ORGANIZATIONAL ENVIRONMENT

ASSESSMENT QUESTION:

Are we internally positioned and prepared as an organization to do what we are seeking to do?

In order to make informed decisions about the organization, a leader must have a full grasp of the organizational environment, or the internal system of the organization, in which he operates. Each organizational environment is built around an organizational design, which is defined in the business world as the manner in which leaders achieve the right combination of subdivided departmental units and the linking of these units to achieve unity of effort in organization's operations, in response to the level of unknown and unpredictable potential outcomes that might occur in its external environment.[13] This complex definition basically boils down to the way that internal aspects within the organization work together to produce certain outcomes.

For a better understanding, think of an organization like the human body. The human body is designed with various parts, or units, that work together to produce certain outcomes, including things like sight, vision, taste, touch, hearing, and motion, as well as our abilities to reason, feel, process, work, and reproduce, among many other functions. However, each of these internal functions is directly impacted by things that happen in our external world.

An organizational design typically features the following units, which, when linked, work together to produce certain outcomes for the organization:

1) Strategy
2) Structure
3) Processes
4) People
5) Rewards

Issue Triad Side 1 | Organizational Environment
CATEGORY 1:

STRATEGY

Strategies are the choices that position an organization for competitive advantage.[14] They address what the organization wants to do and how it will go about doing it. Strategies must be supported by a structure that will bring the mission or vision to pass.

Issue Triad Side 1 | Organizational Environment
CATEGORY 2:

STRUCTURE

Structures determine the placement of power and authority in an organization. [15] It addresses how the organization should be put together in order to be able to effectively execute the strategy by deciding who can make decisions and what decisions they can make. Structures must have processes that coincide with the strategy.

In the case of the CCC, for example, the president, John, put together a structure that included the volunteer coordinator, who was responsible for mobilizing the human resources necessary to run the events; the community coordinator, who was responsible for mobilizing organizations and key partners in the community to support the goals and programs of the CCC; the marketing coordinator, who was responsible for making the community aware of the events and programs offered and helping to build the organization's brand in the community; the accounting manager, who was responsible for maintaining an accurate record of revenue, expenditures, accounts payable, accounts receivable, and financial statements; and the operations manager, who was responsible for overseeing the day-to-day functions of the CCC and its programs and activities.

When John put this dream team together, he really felt like he made very clear distinctions regarding what everyone's role, function, and responsibilities were in the organization. However, this was clearly not the case! The marketing coordinator, Carl, grew frustrated because he felt like he should have more power to increase the marketing budget to be able to effectively market the program. He felt like the accounting manager, Blake, was unfairly handcuffing him because of his stringent budgetary tactics and that Blake should not be allowed to make such a call when the success of the program depended so heavily upon increased funds to marketing! Upon seeing this breakdown in his organizational structure, it was up to John, as the leader, to go back and clearly establish what the limits were to each individual's authority at the CCC, including what decisions each one had the authority to make and how the various departments could shake hands and work together for the overall good of the organization.

John's organizational example teaches us an important lesson: it is never enough to merely assign tasks and job descriptions to personnel within an organization, no matter how clear their job titles might be or how much power and authority are implied or assumed to accompany the job title. Instead, it is the work of the leader to plan out how each of the job positions interact, their respective levels of power and authority to make decisions, the limits of their decision making power and authority, and where they shake hands or intersect. Never assume that such relationships are clear. Instead, the leader must deliberately design and communicate them.

PROCESSES

Processes define how activities in the organization are coordinated.[16] They address what steps will be taken, in what order they will be taken, and when they will be taken to execute the strategic vision. There must be people to drive the processes.

The story of the CCC gives us a good glimpse into the value of processes. At the CCC, the job of the community coordinator, Pam, was to get buy-in from other community entities so that there would be enough medical partners to provide screenings at the upcoming health event. It was only after things fell apart that John realized that Pam did not have an adequate understanding of what kind of process to undertake that would result in real buy-in from community partners. To Pam, simply sending an e-mail inviting the partners to participate or sending a letter of support was enough of a process to convince Pam that these community entities were going to engage. However, to John, a complete process of generating buy-in would include:

Define the process. Refine the process. Ensure that everyone is operating based upon shared definitions of the process.

- Sending an invitation letter or e-mail
- Waiting for a written confirmation of participation
- Following up on organizations that did not respond in order to confirm or deny their participation
- Having coordination meetings that brought each of the confirmed entities together for planning
- Having the participating entities submit the plans and details of their screening in writing
- Training the people on the workings of the event

- Certifying that the people who would participate were trained
- Coordinating arrival times for each of the entities at the event
- Staggering the arrival of each entity's volunteers so that the event would remain fully staffed throughout the day
- Following up with each group to ensure that each had what it needed to function effectively at the event.

Needless to say, what John had in mind as a complete process was not what Pam had in mind. The failed health event helped him to see, in retrospect, that he should not only have *defined* the buy-in process with Pam; he should have gone back to *refine* the process with her, ensuring that they were operating based upon shared definitions of the process, what it meant, how it was measured, and how its execution would impact the overall strategy.

Many leaders make the mistake of believing that the words they use to define their process have shared meaning with the workers with whom they use them. For example, even though John would ask Pam throughout the planning process whether or not she had managed to get buy-in from the community partners, and she affirmed this to be true each time, they were clearly not speaking the same language. Leaders must do the work of taking the time of investigating the processes that they set into place in order to ensure that they are being followed. A process without such follow up or accountability will always end in miscommunication, disappointment, and failure.

> *A process without accountability will always end in miscommunication, disappointment, and failure.*

Issue Triad Side 1 | Organizational Environment
CATEGORY 4:

PEOPLE

People are the human resources that put legs to the strategic vision. This element addresses which people will do the work, what work they will do, and how they are driven. The people must be driven by rewards.

People make things – processes, systems, technology, hardware, events, etc. – work! They put legs on ideas and wheels on processes and initiatives to make them go! Without people, nothing in an organization can move. Organizations often make the mistake of investing in the latest and greatest technology; however, having technology in and of itself has never been the answer to any organizational problem. It is the maximization of technology that can provide solutions for the organization, and technology can only be maximized by people! Think about it: your computer sitting on the desk alone will never produce any file or document. A person must act upon the technology, planning and structuring the actions that are necessary in order for the computer to do what it needs to do! Nothing works without people, because people do the work!

Issue Triad Side 1 | Organizational Environment
CATEGORY 5:

Rewards

Rewards are incentives and schemes that are designed to support and reinforce desirable behavior among people. [17] They address how to motivate people to accomplish the work and execute the strategy that is laid out by the leader, and they help people to see the benefit of engaging in certain behaviors – those that are rewarded by the organization and its leader. In organizations that rely heavily upon volunteerism, rewards systems must revolve around something other than monetary compensation.

Regardless of whether you lead a for-profit or a non-profit organization, part of your work as a leader is to discover what motivates each of your workers or volunteers and provide that motivation in order to keep them fully engaged. This is critical for the success of the leader. Sometimes, this means simply recognizing the work that they have done and saying "Thank you." Other times, it might mean a personal touch – resting your hand on their shoulder while looking them in the eye and expressing your appreciation for something specific that they have done. In my church organization setting, I have found one of the most effective motivators to be public acknowledgement of my volunteers' efforts over the pulpit. Receiving accolades from the pastor for a job well done in front of their fellow congregants can leave my volunteers bursting with pride and feeling a great sense of appreciation, worth, and significance. Even better, this can translate into them being willing to pour their high level energy into doing more work for the church for the next several months – or even the next several years!

In the case of the CCC, Juan, the volunteer coordinator, would need to not only become skilled at recruiting volunteers; he would need to become masterful at motivating his volunteers so that they would feel valued and appreciated for their contributions and be willing to return to volunteer for future events. This has everything to do with creating an environment for volunteers that says, "We see you!" "You are welcome!" and "We appreciate your help!" Juan can begin developing this atmosphere by merely having simple refreshments like doughnuts and coffee upon the volunteers' arrival. Once the volunteers are up and running, performing their various functions, Juan could motivate volunteers by walking from room to room and personally thanking them by name and giving each and every one a personal smile. He could ask them how their families were doing, and if he was savvy enough to have learned and remembered their children's names, he could ask about their children by name, including how they are faring in their extracurricular activities. People like it when you remember their names, but they *love* it when you are caring and intentional enough to remember their children's names! Something as simple as this is a great motivator! It is prone to make a volunteer say, "Wow! He remembered my kids' names and that each of them plays a different sport! I like this place. They really care about me. I'll definitely be back!" Scientific research shows that when people feel cared for, significant and valued, the physiological reaction that they experience is like an injection of feel-good drugs – literally! You see, these motivating gestures stimulate the brain and trigger the release of dopamine, the "feel-good hormone," in the body. Thus, as the volunteers are receiving motivational feedback from their leader, they are literally getting "doped up" and feeling good about it! When the mind produces positive hormones, positive reactions are sure to follow; because they associate volunteering for your organization with "feeling really good for some reason," they will inevitably return when you call to request their services again!

Most of all, Juan's ability to keep his volunteers motivated is tied to his ability to maintain a volunteer-friendly environment. This means keeping things enthusiastic, upbeat, and positive. Music should be playing, lighting should be ample, and the atmosphere should be vibrant. As the volunteer coordinator, Juan should not be locked up in his office; he should be walking around with a big smile, because our smiles have a subconscious way of drawing people closer to us, as opposed to frowns, which tend to push people away. He should be constantly on the move, encouraging people and giving them good feelings, always ensuring that his body language and facial expression are open, lively, positive, and energetic. If he sees a volunteer with negative body language or a negative facial expression, he should immediately work to extinguish it , because a such a vibe can easily become contagious in a volunteer atmosphere if left unaddressed.

Essentially, the "people side" of the job of leader is that of regulating the atmosphere by doing things that make people feel inspired, motivated, and willing to pour their efforts – both required and discretionary – into the work that needs to be done.

Issue Triad Side 1 | Organizational Environment
SUMMARY & CONCLUSIONS

Without Evaluating Proper Position and Preparation, Potentials for Success Are Slim!

In summary, leaders must become skillful in answering the question posed by the Organizational Environment side of the Issue Pyramid, "Are we internally positioned and prepared as an organization to do what we are seeking to do?" In order to be properly positioned, an organization must have all of the components in place necessary to execute the idea or the initiative. In order to be properly prepared, an organization must have the people who understand the processes and sufficient rewards in place to keep them engaged. If the answer to the question is "No," the leader must then ask, "Are we able to make the necessary adjustments to position ourselves to do what we are seeking to do?" Without answering this critical question, leaders will undertake ideas and initiatives without a full awareness of whether their organizations can bring them to completion or not and whether the organization actually has the strength to meet the goals.

When Internal Units Do Not Work Together, Ideas and Initiatives Fail - Miserably!

An organization's strength to be able to meet its goals is directly tied to each unit of its organizational design's ability to work collectively towards a certain strategic goal. Although each of the elements of organizational design (strategy, structure, processes, people, and rewards) is an individual unit, each unit works in concert with the others to create an organizational environment in which ideas and initiatives can succeed or fail. If working effectively to support one another, ideas and initiatives will succeed, helping the organization to grow, thrive, and survive. However, if the units are not working effectively to support one another, ideas and initiatives will fail. Eventually, after a series of failures, the organization will come to its ruin.

For an example of how the elements of organizational design should work together, consider my own personal example of being a leader who was driven to increase his organization's online presence. First, I had to make a strategic choice to undertake this initiative for the sake of my organization's benefit. I assembled a strategy for the development of a website that was not only user-friendly and eye-friendly, but one that was also dynamic and mobile-friendly; one that would engage the customer and draw him in to interact with the various features of the website versus merely informing him. Next, I had to structure my organization in such a way that it could support my strategy. To accomplish this, I put together structured plans for content development, refinement, and insertion, data mining (to capture data from customers), media exchange, delivery, and rewards. Following this step, for each structural component, I mapped out a step-by-step, clearly-defined process of how to execute one, from start to finish. Then, I assigned people to each of the steps contained within the processes, and provided careful instructions on how to oversee and run each area along with checkpoints for accountability – moments when they would be expected to provide detailed updates of their progress. Finally, once the project was complete and all goals had been met, I executed the rewards component of the process by having a celebratory lunch for the team.

Things did not flow as smoothly for players in our story of the CCC. Juan, the volunteer coordinator, needed Carl, the marketing coordinator's assistance with bringing in volunteers to work the health screening event. Carl was responsible for designing and producing the promotional marketing pieces that Juan would use throughout the community to recruit volunteers. However, Blake, the accounting manager, limited Carl's budget, so he could only produce about a quarter of the materials that Juan would need to take into the community to recruit volunteers. Therefore, Blake and Carl's budget disagreement directly impacted Juan's ability to recruit enough volunteers to work the event. This wholeheartedly affected Jenny, the operations manager, who literally watched the program fall to pieces. Ultimately, this disappointing outcome worked its way up to John, who, despite all of his planning, skills, and experience, felt like he himself had failed in leading the organization in this project. The reality is that the event failed because of a systemic lack of coordination among each of the units in the organization's internal environment. Misalignments and unsupported processes often lead to failure, despite the skills and abilities of the leader.

If the Systems of Your Organizational Body Are Not Working Together, You've Got Issues!

When the individual units of organizational design are working together and supporting one another, everything flows smoothly in the organization, and many healthy outputs are produced. However, what happens when the units do not operate efficiently and support one another? The answer: the same thing that happens to the human body when its systems do not work together and support one another. To help you understand this, consider another personal example of mine. Some years ago, I had an appendectomy. After my surgery, as I lay in my hospital bed recovering, I experienced great abdominal pain – pain that was uncharacteristic following a procedure of this nature. Upon further investigation, my doctors realized that my colon and my intestines had folded on top of one another and formed adhesions, which were causing my digestive system to shut down. Although digestive enzymes were still being pumped into my stomach, my systems were not working together to move anything out of my stomach, and since food and water could not go down, after I ate and drank, it would all come right back up! My systems were doing more than not working with and supporting one another; they were fighting against one another! Eventually, I had to have surgery to remove the blockage in my intestines, and I had to go through a therapeutic process designed to help my systems cooperate. Only after this therapeutic intervention were my systems able to work together and support one another to the point that I could function healthily and, after one month, leave the hospital.

The Bible says that the whole body, being fitted and held together by what every joint supplies, according to the proper working of each individual part, causes the growth of the body for the building up of itself in love.[18] In essence, the Bible refers to the body as an organization which can only function if every joint, or unit, does its part to supply what ever resources it is designed to supply and if all of the joints, or units, work together to support one another. When they do, the body functions optimally and grows into what it has been destined to become. Just as the body is an

> *When things do not cooperate, they generally complicate!*

organization comprised of parts working cooperatively to achieve a certain outcome, so are our organizations. The work of the leader is to ensure that there is cooperation amongst all of the moving parts within the internal organization. Without cooperation in the internal environment, systems will become backed up, lines will become clogged, units will become frustrated, structures will break down, and the organization will begin to fail! Remember: when things do not cooperate, they generally complicate!

Good Ideas Rarely Fail, but People and Processes Do!

Good leaders stay aware of the internal workings of their organizations in order to lead them effectively. When leaders do not operate with such awareness, they tend to charge full steam ahead with their strategic choices, but because their organization's internal environment is not set up to support the strategic choice that has been made to push an idea or initiative forward, the strategy will fail before it can even get started. I have seen this happen often: a community expresses the desire for something and its willingness to pay for or patronize it, and consequently, the leader becomes passionate about it and leads the organization in attempting to provide the product or service. However, as they went along, they realized that this idea was beyond their organization's current capacity to produce. No preliminary assessment had been made concerning whether the internal environment was designed to effectively render the product at a certain cost or quality, and it was not until they were halfway into the production process that they realized that the undertaking was too ambitious of a goal and that the organization had an inability to produce what was demanded by the community. Therefore, the organization had to scrap its plans, midstream, and swallow the losses that it suffered in time, energy, money, and morale.

Before launching strategic ideas and initiatives, good leaders ensure that they are aware of the organizational environment into which they are launching them, and if sufficient support is not available to execute them, either adjustments to the organizational design must be made, or the idea or initiative must be tossed out of the window! For example, consider again the case of John, the CCC, and the failed health screening event. As the leader, John had discovered and was very clear on what was needed in the community: a health event that provided free screenings, consultations, and health information for those who could not afford them. Therefore, the idea was actually good. The problem with the event was not the need; the problem was that the CCC organization could not supply the need.

The CCC's failure to supply the need boiled down to various individuals within the organization running into roadblocks. Rather than making the necessary adjustments and finding detours around these obstacles, they simply stopped the process. For example:

- Could Carl, the marketing coordinator, not have come up with an innovative solution to be able to provide more marketing literature for Juan, the volunteer coordinator, to use when recruiting volunteers for the event?
- Could Carl not have reduced the size of the marketing literature so that he could produce more for the same cost? Could he not have sought out to get some of the printing donated by various

local printers in exchange for certain promotional opportunities at the event?

- Could Juan not have utilized a combination of handout literature and e-mails, which are free to send? Could he not have made community presentations, had interested people sign up on an interest list with their names and e-mails, and sent a series of flyers that Carl designed out to them?
- Were there any other innovative approaches that the individuals could have taken to ensure that their jobs were effectively completed, even in the presence of obstacles?

Most of the time, it is not the good strategic ideas that fail; the people who work the processes do. The ability to adjust or adapt to limitations or hindrances – also known as "issues" – in the internal environment can make all of the difference in whether processes fail or succeed and whether

> *It is not the good strategic ideas that fail; the people who work the processes do.*

visions crumble or manifest. When processes fail and visions crumble, it is typically because the people within the organization are not rewarded enough for thinking critically and finding their way around obstacles to get the job done.

Be Aware of Your Team's "Issues" when Crafting Your Game Plan!

Always keep in mind that regardless of how skilled and passionate the leader is, if the organization is not in a position to drive towards the goal or to readjust the goal, then the idea should be taken off of the table. Good leaders never put themselves in the position of undertaking strategic goals that their organizations cannot handle!

In the world of football, each football team possesses unique attributes that give them a competitive edge in some way over their opponents. It is the coach's responsibility to understand his organization's internal strengths and weaknesses. If the team's internal strength is its offensive line because it has a good running back, it is up to the coach to put together a game plan that makes full use of this strength – a running game. He should never put together a game plan that ignores his organization's internal strength – if he wants to win the game, that is. Therefore, I urge you as leaders to not only understand the internal workings of your organizational environment, but to establish a game plan – the strategic ideas that you undertake – according to your strengths. In approaching ideas and initiatives with full knowledge of how your internal environment operates and choosing to undertake only those that you are equipped to handle, you will always set yourself – and your organization – up to win the game!

> *Good leaders never put themselves in the position of undertaking strategic goals that their organizations cannot handle!*

CHAPTER 8

ISSUE TRIAD SIDE 2: EXTERNAL ENVIRONMENT

ASSESSMENT QUESTION:

What forces or considerations outside of my organization affect my cost and ability to do what I do inside of my organization – and my ability to continue doing it in the future?

While every organization possesses an internal organizational environment, every organization operates in an external environment.

The external environment is the market in which products and services are offered and sales are made, and a place where organizations compete to be selected over and above others by the consumers. Simply put, the external environment is where the "actions" – the transactions, that is – actually take place! These transactions can be between the organization and its suppliers, between the organization and its customers, or both!

Leaders must have a good understanding of where their organizations are positioned in the "environmental food chain." The environmental food chain helps us to understand how the various facets of the marketplace interact with one another, and it ultimately addresses how customers' needs are met by product and service providers, and at what cost. The environmental food chain consists of: 1) Needs, 2) Customers, 3) Product or services, and 4) Providers. Organizations can either be providers, or they can be the actual products or services themselves; in either case, they are helping to meet the needs of the customers that are in their environment. In order to be able to compete effectively in the external environment, leaders need to know exactly where they fall on the spectrum of the environmental food chain.

Leaders who are not aware of exactly where their organization's position is in the environmental food chain will find themselves being misguided in their efforts, trying to execute things that have nothing to do with their purpose in the market. Furthermore, they will be unaware of how changes in the external environment directly impact their ability to provide their products and services. Consequently, their customers will no longer choose them, money will no longer be flowing, the profits will stop, the business will be unable to sustain its operations, and the organization will be forced to close its doors.

For example, consider an organization that sells cassette tapes and compact disc (CD) products to the market. Based upon their positioning in the environmental food chain, they exist to provide a product to meet consumers' needs. However, the fact that they are still selling cassettes and compact discs suggests that they are clearly unaware that the needs of the market have changed; people rarely listen to these mediums of music anymore and opt to enjoy their tunes via

MP3's instead. Because this organization has forgotten that it exists to meet customers' needs in the external environment, it is not watching and closely monitoring the shifting changes in customers' needs. Therefore, because they are not keeping up with the customers' needs, they are sure to be out of business – obsolete and extinct – sooner rather than later. However, there are also many people who have extensive cassette tape and compact disc collections and who do not desire to just throw them away because music formats have changed. Organizations that are aware that they exist on the environmental food chain to meet customers' needs have noticed that this need is present, so they have shifted their services to meet customers' shifting needs: they provide a digital conversion service in which they take customers' collections of music on cassette and CD and digitize them into an MP3 format. Their keen awareness of where they fall in the environmental food chain and their ability to maintain an awareness of shifts in the external environment has helped them to adapt and excel in the marketplace!

Customers' changing needs are not the only thing that leaders must pay attention to in order to lead their organizations successfully in a constantly changing external environment; a number of other factors also play a significant role. Each and every one of these elements – and the changes that occur among them – plays a part in how efficiently and effectively an organization can produce its products or services and how relevant an organization is to consumers. This is the greatest consideration in whether the organization will be able to sustain itself and keep its doors open. As a rule of thumb, in order for the organization to be able to succeed, the rate of change inside of the organization must equal the rate of change outside of the organization. In essence, when changes occur in the external environment, good leaders see them happening and make whatever shifts are necessary in

> *As a rule of thumb, in order for the organization to be able to succeed, the rate of change inside of the organization must equal the rate of change outside of the organization.*

their internal environment to keep up with the environmental shifts! These leaders recognize that if they do not make the shift on the inside along with what is occurring on the outside, they will soon be without an organization to lead, because the need for what their organization offers will become extinct!

Perhaps one of the most prevalent examples of how changes in the external environment are affecting organizations' ability to stay relevant is that of what I like to call the "movie watching war"! It all started with Blockbuster Video, a brick and mortar chain of video stores into which consumers could go to rent movies on DVD. After so many years, Netflix entered the market, allowing consumers to order DVDs online and have them mailed to their homes; when they finished watching the videos, they would place them into the mail to return them and then wait for more videos to arrive in their mailbox. Netflix saved people a trip to the video store and offered the convenience of simply using the mail to receive and return their movies. When Blockbuster saw what Netflix was offering, it made the shift and also began offering movies in the mail!

Before long, Redbox emerged on the market. This company placed large, distinctive "red boxes" throughout communities so that people could walk up to the Redbox module, rent movies on DVD, receive them instantly, and only pay one dollar for them! Thus, not only did Redbox shorten the distance that consumers had to drive to rent movies from Blockbuster, but it offered them at a rental fee that was 75 percent less! Redbox also impacted Netflix, who realized that it had to lessen the amount of time that it took for consumers to receive their video rentals; since consumers could get their movies from Redbox on the spot; compared to Redbox, the two to four day turnaround that Netflix currently offered was now way too long!

Soon, Netflix had a genius idea, which marked an innovative turn in how our society would consume movies: on-demand video streaming. Netflix would now offer its customers the opportunity to bypass having to drive to the nearest Redbox in their community, and instead, simply log on to their computer, choose a movie, and begin viewing instantly! All of a sudden, the 10 minute round trip to the nearest Redbox became a 30-second trip to the Netflix website!

This latest advancement tapped into customers' need to have instant access to products; they valued the cost, convenience, and access to unlimited movie watching from the comfort of their own living rooms, and the service became a big hit! Trying to keep up with the trend, Blockbuster attempted to offer video streaming as well, but it was too late; the company could not make the necessary shifts quickly enough, and for the most part, its brand is retired. However, other companies, particularly cable companies, have followed Netflix's video streaming example. Now, most, if not all cable and satellite providers, offer video streaming so that customers can order videos from the comfort of their sofas and watch movies on demand. What will the next innovation in the movie watching wars be? Who knows? However, it sure is interesting to watch how changes in the external environment are affecting the way that these movie and entertainment organizations do business! For the most part, each of them is watching the external environment and making the necessary shifts, just as good leaders should!

Perhaps the greatest aspect of the external environment affecting the internal operations of organizations today is that of the mobile phone industry and wearable technology. They are completely altering the way that organizations must operate in order to remain relevant and maintain a foothold in today's marketplace! Rapid advancements in mobile phone and wearable technologies are resulting in the creation of a society that is totally customer-focused. For example, most of the younger generation spends its time not sitting in front of the television but in consuming media and entertainment using laptop computers, mobile phones, and tablet devices. As a result, when organizations create online media such as websites, they must make them mobile ready. This includes paying careful attention to how the website looks when it is viewed on a mobile phone, how the content appears as it is scrolled on the smaller screen of a phone as opposed to a computer monitor, how well the buttons can be accessed for fingers versus a computer mouse, etc. If leaders are not taking such things into consideration, they can easily find themselves leading their organizations in spending a lot of time, energy, and most of all money, doing the wrong things!

There are various aspects of the external environment that affect an organization's ability to compete successfully, and they typically fall into the following categories:

1) Market Trends
2) Technology
3) Demographics
4) Porter's Five Forces

Issue Triad Side 2 | External Environment
CATEGORY 1:

MARKET TRENDS

A trend is simply a pattern of gradual changes in a condition, output, or process over time[19], and a market trend simply refers to these shifts, changes, and developments in a general direction within the external environment. Simply stated, a market trend is a measure of how things are changing in the market. Organizational leaders must always be aware of these changes and shifts, because market trends will inevitably affect the organization's ability to compete in the external environment.

Knowing what to look for in terms of defining market trends and where they are headed is key in order for a leader to be successful. Many people tend to think that trends are always directly related to technology; as long as they keep up with the latest cutting-edge technology, they think they have a complete view of how society is changing. However, don't get locked into relying on what is happening in the high-tech world to be your major source of understanding how the markets are changing and in what direction they are heading! While technological advancements are major players in determining the shifts in the external environment, market trends are also driven by various other factors. For example, trends can be driven by new building projects, community or regional development, the local or national political climate, scientific developments, and even major current events.

One of the hottest means of determining what is trending in society is the medium of social media. Social media serves as a real time indicator of what has people's minds engaged and what they are thinking and feeling. It helps you to see what society is "buzzing" about! This is important, because you can be sure that whatever society is buzzing about will eventually affect your organization in one way or another. Why? Because the people in society are your market, what matters most to them should also matter most to you! Your ability to continue being relevant and appealing to them is largely determined by your understanding of who they are, and social media helps you to deepen this understanding by giving you a glimpse into what they are saying, where their thought processes are going, and who they are becoming!

Social media is a great way to get a glimpse into market trends, but it is not the only place a leader should look by far. Leaders should do their work, constantly gauging market trends through examining periodicals, perusing the internet, reading and watching the news, and reading local and national newspapers, either online or in print. Each of these will provide leaders with a different glimpse into what is happening in the world and how these trends stand to impact their organization, not only today, but in the future.

People in society are your market, so what matters most to them should also matter most to you!

Once smart leaders have a thorough understanding of what trends are occurring in the external environment, they ask themselves:

- How are these trends impacting my organization today?
- How will these trends impact me tomorrow?
- How can I capitalize on these trends?

While making these necessary assessments, I encourage leaders to think outside of the box. Rather than looking for the obvious, surface connections, seek out less conspicuous relationships between how market trends will affect the organization. For example, no one would think that the price of gas would directly impact financial donations to the church, but it does; I know this to be a fact from first-hand experience! When gas prices begin to soar, people are forced to make tough choices about where to cut back in their budget, and unfortunately, the very first place they tend to choose to cut back is in the area of their charitable contributions. Here's another one: few would consider that the weather could impact people's restaurant dining habits, but it does! In fact, research shows that 75 percent of U.S. restaurants report a sales plunge because of adverse changes in the weather.[20] Here's a trend that might surprise you. Few would consider that a presidential election year could impact the cost of gasoline.

However, research has repeatedly shown that during the July 4th weekend and the first week of November before Election Day, gas prices tend to decline more than twice as much as any other time![21] What's my point here? It's simple. Look for unconventional ways that issues in the external environment can impact the organization internally. This will take some research on the leader's part, but it will be well worth it. Think of it this way: your competitors are doing the research even if you are not, and this gives them the upper hand to be able to take advantage of trends and capitalize in a major way on them. Therefore, do your research and don't get left behind!

Issue Triad Side 2 | External Environment
CATEGORY 2:

TECHNOLOGY

Technology can best be described as the purposeful application of information in the design, production, and utilization of goods and services, and in the organization of human activities.[22] In layman's terms, it is simply applying what we know about science to some tool, machine, or practice that humans use in order to enhance it or advance it in some way. In today's society, technology is moving and evolving faster than at any point in human history, and its affects are having more of an effect on the internal workings of our organizations than ever before.

Any leader who is paying attention can see that technology is changing what consumers demand and how quickly they demand it. For example, advancements in technology in the external environment have completely reshaped people's expectation demands. Because technology trends have resulted in making things more accessible upon demand, people's expectations of how long they should have to wait to receive certain products and services are increasingly becoming shorter. As consumers, they expect to be able to access everything that they pay for "right now," and they do not want to wait! Thus, immediacy is no longer a luxury; it is an expectation. As much as having to alter the time it takes to deliver a product or service challenges the internal workings of an organization, savvy leaders will not fight this trend; they will adapt to these technology-driven changes and do what is necessary to meet the need!

Another means by which technology has altered people's expectations is that of connection. Whereas before, the terms "relationship connection" and "technology" were mutually exclusive, as a result of technology-driven changes in the external environment, today, they go hand in hand. What's more, this trend has taught us that it is indeed possible to get a genuine touch from an organization and build a strong, committed relationship through technology. Thus, organizations must find ways to connect and build relationships with people through technology. No organizations – not even churches – are exempt from this transition! Traditionally, church assemblies have been defined according to the number of people who travel to their brick and mortar structures for worship services. However, these days, our technology-driven society demands that churches offer opportunities to not only provide a constant flow of updated information and to receive donations, but to connect and build strong relationships through digital media in order to remain relevant. Try as they may to resist this trend, traditional churches that do not engage those in the online community will eventually find themselves among the relics of society!

How can I take advantage of this trend to make things more convenient, connected, and comfortable for consumers?

Smart leaders actively seek out opportunities to expand their offerings to fit the changing needs of their consumers, and their consumers' needs evolve as rapidly as technology does! This marks the need for organizations to remain flexible – fluid, dynamic, and readily able to adapt to changes as they become necessary. When good leaders see connections between how technology is driving change in the society, they ask themselves, "What is the connection between this technological change and what my organization can offer? How can I take advantage of this trend to make things more convenient, connected, and comfortable for consumers?" In answering these questions, the leader opens the door for innovation and for repositioning the entire organization for success!

As you assess the various uses of technology within your organization, do not be afraid to set your sights on what has not been done! Expand your "idea and initiative" filter so that you do not allow great ideas to be easily dismissed! I can recall one instance in which I allowed this to happen, and I have regretted it ever since. I have always had a heart to help those struggling with diabetes as a community initiative of my church. When Google Fiber, a super high-speed internet network became active in my city, the opportunities to integrate technology with various initiatives became unlimited! I developed what I considered to be a great idea that, if we could pull it off, would make us major players in the area of blood testing and diabetes management: have people wear some type of small technological device – wearable technology – that could monitor their blood sugar and report the results back to their medical service providers. When I presented the idea at a community meeting, the people at the table literally laughed at me – out loud – because they thought that such an idea was impossible! After all, it had never been done, so in their eyes, it could not be done. Recently, I saw an article online that reported how medical practitioners were using a trans-dermal tattoo that tests the blood sugar through the surface of the skin and transmits the readings to medical providers. As I read the article, I shook my head as I exclaimed, "Hey! That was my idea!" The idea was birthed out of my awareness of where technology was going and my desire to see the services provided to the diabetic community adapt to where society was headed. Unfortunately, I let it slip through the cracks, because I allowed people who were not adapting with technological changes to influence my perspective – the same people who are resistant to change and on their way to becoming obsolete!

> *People who are resistant to change are on their way to becoming obsolete!*

Leaders who resist adapting to technology-driven changes in the external environment run the risk of becoming like the famous red telephone booths that dot the city's landscape in London, England. If you have never traveled to London to see them, surely you have seen these familiar fixtures in photographs or even in movies. In fact, nowadays, you might even see them used as decoration in someone's house. Why? Because they have become a relic of times past and are now repurposed for different uses. In the past, their purpose was a functional one: people could stop in and make a phone call in the privacy of the convenient booths. However, with a society that has increasingly moved towards the use of mobile phones, there is now no longer a need for the red telephone booth.

Although these telephone booths are still seen as a British cultural icon throughout the world, they are rarely, if ever used for making phone calls. At most, a few of the boxes have been painted green and converted to free mobile phone charging stations, but for the most part, the days of their usefulness have expired; the need for the original service for which they were designed is obsolete. Therefore, I caution every leader: do not allow your organization to become a relic like the red telephone booth. Adapt to the changing trends of technology so that there will always be a need for what you have to offer! Remember: technology has not only become a part of our society and changed our society; it *is* our society!

> *Technology has not only become a part of our society and changed our society; it is our society!*

Issue Triad Side 2 | External Environment
CATEGORY 3:

DEMOGRAPHICS

Demographics are simply the characteristics that identify the people in a specific population. These factors include age, race and ethnicity, gender, socioeconomic status, employment status, education levels, and any other identifying characteristic that helps us to understand what type of people comprise a group of individuals. The demographics of a market are some of the first things that a leader should study. After all, before the organization can attempt to serve the people effectively, it has to know who the people are and how the people interact in the market.

Among the demographic factors that leaders should closely examine are trends like birth rates. This will help the leader understand where growth is occurring and where people who are having babies are choosing to live. Then, along with birth rates, leaders should also be examining death rates, because these numbers can also provide key insights into what is happening in the market.

Leaders should examine gender trends: what are the men and women like, what do they want, where do they buy, what is their preferred sales method (full-service at a brick and mortar store, online, or by mail), etc.? In fact, leaders should consider trends occurring among each segment of a market's demographics individually, for each characteristic of these potential consumers in the external environment will have a bearing on an organization's internal strategy. Are there any specific needs by age, class, gender, or educational level? What demographic segment is emerging as the big time players in the community?

As leaders continue to examine and periodically re-examine the demographics of their market, they will need to become skillful at identifying trends among these respective groups, assessing the needs associated with these trends, and getting in front of the trend by altering their organization's strategy to keep up with the needs of their target demographic group. For example, if the leader sees that the area in which the organization is situated has a Hispanic population that is growing larger and larger, in order to serve this population, the organization might consider adding on bilingual employees, developing its marketing materials in both English and Spanish, producing bilingual commercials, and undergoing some specific training on how to sell to and effectively connect with this market.

Most importantly, good leaders get in front of the trend and make the necessary adjustments so that when the growth actually happens, it is ready to meet the need. Waiting until the market appears and has already become established before the organization begins its shift will always be too late!

PORTER'S FIVE FORCES

Harvard Business School professor and leading authority on competitive strategy, Michael Porter, is known for developing a Five Forces Analysis that is commonly used throughout the business world as a means of helping leaders to determine the market strength of their organization and to make strategic decisions.[23] Generally speaking, Porter's Five Forces help leaders to measure how strong of a position their organizations occupy in the environmental food chain by answering questions regarding competitors, suppliers, potential entrants, substitutes, and buyers.

Force 1: Competitors

Your competitors are organizations within your market that offer the same or similar product that you offer to the same or a similar customer base. The fewer organizations there are providing the products and services that your organization provides, the better position you occupy. Conversely, the more competitors there are in your market, the harder you will have to work to maintain your share of the market. The presence of competitors means that people have options, so if you do not meet their needs, they can easily go to another organization to have their needs met. If you are the only organization in the market that provides the products and services that you offer, you occupy the best possible and strongest position; you can control the cost of what you offer without the fear of any other organization offering the same product or service at a lower cost.

In order to compete in the best way possible, ensure that you are clear about the basis upon which you are competing: differentiation or price. If your organization is competing on differentiation, you are saying to the consumer that you have a better product than your competitors or that your product is so different from what your competitor has to offer that people must come to you to get it. If you are competing on price, you are saying to the consumer that you can offer the same or very similar product or service that your competitors offer, but you can offer it at a lower price. Both are good ways to compete; however, as a leader, you must simply be clear on exactly how you – and your competitors – are competing.

When you do not understand your competition, you are prone to: 1) assume that everyone in your industry is your competitor, when they really are not, because they have different selling points or a different customer base; 2) erroneously believe that you are competing with a certain organization because they might be selling a similar product but competing with a different strategy; or 3) find yourself spending a lot of time, energy, and money against an organization trying to compete against something that does not call for the use of such valuable resources.

In order to be a successful leader, you must not only know your consumers, but you should always keep one eye on your competitors. If you do not, you will turn around one day and see that your competitors have invaded your share of the market! By maintaining a constant awareness of your competitors, what they are doing, and how they are adapting, you will always see them coming, and there will not be any surprises!

Force 2: Suppliers

Suppliers are those who furnish you with the raw materials that you need to produce your product or service. For example, if you are in the hamburger business, your suppliers would be those who sell you with the buns, ground beef, veggies, and equipment, but they would also include those who fix the equipment, process the payroll, provide the internet service, and power wash the parking lot. Anyone who sources you in any way that allows you to offer your quality of product or service to consumers is your supplier!

Wise leaders never underestimate the power and influence that suppliers have over what they produce. With one decision, suppliers could easily change the game and leave organizations scrambling for survival. When a supplier raises the price of a certain raw material that an organization needs to produce its products or offer its services, the organization must either pay the higher price or try to find a supplier who offers that same raw material for less. A prime example of this force in action is that of how crude oil suppliers can affect the price of air travel among various airlines. Crude oil is a major input cost for airlines – a necessary raw material that they need to run their operations. When the industry price-per-barrel of crude oil is on the rise, airlines must purchase the oil at the higher price; they do not have the option of going elsewhere to other suppliers to purchase the oil for less. Because the airlines must pay more to its oil suppliers, these expenses are passed on to the consumer through higher airfares.

If a particular supplier is the only source of a raw material and there is no other alternative from which the organization can obtain the raw material, the supplier holds all of the power in the relationship! The organization has to either pay whatever price the supplier demands, which will result in having to raise the price of the products it produces, or it must cease production on whatever products it makes using that specific raw material. Because suppliers have a direct impact on how much it costs organizations to do what they do and on their ability to impact organizations' bottom lines, suppliers have some real power.

Force 3: Potential entrants

A potential entrant is any other organization that could possibly enter the market to offer a same or similar product or service that you offer to the same or similar consumers. The easier it is for a potential competitor to enter the market that you are in, the harder you will have to work to maintain your market share. "Easy entry" suggests that there are few barriers between another organization's desire to do what you do and their ability to start doing it. Thus, there are potentially many other organizations that could easily enter the market and start selling the same products and services that you sell to the same customer base.

Typically, people will choose markets with lower "barriers to entry" rather than choosing to enter markets with higher "barriers to entry." For example, there will always be a lot of barber shops and hair salons in the marketplace, because getting these types of businesses up and running does not take a lot. All you really need is a lease space, chairs, mirrors, a shampoo basin, some styling tools, and hair products. However, there will not be a lot of automobile manufacturing companies or chemical processing plants, because these types of businesses take a more substantial investment to get up and running. Thus, there will be fewer potential entrants in this market, and as a result, less competition.

I have a friend who offers personal fitness services. Each day of his week is filled with one-on-one personal training in the gym, where he makes $25 per hour. A while back, I warned my friend that he was going to need to shift his business strategy, because it is too easy for potential entrants to enter into his market and take some of his market share. After all, if a person wants to become a personal trainer, all he needs to do is take a self-study course, take an exam, and receive a certificate identifying him as a certified personal trainer. This low barrier to entering the field meant that my friend would be facing a lot of competition in the near future. Thus, I encouraged him to go to a different format: group training. By offering personal training sessions in a group, he could stand to make upwards of $500 an hour versus training one person every hour for eight hours a day. Even better, he could make more efficient use of his time and offer several group training sessions a day to make significantly more money! Sad to say, my friend was reluctant to make this shift that I'd recommended. Five years later, he saw the market change, and unfortunately, he was behind the trend instead of in front of it.

As leaders, especially if you are in a market that is easy for potential entrants because the cost for entry is relatively low, it is important that you find ways to stand out and maximize your ability to profit! Continue to build a higher quality product, a competitive quality but less expensive product, and a loyal customer base, and as the new entrants enter the game, look for new and creative means to compete among them in order to win and maintain the upper hand!

Force 4: Substitutes

Substitutes are products or services that can meet or satisfy the same consumer needs that are met by the products and services that you have to offer. As a result of their ability to offer what you can offer, these products and services can easily be substituted for yours. Various things in the marketplace can be threatened by substitutes; substitutes are not just limited to products and services. For example, a new delivery method can be a substitute for the traditional method of delivering products in the mail. Companies like Amazon are aggressively researching the feasibility of using drones to deliver their goods so that consumers can receive their product orders that much more quickly – faster even, than companies like Federal Express, who must still deal with such uncontrollables as gas prices, the number of stoplights on the delivery route, and traffic! Thus, this substitute delivery method threatens to cut in on Federal Express' market share of the expedited delivery market. Anytime an organization can provide a product or service that is already being offered but with greater quality, speed, and convenience at an affordable price, their competitors better look out; a substitute is on the way!

I have heard people say, "You pastor a church! You're lucky that you don't have to always be on the lookout for someone who might try to come in with a substitute for what you have to offer! It must be nice to not have to operate with such a threat looming over your head." Oh, how wrong they are! Substitutes can pop up in *any* industry, and they will differ by market. For instance, in my case, people have indeed found substitutes for the church. Churches represent a physical gathering place where people can go to connect with one another, be encouraged, and feel a sense of care, community, and belonging. People have managed to come up with substitutes like book clubs, support groups, and even an atheist church – a church that includes every aspect of worship except God! This might sound strange, but places like these pop up all over our society, and because they meet most of the same needs that the church meets, people patronize them regularly!

Smart leaders not only look out for potential substitutes on the horizon; they look for ways to *become* a substitute! If you can develop a substitute – an alternative product, service, process, delivery method, etc. – that offers consumers more for their money, the key to maximizing the substitute is to get it out on the market first, because first is a great place to be!

Force 5: Buyers

Buyers are simply what their name suggests: those who offer you money in exchange for your product or service. You might be inclined to wonder, "Why would buyers be considered as one of the forces in the external environment that affect the way my organization does business?" The answer is easy: buyers are fickle! In most industries, loyalty is a thing of the past. Therefore, rather than sticking to consuming products and services from one exclusive provider, people shop around to look for what is most convenient or cheaper for them. Because of the lack of consumer loyalty in today's market, an organization can fare very well in its profitability in one quarter and then take a nose dive in the next, even though it has not changed anything about its product or service. Consumers have simply opted to choose something that met their needs in a better way!

Buyers have a lot of power these days as a result of their ability to drive costs up or down in a particular market. If they can find the product or service that you offer at a lower price, they will force your organization to either lower your price or improve the quality of your product in order for them to continue to choose you over your competitor's lower priced product. Simply put, organizations must do a lot to hold on to their customers these days, because these buyers have so many options! This dynamic is especially influential on organizations in the age of the internet. Rather than being restricted to shopping around the neighborhood or even around the country, people can now shop online, making the world their marketplace – and thousands of other companies internationally your competitors!

Each of Porter's Five Forces is a tool by which a leader can assess his organization's strength in the external environment. When I consult with clients about how to practically understand these forces, I often use the example of being a girl in high school during prom season. If you are the only girl in school, your choices for the prom are unlimited, because you have no competition: no other suppliers, high barriers to entry, and no substitutes to meet the demands of buyers. However, if you are *not* the only girl at the school during prom season, you will have competitors, each with something different to offer than you. For example, some girls might be taller, some shorter, some curvier, some slimmer, some smarter, some funnier, some more athletic, etc. Each of these characteristics might appeal to the boys in the school who are seeking a prom date in ways that you are not able to offer. Thus, you will have to work harder to get a prom date because you are competing against other girls for the same resources – a date to the prom.

The key to your organizational success is ensuring that you always have some level of strength in the environment. You don't need to be the best and strongest at *everything*; you just need to be the best and strongest at *something* if you will maintain a strong position in the external environment. If you are the prettiest girl, do all you can to remain the prettiest. If you are the strongest guy, do all you can to ensure that you remain the strongest. If you are the organization that provides the best quality service for the lowest price, ensure that you continue to do so. Then, even when you occupy such a position in the external environment, you should always keep a lookout for those who are bigger, faster, better, and stronger than you and your organization, because ultimately, these are going to be the ones that threaten to knock you out of your top position!

You might ask, "Is it really that important for my organization to try to occupy a strong position in the external environment?" My answer is a loud and resounding "Yes!" However, being the only choice or the best of multiple choices from which consumers can select to purchase a product or service among the competition is only part of the equation. Another means by which you can enhance your strength in the external environment is by increasing the level of control that your organization has over what it produces – its supplies.

The more elements, or supplies, that are necessary to produce your product or service that you can control in the external environment, the more power you will have over how much you can charge for what you have to offer. For example, if you are in the cattle business, and you own the land where the cattle are raised, which also means you own a place where you can grow hay and feed the cows, and you own an ample supply of water on the land, you have an advantage; you not only own the cattle, but you own all of the elements that are necessary to help them to grow and thrive. Contrast this with a cattle business that does not own much land where it can grow hay and that does not have a sufficient supply of water on its own land. This business will have to go out and purchase hay and water at whatever price the suppliers choose to charge. Even if the suppliers raise their prices sky high, the cattle business will have to pay, because the suppliers are in control of food and water, which are necessary for the cattle business to produce its product – healthy cattle.

The business that is not in control of its own supplies will pay a higher cost to produce cattle, while the business that is in complete control of its supplies of food and water will pay a lower cost. As a result, this same business can charge less for its cattle, which will result in more sales, and this can result in the business holding a very strong market position! Therefore, as a leader, as much as you are able, you should strive to be in control of as many of the supplies as possible that are necessary to produce your product.

Among discussions of how competitors and suppliers can affect one's position in the external environment, we cannot neglect the discussion of another force that makes a big difference in market position: potential entrants. When you consider an international behemoth of an organization such as Walmart, you are looking at a prime example of an organization that has grown so massive that it has virtually rendered potential entry into its field unattainable. Walmart was able to reach the highest possible market position among major departmental big box stores by squeezing out the competition. It achieved this position by growing the volume of the products it has to offer, not only throughout the U.S., but around the world!

While other stores might order ten thousand products to put into their stores, Walmart can order one million! In doing so, Walmart is able to get bulk pricing and volume discounts which result in the organization paying only a small fraction of what other stores have to pay in order to offer the same products. For example, while other stores might pay $1 for a sweater, Walmart can pay $0.79. Consequently, they can charge much less for their products, make a lot more sales, and maintain their position among consumers as the store of choice when it comes to purchasing general merchandise. This also means that any potential entrants that might desire to enter the retail game, of which this retail giant is the clear leader, should think again... and again and again! A business would have to have quite a bit of capital, quite a large network of stores – and let's face it – quite a huge ego to think that it could potentially enter into the big box general merchandising industry and successfully compete with Walmart! Walmart has a near monopoly on this sector of the retail industry. They don't only control the cost of products in the industry, but as a result of their size, they control what it takes to enter into the industry itself! Therefore, potential entry into the field is improbable. Walmart will not likely see any new competitors trying to creep into their field anytime soon! By the way, can you imagine your organization having this much control in an industry? What a market position *that* would be!

Issue Triad Side 2 | External Environment
SUMMARY & CONCLUSIONS

Get Things under Control if You Want to Occupy a Top Market Position!

In summary, leaders must become skillful in answering the question, "What forces or considerations outside of my organization affect my cost and ability to do what I do inside of my organization – and my ability to continue doing it in the future?" Leaders must know how much it costs for their organizations to do what they do, how their suppliers impact their ability to produce their products or services, what other organizations in the environment can do what they do, how easily other competitors can enter the same playing field, and how changes in society can impact what consumers choose to buy. These factors, or issues, in the environment help to equip leaders with the perspectives they need to make informed decisions about their organizations' future.

Consider this: if a leader examines his suppliers and says, "Wow! Our materials costs are way too high," this can prompt the organization to seek out other suppliers or service providers who can offer materials at a lower cost. Based upon the reduced cost of production, the organization is now in the position, if it desires, to lower the cost of its product in the external market, which could result in increased sales and a stronger market position. Ultimately, this results in a competitive edge for the organization; as long as the leader pays close attention to the external environment and maintains pace with it, it can continue to hold its edge in the market.

The less control you have over what you do, the greater the cost you will have to pay as an organization. This does not only apply to businesses; it also applies to organizations like mine – a church! For instance, my church and I put on a theatrical production every year. We are a mid-size church with a very tight budget, so we do not own our own big-budget theatrical equipment. Instead, when we put on our grand productions, we must go out to rent the lighting, sound equipment, and other materials and technology that are necessary to produce the event. Only twenty minutes away, there is another church – a mega church with a mega budget – that also puts on theatrical productions. However, because of their budget, they own their own high-definition cameras, lighting, sound equipment, theatrical supplies, and everything they need to put on a big show. Though we put on the same type of event, my smaller church has to work three times harder – and spend three times more – than the mega church down the street to produce the same product, and we still get a lower yield for the same event. Based on this, can you guess which of us has the stronger market position? I'm sure you guessed right!

Staying Aware of "What's Out There" in the External Environment Helps Leaders to Stay Relevant... and Stay in Business!

Successful leaders do not dare operate without knowledge of what is happening in the external environment, because they know that these issues can easily disrupt and compromise their organization's ability to function today and keep functioning tomorrow! They are always examining each factor and force in the external environment, because they understand that the slightest shift "out there" can make a big difference in how they do what they do in house. When they see things coming, they can make the necessary adjustments to their strategy so that their product or service continues to be relevant to consumers and so that they maintain or increase whatever position they occupy in the food chain within the external market.

Part of knowing what is going on in the external environment is having a clear picture of where one's organization falls on the food chain. We must face reality: not everyone can be on top! It is possible that a leader might realize that in one area of his business, his organization fares less than average in sales in the external environment due to forces beyond his ability to influence. In such cases, he might accept this as his reality; he could put less emphasis on this particular area of the business and place more focus on areas of the business that are doing much better in sales and that occupy a much stronger market position. In any case, once a leader is aware of what is happening in the external environment and how it is affecting his cost and ability to produce a particular product or service, he can make changes or modifications that are informed and realistic. In addition to adjusting his organization's strategy, he can also adjust his own expectations so that they are more realistic.

Smart Leaders Use the Forces in the External Environment to Push Them where They Want to Go!

I always stress to leaders the importance of being aware of what is happening outside of their organization's doors, because they must survive in this environment! These issues impact them, their bottom line, the people in their company, and even their brand, so they must remain constantly aware of them and be willing to make the right adjustments at the right times in order to move their organizations into the best possible position. While they might think that undertaking extensive strategic plans and exercising a lot of effort to pull their organizations into a good market position, I offer them another alternative: allow the market to push you there!

Leaders can use the force of current market trends to push them and their organizations to where they desire to be. In other words, they can use the momentum from forces that are already active in the environment to push them forward. My favorite example of making use of external forces in this way is that of a sailor navigating a sailboat as it glides through the ocean waters. All a smart sailor has to do is adjust the boat's sails so that the force of the wind can push the boat forward. As a leader, you need only to adjust your organizational sails so that the forces in the environment can push you out and propel you forward!

Stay in your lane, stay in your game, and stay focused!

128

Most importantly, as you glide through the waters, do not try to compete with the size and speed of the boats with the big motors, because you are in a different league; you are not playing with the same set of tools. Stay in your lane, stay in your game, and stay focused on leveraging the changing winds of the external environment so that you can use them to your advantage by allowing them to propel you forward!

These Days, Strategy is Dynamic, *Not* Static!

The various elements that we deal with in today's climate have made the external environment a volatile one! It is always changing and never staying the same for long. In light of this, for you to remain static in your approaches to strategy is foolish. Why would you remain standing still and fixed upon your approach when everything around you is moving, changing, shifting, and evolving every single day! In order for an organization to survive today, it must be led by a leader that recognizes that today's strategies must be dynamic, fluid, and flexible, not static. They are to be mobile, not fixed and steady.

You know that you are being dynamic in your strategy when you are intentional about staying aware of trends in the external environment and leading your organization in following the trends. In fact, when wise leaders develop a strategic plan, they develop it with several possible outcomes built into it, and they make adjustments along the way according to changes that occur in the external environment. One of my favorite real world examples of an organization that has successfully made a shift with the trends is that of Marvel Worldwide, which is commonly referred to as "Marvel Comics." Marvel began as a comic book company in the 1950's; it published paper comic books that youngsters, a small segment of older aficionados, and collectors would purchase from the local convenience store. Over time, however, comic books lost their appeal and popularity among a high-tech generation. Sales tanked, and Marvel was losing money year after year. Marvel's leaders realized that although the comic book had become a dinosaur, its characters were still exciting, engaging, and marketable. People loved the stories of Marvel's heroes like Spider Man, the Fantastic Four, the X-Men, and Iron Man, among many others. However, because consumers were no longer purchasing comic books, Marvel would have to find another market-appropriate way to deliver these entertaining stories. In 2009, The Walt Disney Company acquired Marvel, and the rest, as they say, is history! Working together, the team turned the entire superhero industry around, producing action-packed cinematic blockbuster after blockbuster based upon the beloved Marvel characters and grossing billions of dollars in theatre receipts over the years![24] All it took was a shift in the strategy of how they delivered their product in order to make the consumption of their characters appealing. Once they tapped into the trends of how the market was consuming entertainment and were able to effectively connect to their customer base, they hit the entertainment jackpot!

As you consider how to keep your organization moving with the trends in the external environment, take special note that following trends is *not* the same as being trendy! Organizations that follow trends strategically adapt what they are already doing to fit the needs of consumers, which are changing with the trends. Organizations that are trendy see something happening in the market, adopt an entirely new strategy, and continue executing this strategy, riding it out until the trend is no longer popular. My encouragement to you is to not be trendy. Instead, be strategic as you follow trends in the external environment! However, do not be committed to a fixed strategy; be only committed to the success that comes with being able to ebb and flow with the trends and make the necessary changes and shifts along the way!

CHAPTER 9

ISSUE TRIAD SIDE 3: ORGANIZATIONAL CULTURE

ASSESSMENT QUESTION:

What is the structure and style of this organization's culture, and am I working with it or against it as I implement change?

In order to operate effectively, leaders must understand the distinctions between their organizational environment and their organizational culture. There are real differences that must be dealt with here! The culture of an organization refers to the values and behaviors that contribute to the unique social and psychological environment of an organization.[25] It encompasses the shared ways in which the people within your organization talk to one another, the language you use, the ways in which you move amongst each other and interact, what you believe, what you value, and how you get things done. Culture details not what you do as an organization but how you do it – how you process things and flow together, how you connect and transmit information, how you react and respond to one another, and even how and when you smile at one another. The environment merely refers to the surroundings in which your organization operates. While organizational culture describes the ethos or attitudes that shape your organization, the organizational environment describes the actions that take place around the organization. Thus, the culture is the air upon which the environment lives and thrives!

I recall a particular instance in which the importance of considering an organization's culture into an analysis was impressed upon my psyche like never before. I was brought in as a consultant for a German Lutheran church in my city to do some organizational leadership and church growth work. One of the first areas in which they requested immediate help was that of church growth. After assessing the church's atmosphere, it was very clear that one of the actions that they could immediately take to facilitate church growth was that of being friendlier as they welcomed people into the church. Once we all agreed on this need, I began to recommend several strategic actions that could be easily implemented and that would make them seem warmer, friendlier, hospitable, and a more inviting congregation. After listening intently to my recommendations, they agreed to implement all of them except one: they would not agree to smile at their guests. Now, this might seem like an absurd notion to you, because one of the first things that we recognize as an invitation to friendship in our society is that of a smile. However, I came to learn that a characteristic of German Lutheran culture is that they do not smile much at one another; they are a very stoic group. Even though being friendly made sense to them, and even though they recognized a clear need to be friendlier in order for their church to grow, they simply refused to incorporate smiling into these friendliness efforts, because according to their culture, smiling did not make sense to them. You see, culture, and everything that goes into creating it within an organization, really matters!

In the same way that leaders must be aware of their internal environment and ensure that it keeps pace with continual changes in the external environment, they must also carry the same level of awareness regarding how their external surroundings affect their organization's internal temperature – their organizational culture. Always keep in mind that organizations do not exist in a vacuum; everything that happens "out there" impacts what is going on "in here." Leaders must keep their fingers on the pulse of the external environment, not so that they can know "if" something will affect the way they do business, but "when" and "how"! Without ensuring that the organization's culture matches pace with the external environment, their organizations run the risk of losing their relevance to the base of consumers that they exist to serve.

I have a beautiful Betta fish in my office – you know, the popular, low-maintenance aquarium breed with the large flowing fins and brilliant colors. My fish's internal environment, the aquarium, has to be maintained with lots of free space, clean water, and oxygen. Most importantly, his aquarium must be maintained at a constant temperature of 23°C – 27°C (76°F - 82°F). It is only within a culture of this temperature that he will be able thrive, interact with and respond to people who approach to view him, and even survive. There are also other cultural considerations for my male Betta, like the fact that he cannot live with other male Betta fish, that he prefers to live alone, and that he may kill other fish or snails if they are added to the tank. In addition, Bettas do not like strong water filters, because they can produce currents that are too strong for them. They also dislike jagged rocks, decorations, and hard plants, which can damage their large, free-flowing fins, and mirrors placed along the side of the tank, which can stress out the fish by causing them to think that there is a rival in their territory. Lastly, Bettas enjoy having fresh plants in the tank because they allow them a place to hide and sleep.

I'll bet that you never realized that fish could have such a complex culture, did you? Surprisingly, these details only comprise part of my

Betta's culture! Another significant part of his culture is how changes are made in his internal environment. Like any other organization, my Betta's organizational environment, or culture, does not exist in a vacuum; there is an external environment that impacts it. For example, my fish's external environment is my office. Any changes in the temperature of my office will have an effect on my fish's internal environment and culture – his surroundings and how he acts and interacts within the aquarium. Therefore, I must keep my office at a certain temperature in order for the water in his aquarium to remain optimal for his functioning and survival. Thus, part of my Betta's culture is that he is totally dependent upon me to regulate the temperature of his aquarium. If, by chance, changes in my Betta's external temperature do occur because my office is too cold, it is up to me to make changes in the aquarium – by installing a heater, for example – so that my beautiful and beloved Betta can continue to function and stay active and involved.

Successful leaders know that you cannot discuss culture without simultaneously discussing change. Why? Because changes are always occurring in the external environment, and successful organizations are always adapting their environments to accommodate these changes in the internal environment in order to remain relevant; however, the culture of an organization entails a discussion of its structure and style, which dictates *how* these changes can be made within the organization! Depending upon the structure and style of an organization, different strategic approaches must be taken to implement changes within its internal environment in order to keep the organization functioning, thriving, and surviving.

> *An organization that does not change is like stagnant water: the only things that grow in this type of water are bacteria and disease, which lead to death!*

You might wonder about what happens when leaders do not assess their organization's culture and implement changes according to it. The answer is simple: they do not change. Flowing water is always changing, and as a result, it keeps things fresh and gives birth and new life to things. However, an organization that does not change is like stagnant water, and stagnant water is much different; the only things that grow in this type of water are bacteria and disease, which lead to *death*! Thus, when organizations do not do what is necessary to effectively implement changes within their organization – like considering their organizational culture – they become stagnant, and their inevitable demise is likely soon to come!

There are several ways in which the structural and stylistic considerations of culture can impact how changes are made in the internal environment in order to keep pace with changes that occur in the external environment. Per Cameron and Quinn (2006)[26], they typically fall into the following categories:

1) Market
2) Clan
3) Adhocracy
4) Hierarchy

MARKET

Example: Walmart

An organization whose cultural structure or style contains a market orientation operates by taking measurements and assessments of what people are doing in the environment and using this information or research in order to develop strategic approaches to gain more clients, consumers, or customers. This type of structure is heavy on measurement, evaluation, and analysis of the competition and is typically characterized as a statistically-driven organization. It thrives upon winning by being the best, competing at the highest level, and outperforming their competitors.

In order to lead internal change within their organizations as they seek to keep pace with changes in the external environment, leaders of organizations with a market orientation must be fast processors while at the same time being highly analytical; they must make informed, well-researched, and educated choices about the new direction and strategies that the organization will follow in order to remain on top in their industry. They must be able to make quick decisions about important matters, provide their workers with hard guidelines on how to stay competitive, and educate their workers on how to execute with excellence. These types of leaders are demanding, and they lead organizations with a demanding culture. However, the better they are at leading change in this type of culture, the better and more competitive their organizations will be. Organizations with these types of cultures often dominate their industries!

Despite their successes, however, there are potential pitfalls associated with a cultural structure or style that operates according to a market orientation. For example, because the structure is so numbers-driven, analytical, and intent upon competing and demolishing the competition at any cost, it can easily tend to ignore the human element. Consequently, it will not see customers and consumers as people;

rather it will see them as giving units. It will also not see its workers as humans with social and interpersonal needs to be addressed by the organization; it will see them instead as nameless, faceless hirelings – tools or cogs on an assembly line – in a one-sided relationship that meets the needs of and benefits only the organization.

Issue Triad Side 3 | Organizational Culture
CATEGORY 2:

CLAN

Example: Southwest Airlines

An organization whose cultural structure or style contains a clan orientation operates according to a more family-style, highly-relational, and team-centered approach. In this type of organization, it is common to hear people use a lot of "We" and "Our" in their dialogue with one another, because there is a collective sense of ownership of the organization and the mission that it seeks to realize. In a clan-oriented organization, the emphasis is not as much about competition as it is about collaboration and cooperation. Thus, those with knowledge of certain areas seek to mentor those without that knowledge, and those who are a part of the team seek to bring aboard those who are not a part of the team. Ultimately, the culture operates according to the belief that if everyone works together, everyone in the organization will be successful – not just the organization itself.

In order to lead internal change within their organizations as they seek to keep pace with changes in the external environment, leaders of organizations with a clan orientation must be maternal or paternal, into caring for people as individuals rather than just as a group, touchable, approachable, and inviting. They can often be seen smiling, resting a hand on a worker's shoulder while asking about his or her weekend or family members by name, and working alongside the workers themselves to accomplish a certain task or goal.

As warm, personable and appealing as this cultural approach might seem to those within the organization, however, the clan-oriented culture also has its share of potential drawbacks. For example, leaders might become so people-focused that they lose sight of the organization's true goals: maximum productivity, sales, and financial sustainability. Rather than gearing their focus towards doing what is necessary to compete for the top spot in the industry and increase their profits, they might be found spending their time and energy addressing the psycho-social needs and concerns of their workers, trying to make everyone feel okay while they are doing the work. Another potential drawback that leaders of this type of family-like clan-oriented structure might face is that of the inability to maintain certain systems or standards. Because the culture is so relationship-oriented, rather than penalize people within the organization for violating certain standards or operating outside of defined systematic procedures, this type of culture is prone to simply let things go. After all, they feel, they are family; because of the love that exists amongst the family members, they do not desire to disappoint or hurt any family member's feelings. In the meanwhile, while everyone's feelings are being preserved, the organization suffers from lack of standardization and is less stable because its systems are consistently being violated!

The culture of the church organization that I lead is actually clan-oriented. When we decide to make a change, we are not faced with navigating through five different layers of approvals, filling out a mountain of paperwork, or obtaining a host of signatures before the change can officially be adopted.

Issue Triad Side 3 | Organizational Culture
CATEGORY 3:

ADHOCRACY

Example: Apple

An organization whose cultural structure or style contains an adhocracy orientation operates according to a highly energetic climate that promotes idea generation, innovation, and new ways of thinking. Such organizations are often contrasted with organizations having a more bureaucratic orientation, because they are more flexible and easily adapt to change as necessary. In light of this, there are not a lot of lines and hurdles to jump over when it is time to make decisions and implement change. They are very "flat" organizations. Adhocracy-oriented organizations do not suffer from change-inhibiting structural inertia, which is characterized by belief systems that say, "We've *always* done things this way, so we are going to *continue* to do things this way!"

In order to lead internal change within their organizations as they seek to keep pace with changes in the external environment, leaders of organizations with an adhocracy orientation must be open and welcoming of ideas, regardless of whether they are modifications of existing ideas or new ideas completely. They must be encouraging of these ideas even if they seem to be completely out of the box, because the last thing that good leaders desire to do is shut down or discourage the idea creation process. Thus, leaders should endeavor to nurture people's willingness to present new ideas without the fear of judgment or criticism.

An adhocracy-oriented leader must not only welcome but test ideas very quickly, because innovation is a process that moves rapidly in today's fast-paced society! Also, because the organization moves to implement change so quickly and easily, many mistakes will be made along the way, particularly in the details that tend to get lost when things are being driven at a hundred miles per hour. Therefore, leaders of this type of organization must know that a lot of mistakes will be made, so they must leave room for them. Such is the price that must be paid for fast-paced innovation. The benefit, however, is that these mistakes or "bugs" can be fixed at a later time, once the work has been done, the product has reached the market, and the billions of dollars have been made!

Like other stylistic and structural cultural orientations, the adhocracy-oriented culture has pitfalls. Although this type of organization can easily implement new ideas in order to remain relevant, it can tend to move so quickly in the process of doing so that it is prone to throw out ideas that have not been given a fair chance. Before allowing an existing idea sufficient opportunity to work for a reasonable amount of time and produce results, they prematurely toss the idea out in order to implement a new and improved approach that promises to work better and produce results more quickly. Thus, this type of organization runs the risk of skipping over the value of things that are fundamental in the system, simply because it values innovation and "new things" to such a large extent.

Issue Triad Side 3 | Organizational Culture
CATEGORY 4:

HIERARCHY

Example: IBM

An organization whose cultural structure or style contains a hierarchical orientation operates according to levels of bureaucracy, from high to low, each with its own level of power to act and decision-making authority; there are clear lines of demarcation and power, and clear, published policies and procedures governing how things are to operate within the organization. Further, these organizations tend to do a lot of training in order to keep the policies and procedures at the top of their workers' consciousness so that they can be consistently maintained. With a hierarchically-oriented organization, the idea is to put as many systems, processes, rules, and procedures into place so that there is standardization throughout the organization; each time something is done, it is done the same way – regardless of who does it – so that the outcome is always the same. Because of the way in which these types of organizations are organized, it is not an easy task for a change to be implemented. Instead, it takes much bureaucratic activity, from introducing the idea according to a formal process, filing applications, allowing the idea to go through the proper channels to be considered, meetings, approvals from various levels of authority, fulfilling requests for more information, paperwork – and then more meetings and approvals! Once the idea has been approved, the process of implementing the change is equally as cumbersome in such an organization. However, there is an upside to organizations that are hierarchically arranged: you can have great confidence that they will produce the same system and output over and over again. This is a great advantage!

In order to lead internal change within their organizations as they seek to keep pace with changes in the external environment, leaders of organizations with a hierarchical orientation must be very strong and organized. They operate at the top of a system comprised of people possessing differing measures of power, so part of their work is that of mitigating the conflicts that can tend to occur between these varying levels of power. Leaders at the helm of these organizations must be very analytical in their thinking, straightforward in their communications, and systematic in their operations. These are the types of characteristics that are most valued, respected, and necessary in order for a hierarchical organizational culture to implement change and function day to day. Because of the need to maintain systemization and standardization of the organization, leaders of hierarchically-oriented organizations must be demanding; there is no room for concessions or compromise, because these are the factors that erode the foundation of what the organization represents.

Considering the functioning of a hierarchical organization, it is no surprise that it comes with a built-in set of potential pitfalls. For example, as a result of the time that it takes to navigate all of the red tape bureaucracy in the organization, ideas about change are less likely to be introduced in these settings. When they are introduced, the time that it takes to go through the proper approvals and be adopted by the organization could easily discourage those attempting to introduce change. In fact, the ways in which these organizations are internally constructed actually discourage the introduction of new ideas and leave very little room for customization or individuality within the organization. The hierarchically-oriented organization operates according to the "We do it this way, we have always done it this way, and we will continue to do it this way!" ethos. As a result, the humanity and individual needs of workers can easily be ignored in this type of organization, as they are often being perceived as simply nameless, faceless slots on an organizational chart.

Issue Triad Side 3 | Organizational Culture
SUMMARY & CONCLUSIONS

In summary, leaders must become skillful in answering the question posed by the Organizational Culture side of the Issue Pyramid, "What are the structure and style of this organization's culture, and am I working with it or against it as I implement change?" Without answering these critical questions, leaders will find themselves ineffective at leading change within their organizations. Rather than implementing strategic change in a way that is best received by the culture, they will attempt to "force fit" change in a way that does not match the way their culture operates. As a result, their efforts to change in order to keep pace with the external society will be unsuccessful, and they will feel ineffective as leaders.

Despite all of their plans and strategies, they will often end up sitting at their desk behind the closed door of their office totally shocked by their inability to get their people to move and implement change. They feel like a character in an old-time western movie, a newcomer who comes into town with new approaches to doing things, only to receive the response from the resistant townspeople, "We don't operate like that around here in these parts!" As they assess their ineffectiveness, leaders might even begin to think that their people are simply resistant or that they are outright and overtly rebelling against leadership. Other feelings, like frustration, resentment, and feeling blocked by some powerful yet invisible force, are sure to follow. However, most often, the reality is that leaders simply do not understand the culture of the organization – how the organization operates. Leaders should take the time to assess the culture of their organization to ensure that their efforts to bring change match the way in which the culture receives change.

The Culture is the Air that
We Breathe in the Organization!

Effective leaders must have an accurate understanding of what culture actually is in order to be able to properly relate to an organization. One of the clearest examples that I offer to my clients in an effort to assist them with understanding this notion is that the culture is the air that everyone breathes in an organization. Culture is widespread and pervasive, and whether they recognize it or not, it affects every single person in the organization. They cannot see it, because while some aspects of culture are visible, other aspects are invisible. However, it is there, and it is what keeps the people and the organization breathing and functioning!

Without understanding the culture, a leader could make some critical moves that are incongruent with the organizational culture, and these moves could ultimately cause the organization to suffocate and die. For instance, consider a Siberian tiger. These powerful and majestic felines are among the largest cats walking the earth. They are savvy hunters and feared by prey of all sizes, from moose, wild pigs, and rabbits, to the salmon that they skillfully pick out of a stream. On land, there is little that can compete with the Siberian tiger; however, if you throw that same animal into the middle of an ocean, what would happen? The Siberian tiger is able to be a major competitor on land because this is the culture that is most advantageous to the way that it functions. However, just because it is a major competitor on land, we cannot assume that it will be as equally competitive in another context or culture.

So it goes with leaders. Without an adequate understanding of their culture, leaders will assume that their organization is able to do things that it is not designed to do! Consequently, when they try to implement new, strategic moves that are not congruent with the culture, although their organizations are staffed with great people, the culture does not allow them to do what they were hired to do! People – at least, those who are healthy and functional – possess an inherent need to feel a sense of efficacy; they want to feel a sense of worth, value, and effectiveness. When people are constantly engaged in activities in which their efforts are hindered or obstructed and in which they are unable to maximize the skills and talents they possess in order to accomplish a goal, they will eventually become discouraged, restless, and unproductive. In turn, these negative feelings will feed back into the culture, creating workers who have lost their motivation to move forward because they feel that their efforts are futile! Isn't it interesting that such a "small" thing like a leader's inability to consider the organization's culture when making strategic decisions can have such a huge impact on the organization? This goes to show that everything, even the "little" things, matters in the leader's assessment when approaching an organizational issue!

Alignment between the Leader and the Culture Is SO Important!

Alignment simply refers to being able to see eye to eye and operate the same way, both of which are necessary in order for an organization to function efficiently and effectively. Simply stated, the leader's style of leadership and of making decisions must be congruent with the way that the organization operates – its culture. When leaders implement methodologies that are deemed feasible after a careful consideration of the organization's culture, there is a greater sense of alignment, and consequently, a greater level of productivity within the organization. On the other hand, when leaders attempt to implement methodologies that do not take the organization's culture into consideration, much anger and frustration will result. The people will neither react to the leader's ideas the way that he or she thought they should react nor execute the new methodologies according to the leader's expectations. In fact, when leaders try to move against the culture of the organization, they can expect a lot of pushback from the people.

Surely you've seen the movies or television shows in which the company hires a new leader – one very different from the way the company currently operates – to come in and "whip the business into shape"! As the confident, high-powered executive stands at the front of the conference room and announces that "This is the way that things are going to work around here from now on" and goes on to spell out all of the new changes that are about to take place, the workers silently shoot glances across the table at each other with looks that clearly ask, "Who does this guy think he *is*? That's not the way things work around here!" Then, when they break from the meeting, as they huddle in their small clusters around the lunch room, they openly discuss the new suit that has come to completely disrupt their work lives, making statements like, "If that woman thinks that she can just come in here and take over the way we operate, she has another thing coming!" or "That guy might think that he can just saunter in here and start shooting around orders and commands, but I'll bet you *I'm* not going to do *a thing* he says!"

When there is a lack of alignment between the leader and the organizational culture, inevitably, one of two things will happen: either the workers will sabotage the new leader, or the new leader will have to fire the workers. Be clear to understand that the message here is not that an organization can never bring in a new leader to make changes. Instead, the message is that when a new leader is brought into an organization, he or she must seek to operate in alignment with the ways in which the culture already operates. After the leader has earned the people's trust, learned about the people and the ways in which they operate, and become intimately familiar with the culture, *then* subtle changes can continually be made until the organization is functioning the way that the leader desires!

One of the most interesting examples of a lack of alignment that I have come across in my research is that of Walmart, when it attempted to expand its retail operations into the Asian market. These efforts initially failed because of a lack of understanding of Asian culture! You see, in the United States, just before a shift begins, the leader will call all of the store's employees together for a rally to get everyone motivated. Leaders begin by clapping their hands, getting the workers riled up, and pumping up the people by saying, "Come on! This is our day! We're going to make it happen! We're going to meet our sales goals! Let's work together! We can do it!" By the end of the pre-shift rally, there is lots of clapping, shouting, and cheering, and all of the employees are excited, encouraged, and eager to get on their posts!

However, remember: that's the way things are done in the U.S. culture. What Walmart did not realize is that in the Asian culture, the clapping and such boisterous expressions were offensive! In fact, the workers were *really* disturbed, as they wondered why their managers were yelling at them every day! What was effective for Walmart in the U.S. culture clearly did not transfer with the same level of effectiveness to the Asian culture!

We can also examine the same principle of "one size does not fit all" in regards to the non-profit sector and the for-profit sector; what works well in one does not necessarily work as effectively in the other. For example, a person who thrives as an employee or leader in the for-profit sector might fail miserably in the non-profit sector, and vice versa. The cultures tend to be completely different! When a people's cultural orientations are that of the for-profit sector, leaders are accustomed to using money to motivate their workers, and workers are accustomed to being motivated by money. Further, they are often both accustomed to having budgets to getting things done, the latest technology, resources, and equipment, and some of the best skilled labor money can buy to pull their weight on the team and get things done. However, when people's cultural orientations are that of the non-profit sector, leaders must find other creative ways other than money to motivate their workers (because money is typically scarce in non-profits), and workers must discover some other intrinsic means of being motivated outside of money. They must also tap into their sense of innovation to compensate for a lack of budget, technology, resources, and top-level labor, because there is no money available to pay for such "luxuries." In light of these considerations, what works in the culture of the for-profit world, including people and ideas, might not work in the culture of the non-profit world, and the opposite is also true. There must be alignment between the leaders, the workers, the ideas, and the culture in order for the organization to perform at its maximum level of productivity!

When a Leader is a Mismatch with the Culture's Structural Orientation, *Somebody's* Got to Go!

Every culture has a leadership style that works best with it. Ideally, a leader must be able to flow with the way that the organization's culture operates. When you think about it, to have such an expectation makes perfect sense! Let's say that recent advancements in the external environment call for changes to be made in the internal environment. There are many aspects of culture, but in such a case, it is the structural orientation of the culture that must be considered. If the internal environment is hierarchically-oriented but the leader is clan-oriented, the leader will attempt to push strategic changes through while violating a host of systems, policies, and procedures. To share the strategic changes, rather than follow the organization's formal communication process (which usually consists of a memo disseminated through an e-mail or interoffice mail in a hierarchical culture), the leader would hold several office meetings with various individuals and small groups of workers or even take a few workers to lunch to discuss the changes. Once enough people have signaled their buy-in, the leader will simply hold a meeting with all of the workers to introduce the new strategic change and how everyone should begin operating according to the new change immediately – no revisions of policy and procedure manuals, no formal presentation, no series of trainings – just a conversation. This approach might sound harmless, but the clan-oriented leader has completely violated the hierarchically-oriented organizational culture, and workers at every level of the organization are throwing flags on the play, setting off alarms, expressing their frustration, and calling for immediate corrective action – even termination – to be taken with the leader! To add to the frustration, the leader cannot understand what the big deal is.

The big deal is the mismatch between the leader and the cultural structure and style of the organization that he or she leads. It is important for the leader's and the organization's orientations to line up, because this will result in greater compatibility, workability, cooperation, and productivity within the organization. In the corporate world, if a new leader is brought in to run a company and there is a mismatch between the leader's orientation and the organization's orientation, the power brokers usually decide that the leader has to go! However, if the leader is the founder or holds a great deal of power and influence in the organization and the staff is a smaller one, it might be the staff that has to go. It's kind of like politics: whenever a new leader, like a president, governor, or mayor is elected, once he or she moves into office, all of those who worked for the former public official are out, and all of those that the new leader has hand-selected to be a part of the new regime of leadership take their places. They surround themselves with people that they can work with, flow with, and who are accustomed to working with their style of leadership. They and other successful leaders recognize how critical a leader's ability to flow with the organization is to their effectiveness!

One particular organization that I know of, a national chain of pawn shops with nearly 900 stores throughout the U.S. and internationally, is currently dealing with the challenges that go hand in hand with a leadership and organizational culture mismatch. You see, the organization has operated with a clan-oriented culture since opening its very first store in 1983. Just recently, more than 30 years later, the organization realized that operating with a clan-oriented culture was not birthing the results it desired. Thus, the decision makers decided to move towards a more corporate, hierarchical structure. In light of this, the corporate brass is actually firing everyone associated with the clan-oriented culture, from the top down – from the Vice Presidents on down to the local store managers. It might seem like a brutal move to make, but corporations do what corporations do in order to move forward and implement the types of changes that will ultimately maximize their bottom line – profit!

You Cannot Assess a Culture that You Cannot *Fully* See!

As a professional consultant, I always advise my clients to bring in an independent company that specializes in organizational leadership and change to assess their organizational culture. These experts are masterful in utilizing tools like cultural assessments, observation, and other research methods that are instrumental in helping leaders to see the culture to which many of them have become blind. The reality is that leaders often only see the surface of their organizations; because they are a part of the culture, and because they helped to create the culture, they cannot really see it. In fact, if they have been with the organization for any length of time, the culture that they are attempting to appraise reflects them, including their strengths and weaknesses. Thus, the fact that they are so close to the culture of the organization makes it nearly impossible for them to make an initial assessment of it objectively.

If you have ever sold a house, you undoubtedly brought in an external appraiser to determine the value of your house to price it competitively. If you are like most homeowners, the value of the house suggested by the appraiser was significantly lower than what you would have valued your house to be. After all, your custom pink marble floor in the foyer, the teak wood floor in the dining room, and the life-sized lions meticulously carved into the wooden staircase make your house special, unique, and priceless – to you and only you! As a result, you feel that people should pay an extra $50,000 to $100,000 for all of the "special features" that you have added to enhance the house, and you ask the realtor to price it accordingly. However, as the realtor will explain, these special features are attractive only to you – not to a buyer. The point here is that when we are too close to something, it is easy for us to be biased about it, either positively or negatively.

> *When we are too close to something, it is easy for us to be biased about it, either positively or negatively.*

The benefit of bringing in an independent appraiser is that this professional will provide you with an honest, objective appraisal of what your home is worth based on what is happening in the real estate market.

In the same way that you can be so in love with your house that you list it according to a "fantasy price," you can be so in love with your organization that you characterize it according to a "fantasy culture," viewing it as something that it is not. However, when you bring in an independent consultant to appraise your organization, the appraiser will assess every aspect of your organizational culture, including the structure and style of your organization. Oftentimes, leaders discover through these third party appraisals that things are not as bad as they think in the organization!

The 720° Snapshot

PART 4:
THE LEADER TRIAD

Building an Awareness of Who You Are,
What You Have to Offer, and How It All
Affects the Way You Approach a Task

Leader Triad Side 1:
Personal Influences

*What known or hidden personal values, motivations, or feelings
are present within me, and how do they affect my perceptions
and interactions, skew my interpretation of the facts surrounding
critical situations, and influence my decisions, actions, and
reactions with others?*

Leader Triad Side 2:
Professional Expertise

*What are my professional capacities and limitations, and how
can they be leveraged or compensated for, respectively, in order
to increase my leadership effectiveness?*

Leader Triad Side 3:
Adaptability

*How far am I willing to go to make shifts in my beliefs and
behaviors in order to connect at a deeper level with others for the
benefit of the organization?*

The 720° Snapshot

THE LEADER TRIAD

PERSONAL

C.O.R.E.

S.T.A.R.C.H.

P.O.R.K.

S.H.O.E.S.

PROFESSIONAL

Skills

Training

Experience

LEADER

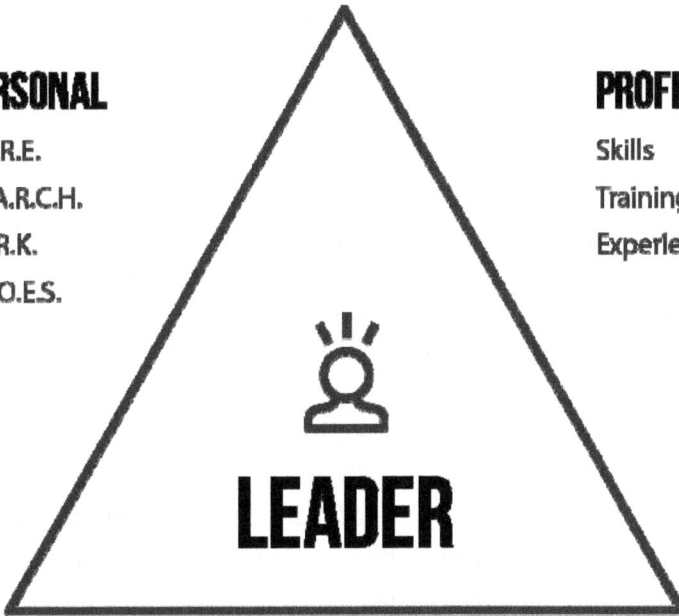

ADAPTABILITY

Emotional Intelligence

Cultural Awareness

Authenticity

LEADER:

A person or thing that holds a dominant or superior position within its field, and is able to exercise a high degree of control or influence over others.[27]

The third triad of *Moody's 720° Leadership Decision-Making Model* is the Leader Triad. It is comprised of three sides about which the leader should be aware when making decisions regarding a given task: Personal, Professional, and Adaptability.

Of all of the considerations of which a leader must be aware when making an organizational decision or approaching the execution of a task, self-awareness of him or herself could possibly be the most important. Sun Tzu, a Chinese military general and philosopher, is noted for saying that the person who understands his enemy can win one out of four fights, but the person who understands both himself and his enemy can win three out of four fights. Tzu was essentially signaling the importance of knowing your personal attributes and characteristics, because your perception, your thoughts, and your past decisions influence your present actions. Once you understand that each of these aspects affects how you think and operate as a leader and understand how they can either work towards or against your success as a leader, the greater part of the battle is already won!

Whether you recognize it or not, you are wearing your very own set of custom-tailored lenses through which you see and interpret life and the world around you – and you never take them off! These lenses, which we all wear, tend to color our opinions. Since our opinions color our decisions and our decisions dictate our behaviors, these lenses through which we view life are *really* important to understand! Understanding how our lenses affect our life – and our leadership – helps us to be aware of all of the various components that influence what we feel, think, and do, usually beyond our own conscious recognition.

Consider one of the dominant players that help to shape our lenses: emotions. It's funny. I've counseled hundreds of people over the years, and they all like to think that they are in full control of their actions, because they are such intelligent creatures. In fact, many of them have invested years of education and training into developing their minds so that they can make decisions in a sure-fire way that would yield the best and most desirable outcomes for their lives. I know this because they explain it to me as they sit back in the comfy chairs located in my office – during a counseling session that they had to request because all or part of their life was in shambles. What's so funny about it is that they do not recognize the irony between their words and where their assessments have landed them. I have learned to simply listen quietly as they attempt to make sense of how their trained, logical minds could consistently produce such undesirable outcomes in their lives. Once they finish their monologue, I break the news to them: our intellect does not determine how we think or behave; our emotions do!

> *Understanding how our lenses affect our life – and our leadership – helps us to be aware of all of the various components that influence what we feel, think, and do, usually beyond our own conscious recognition.*

The brain's language is emotion. As logical as we desire to be, we cannot overlook this fact! You should see the faces of my clients when they finally realize that all the while that they thought they were making logical, rational decisions, they were simply being emotional! These emotions impact our feelings, our feelings impact our decisions, and our decisions impact our actions. Because our emotions impact how we feel about people and situations, what we see, and what we do, it is important that we become aware of them. Once we are aware of how various things trigger our emotions or how anything going on inside of us pushes our buttons, we will be able to better understand why we think the way we think and why we act the way we act.

Our intellect does not determine how we think or behave; our emotions do!

Being aware of how your emotions influence your decision making as a leader and how other internal challenges have similar influences is only part of what is necessary to be a successful leader. The next step is to act upon your awareness by seeking to understand what actions are necessary for you to make leadership decisions that are sounder. For example, I always encourage leaders to slow down when making decisions. I warn them, "Don't be so quick to reach a conclusion!" When a leader acts with immediacy in making important decisions, I can all but guarantee that the decisions that are made are emotional – not logical. However, when they slow down and take time to become aware of what is pushing their buttons, they can make more clear-headed, rational decisions that will result in the best outcomes for the organization. Thus, it is not merely awareness of one's internal workings that make a successful leader; it is the willingness to do whatever it takes in order to apply this awareness that will result in leadership success!

The Leader Triad helps leaders become more aware of their internal workings – what factors are constantly influencing their thoughts, decisions, and actions from the inside out. It is designed to cause leaders to assess to what lengths they are willing to go in order to develop themselves on a personal and professional level. In essence, the

Leader Triad challenges the leader to be holistically introspective, and based upon the results of this self-assessment, challenges leaders to take action to improve or develop themselves for the sake of the organization. When I introduce this concept during training sessions to groups of corporate clients, one of the participants in the session will inevitably ask, "Why don't we just do the 360° Leadership assessment? Doesn't it already provide a clear assessment of us as leaders?" It really is a good question, and I have a good answer. You see, the 360° Leadership assessment focuses upon people from the outside looking in at the leader. Often, receiving the feedback from such assessments will put the leader into a defensive posture, not one that is mature, fluid, and adaptable, which are the types of postures that result in real change. In light of this, many times, 360° feedback results simply end up being costly exercises that yield no real change in how leaders lead. On the other hand, my Leader Triad approaches assessment from a different perspective; it puts the work of assessment on the leader and only supplements the assessment with feedback from people on the outside. Using this style of assessment, leaders are challenged to take a long, hard look at who they are and what they have to do. Then, any additional feedback that comes from the outside helps to further their journey to becoming a more successful leader rather than impede it.

Leaders who do not take the time to engage in a personal assessment of this level will always have blind spots that will inevitably be a detriment to their leadership. They will misconstrue, misinterpret, and misread signals in the organizational environment, and as a result, they will make misguided attempts to address them. The majority of their leadership decisions will be off! While they might think that they are making logical decisions based upon critical thought, the truth is that because they do not fully understand their internal influences, they might not even be involving the areas of their brain that allow them to critically think! Taking the time to make internal assessments through the Leader Triad will help leaders to make clear and level-headed cognitive analyses even in the midst of a myriad of internal factors that are constantly pushing their historical, emotional, psychological, and professional buttons. Because of this ability, both the leader and the organization will experience greater levels of leadership success!

CHAPTER 10

LEADER TRIAD SIDE 1: PERSONAL INFLUENCES

ASSESSMENT QUESTION:

What known or hidden personal values, motivations, or feelings are present within me, and how do they affect my perceptions and interactions, skew my interpretation of the facts surrounding critical situations, and influence my decisions, actions, and reactions with others?

Nothing impacts a leader's ability to lead effectively more than him or herself. The various components of our emotions, psyche, education, exposure, training, and experiences make up who we are as individuals and impact what we think, what we believe, how we arrive at decisions, the choices we make, and how we behave. In fact, if we were to assess the weight of each side of the Leader Triad in terms of how each influences the triad as a whole, Personal Influences would likely comprise 70 percent of the weight. Why? Because who we are as individuals on the inside has *everything* to do with our decisions and actions as leaders! Thus, knowing oneself is essential to leadership effectiveness. This is why I often say that leaders who are self-aware can be their own best friends when leading an organization; those who remain ignorant of who they are can be their own worst enemies – and enemies of their organization as well. It is my aim to help you to become so aware of who you are that you become masterful in managing yourself at any given moment!

Because of the importance for leaders to become self-aware, be trained to recognize their own inner influences (the things that drive them and make them who they are), and be taught how to monitor and mitigate these influences so that they can become more effective leaders, I will address Personal Influences in a later chapter that is solely dedicated to the topic. I know what you're thinking, and the answer is "Yes! It really is that serious, and self-awareness really does deserve that type of focused attention!"

CHAPTER 11

LEADER TRIAD SIDE 2: PROFESSIONAL EXPERTISE

ASSESSMENT QUESTION:

What are my professional capacities and limitations, and how can they be leveraged or compensated for, respectively, in order to increase my leadership effectiveness?

When leaders walk through the doors of an organization for the very first time, they do not enter empty-handed. In one hand, they have a leadership passport, which has been stamped by all of the places that they have served as leaders in any capacity. Simply flipping through their passports and gazing at each distinctive imprint evokes memories of the adventures that they encountered at each place, some enjoyable, educational, and enriching, and others not so enjoyable, distressing, and traumatic. On the other hand, they also carry baggage – "leadership luggage" filled with various things that they have collected along their leadership journey. The contents of this luggage consists of experiences, lessons gained through both positive and negative experiences, skills, trainings, mentalities, ideologies, strategic approaches, research, failures, successes, and a plethora of other things that they will forever carry along with them. Each of the contents in their leadership luggage has made such an impression on them, shaping their Professional Expertise in such an impactful way, that they now travel with these contents in tow wherever they go.

Because no two leaders have traveled to exactly the same places and experienced exactly the same things throughout their leadership journeys, each and every leader's Professional Expertise is unique. Even if, by chance, two leaders have enjoyed exactly the same travel path, because their upbringings were different and unique, what they experienced on their journey undoubtedly differed. For example, two leaders working for the same organization can travel overseas to South Africa, take the same flight, ride in the same transport car, share the same suite in a hotel, attend the same training conference, operate according to the same daily itinerary, and depart on the same flight for home, and yet, both of them will walk away from the trip with distinctly different experiences. This is because though they shared the exact same trip, they saw the trip through distinctly different lenses. Each individual is unique! Every leader has traveled on his or her own personal journey, enjoying rich experiences, collecting passport stamps, accumulating items in their luggage, and picking up valuable souvenirs along the way. Each of these elements adds to the Professional Expertise that the leader has to offer to an organization in a special way that can be offered by no one else!

Possessing an awareness of one's own uniqueness, particularly as it pertains to Professional Expertise, is essential for leadership effectiveness. Such awareness helps leaders to understand what Professional Expertise or proficiencies they possess internally that can be leveraged to accomplish their goals for leading the organization. If an organizational goal calls for a proficiency or expertise that they do not possess, leaders can then assess how to compensate for the lack of it; should they increase their own proficiency and personally address the need themselves or simply pay someone else to fulfill the need? Regardless of the decision made, the important thing is that the leaders are empowered to make it because they possess a clear understanding of the resources contained within their Professional Expertise and can respond to organizational needs accordingly.

There are various aspects of expertise with which leaders should be professionally aware because of the significant impact that they can have on their abilities to lead successfully, and they typically fall into the following categories:

1) Skills
2) Training
3) Experience

SKILLS

A skill is an ability or capacity acquired through deliberate, systematic, and sustained effort to smoothly and adaptively carry out complex activities or job functions involving ideas (cognitive skills), things (technical skills), and/or people (interpersonal skills).[28] Stated in a simpler fashion, a skill is your ability to do something that needs to get done! If I were to take a glance at your resume, I would probably see a set of skills that includes your ability to use certain software applications, to operate certain machinery, to communicate well in writing or verbally, and even your ability to work well with people and be a team player. Each of these is a skill! However, while all skills are valuable for one to possess, there are some specific professional skills that you must possess in order to function effectively as a leader in general, and even more specialized skills – usually technical ones – that you must possess to function effectively as a leader in certain industry-specific organizations.

As you approach a task, it is necessary to not only assess what professional skills are necessary to execute the task but to conduct an honest appraisal of which of these skills you have at your disposal and which of these skills you lack. Understanding both your professional capacities and your limitations to address the task will ensure that you do not "get in over your head" by trying to accomplish more than you have the ability to actually accomplish. Instead, such an appraisal will allow you to devise a proper strategy that relies upon the skills in your arsenal rather than a strategy that calls for skills that you do not possess. In light of this, it is important to not only be aware of the things that you know but to be aware of the things that you do not know – or that you do not know well enough to be able to execute.

Our minds have an amazing way of telling us that we are fully able to do what we simply do not have the skills to do! For example, you might be saying, "I'm going to write a book!" Now, I do not doubt that you have the skills to think and the skills to type out those thoughts on your computer. At the most basic level, this is what it really means to write a book, right? However, as much as you tell yourself that you can write a book, you have been saying it to yourself for the past five or ten years! You might have even attempted to get started; however, instead of producing a book, all you produced were a couple of pages with scribbles and disconnected thoughts and a disposition that was both frustrated and discouraged. What you are failing to acknowledge is that you have hit the wall of one of your skill limitations: you cannot write a book! Do not fool yourself into thinking, "The only reason I haven't written a book is because I don't really want to. If I really wanted to write a book, it would be done!" because the truth is that you really, *really* want to have a completed book! Instead, say to yourself, "I do not have the skill set to write my own book right now. I need to seek outside help!" Admitting that you do not have the skill set to write a book, which includes the ability to sit down and focus on ideas for extended periods of time, convert your ideas into well-expressed words that are arranged in a logical flow, and see the project through to completion is the first step towards your progress. Only then will you empower yourself to make the necessary decisions that will lead to your desired outcome of getting your book done!

Having the ability to honestly admit what skills you have and what skills you do not have does not make you as a failure as a leader. Instead, it positions you for success and can save you lots of time, energy, and frustration! The sooner you are able to determine that you do not have the skills that it takes to get a task done or to address a particular situation, the sooner you can either seek out these skills in someone else (perhaps subcontracting the need to an outside vendor) or take the necessary steps to acquire the new skills and abilities yourself.

When my clients are lacking knowledge in a certain area of skill, they often ask my opinion about whether they should pursue another degree (the vast majority of them already have earned an undergraduate degree, and a large percentage have also earned a graduate degree). I share with them what my mentors have shared with me: consider the cost and time of learning new information, and once you make this assessment, if it makes sense, go for it. However, do not feel that this is the only way to acquire new skills and abilities. This is especially true in the case of those who have already earned degrees. To them, I say, "College has already taught you how to learn, so just go out and learn the information. Why get another degree?" Still, some would rather pay the big bucks to the university and have the calligraphy-inscribed parchment paper on the wall testifying that they went through an official program to acquire their new knowledge and skills. They want the evidence as proof of their skill level. However, the only drawback is that the people that matter almost never ask to see a copy of a leader's college diploma. Instead, they want to see the evidence of their skills reflected through the work that they do everyday, because their ability to proficiently utilize their skills is the only thing that really matters! Considering this, is it really necessary to go get that diploma, or is it more necessary to just go acquire the skills?

Leader Triad Side 2 | Professional Expertise
CATEGORY 2:

TRAINING

Training refers to the organized activity of imparting information and/or instructions into a recipient to improve his or her performance or help him or her attain a required level of knowledge or skill.[29] Every leader has received training, whether formally (i.e., a classroom or seminar), informally (i.e., on the job experience, learning from past mistakes, reading books and articles, etc.), or a combination of both, by which he or she has learned valuable skills, techniques, and information. Each of these training methods equip leaders with valuable knowledge and resources that they accumulate over the years and that they place into their leadership toolbox, accessing them at just the right time to help them accomplish their leadership objectives.

Good leaders are those who recognize that their training never ends. They do not go to college, graduate with a degree, and say, "Well, that's it! I've gotten all of my training done!" They also do not go get graduate degrees, certifications, licensures, or any other advanced training and think that they have arrived at the place called "there." Instead, each level of knowledge that they accumulate through training helps them to realize that there is so much more for them to learn. As a result, they are in constant pursuit of acquiring new knowledge, skills, and techniques that will keep them sharp, current with what is happening in the world around them, and proficient in using all of the new skills and resources that emerge every day in our rapidly changing world. How leaders immerse themselves in new training opportunities is not as important as the fact that they recognize that there always needs to be an element of ongoing training in their lives so that they can maintain their relevance.

I have found that when my busy life does not allow me to set aside time to undergo formal training in a particular area, my training does not have to come to a halt; there are other methods that I use to ensure that I stay on the cutting edge of building my proficiencies. For example, I might do some research online about what executives are reading these days and read the book, spend some time with my colleagues or mentors, stream an online webinar about a current skill or topic, or pop into a conference to hear a session or two. Anything that I can do to receive an impartation of new information will help me as a leader to keep pace with the changes that are happening in society – particularly the ones that affect my organization and its market.

My advice to you is to experiment with formal and informal training methods in order to determine which works best for you. For the sake of accessibility, cost, and convenience, start with informal training and development methods, because these will allow you to learn things in your own time and on your own terms. For example:

- Dedicate at least 60 to 90 minutes a day to reading a book.
- Participate in a webinar online.
- Invite some fellow leaders to lunch once a week to discuss a special challenge or topic that is relevant to the group's interests so that you can pick one another's brains about how each leader is approaching it.

- Watch some Ted Talks online and then write down your reflections about the topic.
- Take a self-paced online class offered by the local community college on a topic about which you need to learn more.

After a while, if you attempt to engage in these informal training methods and find that you are not gaining the advanced skills and knowledge that you need on your own – for whatever reason – you might want to try more formal approaches to training and development. The only real difference between informal training and formal training is that with formal training, you pay an educational institution or organization to provide you with structure, discipline, accountability, and timelines as it provides you with new skills and knowledge, versus informal training, in which you attain the skills and knowledge on your own. In exchange for your investment in their formal training system, they reward you with a degree or certificate at the end of the training process. However, the reality is that both informal and formal training systems offer access to the same knowledge; the knowledge is not hidden! Some people just find that they need the structure and accountability of a formal training context in order to stay on target and maximize their training, while others can gain the same skill and knowledge informally on their own. If you need the structure and accountability of a formal training context in order to ensure that you get what you need, don't knock yourself. Do what is best for you!

One of my favorite sayings surrounding the need for leaders to remain sharp and current through training and development is "As iron sharpens iron, so one person sharpens another."[30] It literally means that when a steel file, which is an iron tool that was used to shape and sharpen a blade in the Iron Age, is sheered across an iron blade, the blade is sharpened; the only way that one can sharpen an iron blade is to use a tool with a different edge or texture. This makes the iron blade better in fulfilling its purpose and function, which is to cut and slice through things easily. Thus, when you place yourself into an environment with strong leaders that can sharpen you with their different proficiencies and areas of expertise, the inevitable result is that these leaders will say and do things that impart wisdom, knowledge, and skills into you as a leader. You, in turn, will do the same for them, because there are some areas in which you have more advanced knowledge, understanding, or skills than them. What results from this interaction is that each leader's life is enhanced and enriched in some way as a result of the "informal training" and development received from the interaction. When each of you walks away from the training, you will do so more equipped and empowered to fulfill your purpose and function as leaders of your respective organizations. Iron has sharpened iron, and all have become the better for it!

Understanding these, however, allow me to caution you about the sharpening process. The Bible distinctly says that "*iron* sharpens *iron.*" Aluminum cannot sharpen iron. Tin cannot sharpen iron. In order for you, the iron, to be sharpened, you need to ensure that you are always fellowshipping and interacting with other leaders – or metals – that are stronger than you are. Otherwise, they will have nothing to offer you in the way of

If you are constantly surrounded by a group of leaders who are not as learned, advanced in their knowledge, skills, training, and development, or as wise as you, you are surrounded by the wrong leaders.

training and development! If you are constantly surrounded by a group of leaders who are not as learned, advanced in their knowledge, skills, training, and development, or as wise as you, you are surrounded by the wrong leaders. Simply put, as you gather with your fellow leaders, if you are the smartest leader in the room, you need to change rooms!

Surrounding yourself with leaders that are ahead of you in some way is essential, because in order for you to grow and develop, you need to be exposed to leaders who think differently and in more advanced ways than you. You need to be in the space of leaders who will challenge your ideas and make you think more deeply about what you are doing and why you are doing it. Only this type of interaction will keep you sharp! If you choose to surround yourself with leaders who are at or below your own level of accomplishment, you might always appear to be the guru in the room. Everyone might look up to you because of your advanced knowledge and ability to impart wisdom. This will surely feed your pride and ego, and you will leave every one of these gatherings feeling like "the man" or "the woman." However, how do *your* leadership skills advance as a result of these interactions? How do *you* get sharpened? How do *you* get to grow as a leader as a result of being in the company of these people? If you cannot find an acceptable answer to these questions, you need to rethink the company that you are keeping. Considering how important it is to stay sharp through the informal training and development that can only come from interacting with other leaders, I encourage you to always ask this question before you accept an invitation to a fellowship gathering or networking event: "What's in it for me?"

If all else fails and you are unable to find a group of leaders with which you can gather to sharpen yourself as a leader, surely you can find at least *one* person in the community from which you can glean some valuable wisdom and knowledge in the informal training process. If not, you might be just a little bit full of yourself and your leadership capacity! Identify a leader in the community who is already where you are trying to go – one whom you respect and admire. Then, seek to connect with the leader through a friendly telephone call or an e-mail. If you regularly see the leader at certain functions in the community, approach him or her and ask to be mentored. Now, I cannot guarantee that you will get a hearty response of, "Oh, I'd love to mentor you! That would be quite a privilege for me!" However, don't be so afraid of receiving an undesirable response that you do not ask! You know, the kind of response where you approach the leader at a public gathering, ask for his or her help, and hear the leader respond in a loud voice with everyone watching, "*You? You?* Who are *you?* Why, you're *nobody!* Why would I want to mentor someone like *you?*" while doubled over in laughter at the ridiculousness of mentoring you. For many people, it is quite a compliment to be asked to help another leader as a mentor, so chances are you won't get as negative a response as the one that you have so creatively envisioned in your mind. Get over your fear and give mentoring a try!

Keep in mind that if a person is worth seeking out as a mentor, that same person is probably quite productive and in high demand, and consequently, quite busy. Therefore, be conscientious of the person's time as you seek out wisdom and advice from him or her to contribute towards your informal training and development as a leader. While you might not be successful at getting an appointment to sit at your mentor's feet for three hours every month, you might be able to treat your mentor to breakfast or lunch every other month and even send him or her an occasional e-mail with a thought or question that you would like to have answered. When all your mentor can offer to you is the opportunity to run something by him or her, do not be discouraged; this too is mentoring and can greatly help to develop your way of thinking as a leader, so take full advantage of it. In fact, take whatever your mentor can offer to you in the form of informal training, and be okay with the fact that it is all he or she has to offer.

Finally, do not make the mistake of thinking that training – formal or informal – is only for leaders who oversee business and corporate organizations. Leaders of non-profit organizations do not receive an exemption from the need to always be engaged in some form of training and development! Every leader who is leading an organization in today's rapidly changing context needs to always ensure that he or she is constantly receiving an inflow of new information – even church leaders! For example, I often tell my pastoral clients that their primary task is to stay aware, because people are depending on them to know what is happening in the world. Thus, pastors need to be not only aware of what is going on with the people inside of their church walls but in the external environment as well. Why? Because what is happening externally will inevitably affect the lives of the people inside of the organization! In order to watch for their souls, the pastor must be aware of new trends, new challenges, and new threats that might affect his sheep, and staying informed through training, whether formal or informal, will ensure that his knowledge of such things remains current.

EXPERIENCE

Experience is simply one's familiarity with a skill or field of knowledge that has been acquired over a period of time in which he or she actually practiced it, resulting in a superior understanding of it.[31] Unlike skills and training, experience produces a knowledge base that cannot easily be transferred from individual to individual. For instance, consider the transference of knowledge and wisdom from a mentor in informal training. Although mentoring has a lot of strengths and benefits, it can in no way replace experience. Experiences make the leader face his own set of unique realities that have not been experienced by anyone else. This is because no two experiences are alike: every one of them is different because it occurs at a unique time, with unique people, in a unique atmosphere, and in a unique context. Further, even you are different each time you go into each experience. Thus, there is something different that can be learned from each experience because each experience is so different.

For example, even though I have been performing premarital counseling for years, I cannot say that when it comes to premarital counseling, "I've been there and done that." Why? Because each time I approach a premarital counseling session, though the context is the same, every session is a different experience that differs from all of the rest. Although the baseline tenets of the counseling session will be the same, each couple comes with its own set of unique circumstances that challenges my abilities to apply those tenets to their particular situation. Considering this, every time I approach this familiar experience, because I am encountering a new context with different players, I have the opportunity to learn something new from the experience.

Each of us is the sum total of our experiences; the things that we have gone through in life have shaped how we think, feel, and behave, both as individuals and as leaders. However, when we refer to experience in terms of professional expertise, we are referring to those things that you have gone through and been subjected to that can have a direct impact on your leadership ability. For example, if you are in an interview with a prospective employer or client, when you are asked about your "experience," you wouldn't launch into a monologue about all of the things that you have experienced since childhood, would you? No! Instead, you would refer only to those experiences that are related in some way to organizations, teams, or groups that you have led and lessons that you have learned as a result of having these experiences. However, be aware that even though when people ask about your "experience," they are referring to your leadership experience, the sum total of your life experiences go into shaping how you conduct yourself as a leader! Thus, every "general" experience that you have ever undergone in life matters, because each one of them has taught you valuable lessons on what to do – and what not to do – to be an effective leader.

Considering this, never downplay your experiences, whether positive or negative, whether large or small, and whether you perceive them to be directly related to your leadership development or not. You would be surprised at all of the rich entries that your experiences register in your leadership portfolio without your even recognizing it! Take pastors, for example. If you were to ask an average pastor what experience he has gained over the past 10 years, he or she might say things like leading and preaching to a congregation, overseeing a small staff of people, and maybe even leading a building project. However, if you take the time to probe a little deeper, that pastor has gained even deeper and richer experiences than he or she thought! How? As a speechwriter from having developed so many sermons, as trainers and facilitators from all of the trainings that they conduct, as community activists from lending their voice and participation in helping to advance various causes and initiatives in the community, as strategists as they map out a plan for increasing their levels of church growth, as financial managers from having to find creative ways to stretch their limited church budgets to cover their expenses, and as counselors from having to meet with people to help them work through their internal and external conflicts in a biblical way. These represent a vast amount of experience that the pastor has gained! However, they can be easily minimized or overlooked if we compartmentalize only certain skills as being relevant to leadership experience. Everything that you have done in the past contributes in some way to the way you perform as a leader today, and everything that you do as a leader today will contribute to your ability to lead more effectively in some way in the future!

Allowing yourself to take part in new experiences can only help you, because they have and uncanny way of challenging your thinking and pushing you beyond your comfort zone as a leader. One of the best examples that I can use to better help you understand this concept is that of weightlifting. One of the most effective methods that trainers use when working out their clients is to keep changing the workout. One day, they will work one part of the body, the next day they will work another, and the day after that, they will work another area of the body. They do this in an effort to make the body more and more unstable. The more unstable you make the body, the more muscles the body uses to stabilize itself. This also makes the exercise more intense, because the person has to engage muscles to stabilize themselves as well as the muscles that are needed to exercise on that particular day. The more they engage in this type of workout regimen, the more developed they become. So it is with the mind of a leader. Constantly seeking out and undertaking new experiences engages different areas of the mind and requires the leader to access different skill sets in order to get certain tasks associated with the new experience done. The more that leaders do this with their mind, the more developed their mind becomes.

Whenever I am coaching new leader clients, it never fails that I end up with one or two who are highly resistant to new experiences. They think that as a result of all of the things that they have done as leaders over the years, they have had enough experiences to last them a lifetime. They have led organizations large and small, traveled around the world, enjoyed numerous adventures, built sizeable budgets, been trained and imparted training into a plethora of leaders, and attended every conference under the sun. I have to work overtime to try to convince these leaders that even though their experiences are rich and plentiful, they are not to be bowed down to; they can still stand to enjoy some new experiences, which will enhance not only their leadership but their lives in general! I also encourage leaders to seek out new lessons from the more familiar experiences that they have on a day to day basis. For example, I advise them to consider what is new about a scenario that they have encountered before. Ask questions like, "What is different about the circumstances of the experience today?" "What do I know about the situation that I did not know before?" "What do I know, what am I not aware of, and how can a consideration of both of these factors help me to arrive at the best decision?" In approaching a familiar situation this way (almost like a new experience) leaders stand to actually gain new insights from a situation rather than simply draw on what they have learned from their past experiences.

When leaders approach tasks and find that their own experiences leave them short of understanding of how to deal with the situation at hand, it might be necessary to on the experiences of others who have greater levels of expertise in the area. In such cases, leaders should ask themselves, "Who can I consult with that might have some relevant guidance or advice to offer about this situation?" In addition to providing you with direction, peers or colleagues in the industry can either validate or invalidate what you are thinking as a leader, or they might even add to your existing perspective by helping you to think about the challenge in a different way. Because others have had different experiences from us, they can provide a perspective on things

Ultimately, the goal of a good leader is not to be the one who is always able to draw off of his or her own experiences and come up with the right answers. Instead, the goal of a good leader should be to access and draw off of the experiences of whoever has the best answers to address the situation at hand – whether their own or someone else's!

that we would never have imagined! Ultimately, the goal of a good leader is not to be the one who is always able to draw off of his or her own experiences and come up with the right answers. Instead, the goal of a good leader should be to access and draw off of the experiences of whoever has the best answers to address the situation at hand – whether their own or someone else's!

Have you ever taken a moment to stop and consider why God is always right? Why does He always make the right decisions? I believe that the reason that God is always right is directly due to His omniscience; He knows all things at all times, and no knowledge is hidden from Him. He is complete in His thought, so He takes everything that can possibly be known about a situation into consideration before making a decision. As a result of always having access to all information at all times, He can neither make a bad decision that He might later regret, nor does He make a mistake. It's impossible! We humans, on the other hand, often get blindsided with the consequences of making bad decisions because we did not have access to the right information, or we did not take certain things into consideration when making a decision because they were not accessible to us at the time we had to make a choice. What's my point here? As you are approaching a task, if you have the answers inside of you as a result of your past experiences, great! Go with them. However, if you find that your lack of experience in a particular area has left you without some valuable knowledge that you need in order to make the best choice possible, seek out the information you need from others who might have had experiences that have taught them the very lessons that you need access to in order to make the best decision for your organization. This is what great leaders do!

Leader Triad Side 2 | Professional Expertise
SUMMARY & CONCLUSIONS

In summary, leaders must become skillful in answering the question, "What are my professional capacities and limitations, and how can they be leveraged or compensated for, respectively, in order to increase my leadership effectiveness?" Without answering this question, you as a leader run the risk of being overconfident in your approach to a task or situation, undertaking strategies that require higher levels of Professional Expertise – skills, training, and experience – than you have the capacity to offer. Approaching situations within the organization in such a manner is sure to result in your leadership ineffectiveness and failure. Thus, for optimal results, you should only undertake strategies and tasks that you have the expertise to undertake on your own merits or that you have access to through the skills, training and experiences of your colleagues, peers, or co-workers. Should you tap into these networks and still see that you are lacking in a vital area of expertise that is needed within the organization, you are well-advised to either develop the proficiency yourself through informal or formal training methods, or outsource the need to someone outside of the organization. After you take a personal inventory of your professional expertise, only you can decide what is best for you!

You Can't *Appreciate* What You Have to Offer if You Don't *Know* What You Have to Offer!

A lot of times, rather than being *over*confident in their levels of professional expertise, leaders lack confidence in their abilities to execute certain tasks or strategies. Not only can they not appreciate their own abilities, but they feel negative emotions anytime the topic arises! Interestingly, the reason for this is rarely because they do not have any professional expertise or abilities; it is because they have never *assessed* them. You see, when you take the time to really list out and assess the length, width, and depth of your professional expertise, such an assessment can evoke feelings of "swag" – cool confidence. When you assess your professional expertise, you might find that you have more of a reason to celebrate your expertise than you thought and that your negative feelings about your professional expertise might be *completely* unfounded! Becoming fully aware of your expertise and capabilities are bound to give you that extra "pick me up" that you need as a leader to stay motivated and keep forging ahead!

"You Complete Me!"... Said No GOOD Leader to Himself... EVER!

Good leaders are not only fully in tune with what skills, training, and experiences they have to offer; they are in tune with the fact that what they do not have can be accessed other ways. Here's a newsflash to you, oh great leader: you are not an island, you are not a fortress, you do not have to be independent, and you do not complete yourself! If you will ever be successful, you must recognize that you need other people and their ideas to complete you and to compensate for the areas of professional expertise that you lack! Saying to a peer or colleague, "I need help," is not a bad thing. It is not the equivalent of saying, "I am a bad leader." Instead, it says, "I am a good leader, and I want to ensure that I access all of the resources available to me as I lead my organization in the best direction possible!" Consider the fact that God calls those who are a part of His church the "body of Christ."

As you endeavor to take your leadership to the next level, cast aside your self-sufficient ways and tap into the resources that lay inside of others around you!

Each individual in the body performs a unique function upon which the rest of the body depends, even as each individual is dependent upon the rest of the body in order to function properly. Again, this gives us a clear indication that God values dependence and community. If God values the interdependence of things, should we not value it as well?

Therefore, as you endeavor to take your leadership to the next level, cast aside your self-sufficient ways and tap into the resources that lay inside of others around you!

A Skilled, Trained, and Experienced Leader Is Priceless to an Organization

Being skilled is one thing. Being trained is another thing. Having experience is yet another thing. However, having skills that have been honed through the combination of training and experience is difficult to replace. In fact, possessing these type of skills make you a force to be reckoned with in the world of leadership! Here's why. Individuals can possess skills based upon the mechanics that they have learned through a textbook, but this is only the introductory level of being skilled. The next level of being skilled, the one that makes you a pro, is that of having your skills honed and sharpened through additional training and through experiences in which you have utilized these skills in various real-time situations. Leadership is both science and art. The science typically comes from a textbook and consists of the technical aspects of how to execute a skill. The art comes in when you have been trained on that skill, both formally and informally, and you have exercised that skill over and over again and have become fully proficient in the use of that skill in various ways depending upon the situation.

For example, consider the application of this concept to my leadership role as a pastor. In my case, the science side of leadership entails the key tenets or components that I always employ, like influencing others, goal setting, conflict resolution, etc. However, the art side of leadership entails how to utilize each of these tenets depending upon the situation. It determines when to apply the tenet, how much pressure to apply when using it, when to stop the pressure and step back. It is the "touch and feel" part of leadership skills. If this example is too abstract for you, consider the application of the same concept to flying an airplane. A pilot flying an airplane has to learn the important mechanical skills of how to navigate such a powerful machine so that it can take off from the ground, fly safely through the air, and land at its desired location smoothly. This is the science side of the skill. However, each take off and landing is different and can be affected by wind, rain, bright sun, runway traffic, the type and size of the plane, etc. Thus, although the pilot clearly possesses the skill of being able to navigate an airplane he or she must know how to adapt those skills when dealing with crosswinds, tailwinds, and even mechanical failure. Each of these unique considerations falls on the art side of the skill of flying an airplane, and they are honed and perfected through additional training and experience. The more that pilots engage their skills in a wide variety of real-life situations and real-time challenges, the better they become with the touch and feel part of flying an airplane.

Fear Not Unfamiliar Territory, for It Can Be Your Best Friend!

If you will ever become the great leader that you know that you are destined to be, you must always be willing to embrace new opportunities to learn new skills, undertake new training, and gain new experiences. To this extent, you must be willing to venture out and try new things, because this is the context in which these new levels of expertise are developed! Most of us are more likely to be comfortable when we have been in a particular environment and dealt with certain problems before. As creatures of comfort, we are programmed to seek out situations or contexts with which we feel comfortable and familiar, because

It is the unfamiliar that leads to our growth and development!

While familiar and comfortable experiences can tend to keep a leader stagnant and complacent, venturing into new and unfamiliar territory can be a leader's best friend!

they breed a sense of self-confidence in our abilities to handle them well. However, rarely do we experience any growth when we are comfortable!

It is the unfamiliar that leads to our growth and development! When we encounter that which is not familiar, it always sends us looking for something; our brains seek to define our new experience based upon what it knows, what it has already been exposed to, and what we have encountered before that is similar to our new experience. In doing so, the brain makes new connections, establishes new links between existing information and new, and causes us to reach beyond what we know in order to accommodate new knowledge. This equates to growth and development, which are critical for the development of a leader! Thus, while familiar and comfortable experiences can tend to keep a leader stagnant and complacent, venturing into new and unfamiliar territory can be a leader's best friend!

CHAPTER 12

LEADER TRIAD SIDE 3: ADAPTABILITY

ASSESSMENT QUESTION:

How far am I willing to go to make shifts in my beliefs and behaviors in order to connect at a deeper level with others for the benefit of the organization?

Among the unique abilities that leaders must possess in order to effectively approach a task or situation is the ability to grow and adjust to the uniqueness of every situation that they encounter as authentic leaders utilizing high levels of emotional intelligence and cultural awareness. One of my most favorite examples of an adaptable leader is from the Bible, of course: the apostle Paul. Paul had been called by Christ to preach God to a Greek society that worshipped many gods. How could he convince a people whose only frame of reference was that of worshiping many gods rather than one exclusive God? How could he make this concept, which would be completely abstract to them, hit home in a way that they would understand? When he went into the midst of the Areopagus, or Mars Hill, a place where men often gathered to discuss philosophy, religion, and law, he saw altars to many Greek gods. Seeing this, Paul adapted to the situation; rather than introduce this new religious concept to them in abstract terms, Paul exercised his understanding of their culture by introducing God to them in a context with which they were already familiar. Thus, the Bible tells us that Paul stood in the midst of the Areopagus and said, "Men of Athens, I perceive that in all things you are very religious; for as I was passing through and considering the objects of your worship, I even found an altar with this inscription: To the unknown god. Therefore, the One whom you worship without knowing, Him I proclaim to you."[32] After his appeal, while some mocked his words, other men joined him and believed! However, Paul would have never experienced such a high level of effectiveness if he had not been knowledgeable about the culture and used this knowledge to his advantage – to adapt his approach to the situation.

John the apostle also showed adaptability. Scholars believe his gospel to have been written A.D. 90-100 for the purpose of confirming and securing Christians in the faith. John understood the Roman culture under which his audience lived, however, and his writing reflected this. John understood that the part of the intellectual lineage of his audience, which included such philosophical greats from Aristotle to Socrates, was the understanding of divine information and man's reason for being. Thus, John did not start his gospel out by explicitly stating that Jesus was God in the flesh. Instead, he takes a more intellectual and philosophical approach in John 1:1 by saying, "In the beginning was the Word, and the Word was with God, and the Word was God." Although there were many ways to which he could have referred to God, John brilliantly used the Greek term *logos* to refer to God the Son as the "Word." He took an incarnational approach in his writing by which he placed himself in their shoes, saw the world through the lens of their perspective, adjusted his approach, and conveyed his message of truth to them using their own language and philosophical constructs so that they could easily understand it. Thus, John was an adaptable leader as well!

Because adaptable leaders are interested in seeing things from the followers' perspectives, they are less inclined to rush to judgments or draw fast conclusions and more inclined to ask questions – to investigate what is really behind *why* individuals are thinking, acting, and responding the ways that they are. Rather than judge, blame, or accuse their followers when they experience an undesirable outcome in a particular situation, adaptable leaders will pause and take a deep breath. Rather than operate out of an automatic decision-making reflex, they will take time to assess not only what caused the negative outcome, but the possible reasons why. Adaptable leaders investigate, ask questions, and even challenge and modify their own internal beliefs based upon the answers that are unearthed through their careful assessment of the situation. As a result of using each undesirable outcome as an opportunity for greater learning about their followers and themselves, each circumstance becomes an opportunity for growth and development, which makes them more effective as leaders. That is to say, when they are not achieving the results that they would like to see, adaptable leaders do not become *bitter* – they become *better* by shifting their approach so that they can produce a different, more desirable outcome!

If you are one out of the 100 million Americans who drink coffee every day, you have likely heard the buzz circulating within the coffee culture about how good McDonald's coffee is. If you are a connoisseur of good coffee, you might have even gone to try it yourself. In fact, you might even have a cup sitting in front of you right now! As you know, McDonald's has not always been known for its good coffee. Of course, since its inception, the McDonald's brand has been about burgers and fries. However, at some point, leadership executives at McDonald's realized that the "coffee club" was not a closed one, and they sought to gain a market share of the $18 billion that Americans spend on coffee annually. [33] McDonald's already had a stronghold on the breakfast market, but understanding that coffee drives a breakfast program, they knew that they could gain an even greater part of the market share if they dedicated more focus to their coffee products. They did their research and realized that not only do 60% of Americans report that they need a cup of coffee to start their day and that out of this percentage, a little over one-third of them traveled to premium places like Starbucks and The Coffee Bean for their daily caffeine fix. What resulted from McDonalds' research was the development of a new premium roast coffee that most of the coffee drinkers I know describe

When they are not achieving the results that they would like to see, adaptable leaders do not become bitter – they become better by shifting their approach so that they can produce a different, more desirable outcome!

as being downright delicious – one of the best out there! McDonald's also developed its McCafé line of coffee-based products that rivals the extensive menu of cappuccinos, lattes, frappes, smoothies, and other drinks offered at rival premium coffee shops. While they could have scoffed and become resentful or bitter at the coffee competition that their competitors presented, leaders at McDonald's chose instead to adapt, by making a subtle shift in its approach to coffee, and take some of that market share for themselves! As a result, McDonald's did $10 billion in breakfast sales alone in 2012. When you compare these breakfast sales to the $7.6 billion that Taco Bell did in *all-day* sales in the same year[34], you can see that McDonalds' adaptability has helped to establish it as the undisputed powerhouse in America's fast-food breakfast industry!

Notice that when I talk about adaptability, I talk in terms of making "shifts" and "adjustments" – not "changes." This is a critical detail for you to note as a leader! The word "change" carries a strong connotation in the mind of most leaders. A loaded term, it tends to conjure up images of abandonment of one's old way of doing things for the sake of taking on a completely new method or approach to something, and it carries along with it feelings of desertion, denouncement, and in some cases, even blame. However, the use of the term "shift" connotes making a slight variation in the way that things are done. It offers a more subtle approach to adaptability that rearranges and modifies existing strategies and techniques rather than abandoning them outright, and these adjustments are always based upon new information that has become available to the leader.

Leaders who are not aware of their own values and beliefs and will never be able to engage in the adaptability that is necessary to be an effective leader. Without this level of awareness, they will allow themselves to feel negatively about people and situations that differ from them, and this will inevitably affect the outcome of the business dealings – that is, *if* they even choose to participate in the business dealings at all. What's worse, they will not understand the reasons why they feel so negatively about others; they will say things like, "There's just something about them that makes me uncomfortable – that I don't like!" not recognizing that there are underlying cultural orientations and differences between them and those with whom they are interacting, and that these differences are making them uncomfortable. However, differences *do not* have to be deal breakers! Many differences can be easily set aside for the sake of having an effective business relationship if the differences do not cause us to compromise our innermost core values and who we are as individuals. Making a subtle shift in the way that we approach things in order to accommodate the beliefs of others is perfectly acceptable in order to establish a friendly and productive business relationship.

Perhaps no leader was more adaptable than the apostle Paul, because he had a "whatever it takes" mentality when it came to accomplishing his goals as a leader: the salvation and discipleship of as many people as possible. In light of this, he was willing to do or become whatever the context called for him to be in order to win people to Christ, as long as this adaptability did not compromise his internal core values. The apostle Paul put it best when he said:

> *Though I am free and belong to no one, I have made myself a slave to everyone, to win as many as possible. To the Jews I became like a Jew, to win the Jews. To those under the law I became like one under the law (though I myself am not under the law), so as to win those under the law. To those not having the law I became like one not having the law (though I am not free from God's law but am under Christ's law), so as to win those not having the law. To the weak I became weak, to win the weak. I have become all things to all people so that by all possible means I might save some. I do all this for the sake of the gospel, that I may share in its blessings.*

Paul was not concerned about sticking to doing things a certain way, being "right," being comfortable in the way he operated, or upholding a particular identity for the sake of his ego. He was concerned only about winning, and to win, he recognized that he had to be adaptable!

There are various aspects of adaptability that can affect a leader's ability to lead successfully, and they typically fall into the following categories:

1) Emotional Intelligence
2) Cultural Awareness
3) Authenticity

Leader Triad Side 3 | Adaptability
CATEGORY 1:

EMOTIONAL INTELLIGENCE

Emotional intelligence is our ability to identify and manage our emotions and the emotions of others, the ability to harness our emotions and apply to tasks like thinking and problem solving, and the ability to regulate our emotions.[35] When leaders develop the ability to clearly understand both what they are feeling and why they are feeling what they are feeling at any given moment, and when they are able to master the ability to manipulate their own emotions at will by regulating them in order to reach a desired emotional state, this ability is a priceless one that will position them heads and shoulders above both their peers and their competitors. After leaders become emotionally intelligent enough to pinpoint, control, and regulate their own emotions, they can also do the same with the emotions of others, including their followers, peers, and others with whom they interact in business.

In the business context of an organization, leaders use emotional intelligence to intuitively connect with other people, inventory the emotional state of the individuals, and then take whatever actions are necessary to manipulate the individuals' emotional states until they reach the emotional state that the leader desires for them to reach. Of course, the desired emotional state that the leader will be guiding the people towards, beyond their knowledge, is a state that will result in a win for the leader! I guess one might say that having a high level of emotional intelligence can help a leader become masterful at influence, so that he or she can get what is needed out of people for the good of the organization. However, you should also be able to see the link here between emotional intelligence and adaptability.

In order to function at a high level of adaptability, leaders must develop their relational capacity; in order to develop their relational capacity, they must develop their emotional intelligence. You see, emotional intelligence reflects our abilities to sense where a person is, see where the person needs to be in terms of a desired emotional state, put ourselves in their shoes, and walk them to this desired state. After we see where they are, the adaptability comes in at the point at which we adapt our thoughts, words, and behaviors in an effort to move them – or walk them – to the desired state that we want them to feel. It's almost like taking things a step further in order to add action to empathy; rather than merely being able to see and relate to what people are currently experiencing, we masterfully move them to a place where they experience something different – something we want them to experience that will ultimately benefit our organization!

When we improve our levels of emotional intelligence, we increase our capacity to grow and maintain relationships – and business is all about relationships, right? Emotional intelligence helps us to know when to push a little harder, when to pull back, when to poke and prod a little more, and even when to offer a person a compliment in order to get the outcomes and results that we desire in a particular business interaction. As we become more and more emotionally intelligent, engaging in these strategic behaviors becomes increasingly more intuitive, almost to the point that we do not even have to concentrate on doing them as much; they become a natural part of how we operate as leaders. That is to say, as soon as we see someone experiencing an emotional state that will not benefit the organization, we automatically adapt our words and behavior in such a way that it will change their emotional state to one more beneficial for the organization.

Best of all, when leaders operate with heightened levels of emotional intelligence, not only do they become more effective in their leadership efforts, but people actually like them! This is because they understand the emotions of those whom they are leading in the organization and those with whom they are working in the business world. By understanding the emotions of other people and how to manage and regulate them, they are able to adapt, doing whatever is necessary to get people's emotions where they need to be in order to produce certain outcomes. They are able to truly lead people by getting them to do things that they would not otherwise get done while feeling good about getting them done in the process. Thus, when a leader operates with emotional intelligence, it results in a win-win for everyone!

As a pastor, it is essential that I operate with a high level of emotional intelligence for a very good reason: feelings are all I have to move my people! Unlike a corporate or for-profit business setting, I do not have a big budget, so I cannot dangle a paycheck or bonus in front of my people to motivate them to do what needs to be done in ministry. Instead, I must lead them in such a way that they are internally motivated and that the intrinsic value that they receive alone is compensation enough to contribute great amounts of their time, talent, and resources to the work of ministry. This means that I am forced to always have the antennae of my "emotion-sensing" radar up as I walk through the ministry environment, zeroing in on anyone feeling emotions that might be a hindrance to the organization.

Verbal and non-verbal emotional cues are always being released into the environment between me as a leader and my followers, and these cues give me a good idea of the underlying emotions that my people are feeling. Sometimes they are positive and healthy. In these cases, I need not adapt or shift my behavior to change their emotional state; I just remain consistent with them. However, other times, they are negative and unhealthy. For example, if I see members whose arms are folded when I approach them, this is a pretty strong cue that they are closed and emotionally shut down. If I see members whose legs are crossed and who are sitting back away from me, this could mean that they are confident; however, if they have an unpleasant look on their face rather than a smile, this could suggest that they are creating distance from me because they are having negative feelings about something. In these cases, it is time for action; I must engage in interpersonal interaction with them, adapting my behavior in an effort to change their emotional state. This must be done quickly and effectively, because bad attitudes are as contagious as the flu and can spread throughout a church like wildfire!

I recall one particular occasion on which my congregants and I were preparing for a special Super Bowl service; we host this special interactive, exciting, and football-themed worship service each year on Super Bowl Sunday as part of our invitation efforts to reach out to football lovers. The night before the service, the planning team had been working all evening, going through rehearsals and running through each aspect of the worship service. After several hours, everyone was completely exhausted and ready to go home, and their body language and energy levels showed it. I had been in my office doing some work, occasionally peeking my head in on the rehearsals to check their progress. Around 10 p.m., I walked out of my office into the sanctuary; I was trying to "taste the air" and sense the atmosphere. As I walked through and observed, I was taking an emotional inventory of the group. Were they physically tired, emotionally fatigued, frustrated, angry, or irritated with one another? Indeed they were. It was time for me to adapt from my current state as a leader and shift into motivator!

I called everyone into my office and invited all to take a seat. I'm sure that they were wondering why I had pulled them away from their worship service run-through, because though they were exhausted, the service still needed work. However, what they did not realize is that they had an emotionally-intelligent, adaptable leader! I proceeded to shower the people with love, issued out specific compliments to individuals and teams, told a few jokes to make everyone laugh, and made them feel good about what they were doing. I explained that we needed just one more really good run-through, because the following day, this worship service would minister to people – both who knew God and especially those who did not know God – in a very special way. I inspired them about the significance of the work that they were doing, noting that it was not about entertaining the people; it was about the bottom line of souls being saved and angels rejoicing in heaven as a result of their hard work. After my words, the entire room erupted in loud applause! Then, they all filed out of my office and went back into the sanctuary fully energized and with a new sense of vigor and determination to complete the best worship run-through of the evening! If I had not adapted my behavior or approached them with an iron fist rather than a kid glove, the outcome would have been quite different! Using emotional intelligence to become adaptable as a leader always results in a win for the organization.

Leader Triad Side 3 | Adaptability
CATEGORY 2:

CULTURAL AWARENESS

Cultural awareness involves the ability to stand back from ourselves and become aware of our personal cultural values, beliefs, and perceptions. It helps us to understand why we do things a certain way, how we see the world the way we do, and why we react to things in a particular way.[36] In order to be adaptable, leaders must not only be aware or cognizant of the beliefs associated with their own cultures; they must also be aware of the beliefs of those whom they work beside and serve. Each of us as leaders holds certain assumptions of what we consider to be right and wrong, and these internal beliefs shape our perceptions about the people and situations with whom we interact. In order to be able to adapt as leaders, at any given moment, we must be conscientious of how our moral compass (our beliefs about what is right and wrong) is shaping our perspective, and if we realize that our compass is pointing us in the wrong direction, we must be able to immediately adapt our approach to the individual or situation in order to lead effectively.

Nowhere is cultural awareness more necessary than in the global context in which we now live and operate more than ever. Based upon the geography in which you were raised, you have undoubtedly developed your own strong orientation of what is right and wrong, appropriate and inappropriate, and acceptable and unacceptable. However, as an American, consider the following[37]:

- In America, is it more than acceptable to give money as a gift. In Bangladesh, it is considered unacceptable and a cultural faux pas.
- In America, it is just fine to use your left hand to do things if you are left handed. However, in Indonesia, it is considered a big cultural no-no to use your left hand. Instead, you must always use your right hand when shaking hands, offering a gift,

handing or receiving something, eating, pointing, or even touching another person.

- In America, showing affection to your loved one is endearing, so it is quite acceptable to greet your partner or spouse with a quick kiss upon greeting one another. However, in Malaysia, it is considered improper to show affection, as this is considered very immodest and impious.

- In America, if someone offers you a business card, you extend your hand to take it, say "Thank you," stick it in your pocket, purse, or portfolio, and offer your own card to the person. However, in Japan, to do such a thing would be offensive – a major cultural faux pas! Instead, in Japan, business cards should be given and accepted with both hands, and when you are given a business card, the cultural expectation is that you will immediately inspect it, admire it, and place it on the table in front of you for the remainder of the meeting. Then, at the end of the meeting, the culture dictates that you store the person's business card respectfully – never in a back pocket.

Were you culturally aware of these practices? Where do your notions of right and wrong or appropriate and inappropriate factor into them? These represent only a few of the myriad examples of how your beliefs and assumptions of what is considered right and wrong might be right and wrong depending upon the context in which you are operating and the individuals with whom you are interacting. The old adage says, "When in Rome, do as the Romans do." However, I add a caveat to the saying: When in Rome, do as the Romans do *if* doing so does not violate your core values, and only *if* you want to win!

If you are a leader interacting in a business context with someone from another culture or country, certain adaptations might need to be made in your thought processes, strategic approaches, and behaviors in order to achieve your desired outcome. However, if you are not an adaptable leader, when your assumptions of what is right and wrong or acceptable and unacceptable collide with those of what others hold to be right or wrong and acceptable or unacceptable, you will hold fast to the direction of your moral compass, ethics, values, and beliefs, and you could quite possibly blow the whole deal! We must become adaptable in order to lead effectively in today's world. Always keep in mind that the goal is to get a win for your organization without compromising your core values and beliefs, and sometimes, accomplishing this goal calls for making a shift in the way we approach things.

Cultural differences might not be as extreme as those that a leader might encounter when working with someone from another country; cultural differences are present between various races and ethnicities in America as within each respective race and ethic group. Differences also exist between people of different ages, different genders, and even different religious orientations. I have found differences in what people of different cultures deem acceptable dating practices. Where I come from, my orientation considers the notion of finding a spouse through an online dating site to be a bit absurd. I was in a meeting with some corporate clients on one particular occasion, and I made a flippant joke about internet dating and marriage as I chuckled at my humor. In an instant, I noticed that everyone in the meeting had grown a little quiet. It was a few minutes later that someone revealed to me that one of the members of the board of directors – who happened to be sitting there at the table with me – had met his current wife over the internet. Needless to say, I had some kissing up to do. I tried to wiggle my way out of the joke I had just told by explaining that internet dating was not wrong – just different! They were gracious towards me, but I could tell that my lack of knowledge about our cultural differences had led me to offend more than a few people that day. They weren't racial, gender, or age differences; they were just cultural mores that differed between my orientation and theirs. Contrary to the popular saying, what I didn't know that day did hurt me, because without knowing about this difference, I did not know to adjust my humor to fit the context of the situation.

My son's basketball team offers another example of how differences in culture can extend beyond race, gender, age, and the like. He plays in one of our city's Christian basketball leagues, which happen to be characterized, of course, by "Christian sportsmanship." Now, where I come from, "Christian sportsmanship" means no cursing, no violence, no fighting, no seeking to injure another player, and playing fairly and with integrity. Other than these, everything else is fair game, because we're out to win the game! However, it is apparent that I am from another culture, because this league's definition of "Christian sportsmanship" is quite different from my own. Part of this league's sportsmanship policy is that both the players and the people watching the game from the bleachers can only say positive, affirming things to the players on the court. There is absolutely no "trash talking" – you know, one of the biggest things that makes the game fun – because saying such words to your opponents might offend them and hurt their feelings. Further, when players and audience members make these positive affirmations to the players, the words must not be yelled; they must be spoken nicely and politely. As you might imagine, the atmosphere at these basketball games is very quiet, very subdued, and very boring (to me, at least!). Despite our cultural differences, however, I adjust my behavior to comply with what is deemed acceptable by the league. Thus, each time I feel myself on the brink of yelling to my son, "Take that rock!" or "Those guys have no game! You run this court! Take them to the hoop!" I have to catch myself, pause for a moment, and calmly and politely say instead, "That was a very nice shot!" Because of this, watching the games is about as interesting as watching paint dry. The entire time I am enduring this type of low-key spectacle of a competition, I am reminded that cultural differences extend far beyond geography, race, and morality.

Regardless of the nature of the differences, leaders who operate at high levels of effectiveness realize the necessity of understanding and adapting to them. In other words, they have high levels of cultural competency, regardless of whether the culture is race-based, gender-based, class-based, morality-based, etc. However, what is it about cultural competency that empowers a leader to be more effective? The answer is contained in one word: empathy.

Empathy is one's ability to psychologically identify with or imaginatively experience someone else's thoughts, feelings, or attitudes.[38] Empathy is not agreement. Rather, it is the ability to feel, as much as possible without experiencing the situation yourself, what another person is feeling, and to put yourself in the other person's shoes so that you can try to understand what they are experiencing at a deeper level and look at life through their eyes. Cultural competence empowers us to have greater levels of empathy for other people, because the more we understand how people who are different from us process, think, and feel and how and why they operate the way they do, the more we are able to see things from their perspective by putting ourselves in their shoes. The more we are able to see things from their perspective and feel a sense of being in their shoes, the more knowledgeable we become about how they specifically differ from us. In turn, as we anticipate the potential collision of our own culture and orientation with theirs, we can become proactive in making the necessary adjustments to our beliefs and strategic approaches to a situation so that, rather than end in conflict, the interaction will result in a positive win-win for our organization as well as for the other party. Not to mention, being aware of the culture and context of others can give us a great edge in business, because we can better understand the motivations behind how they think and what they do, and consequently, predict how they will operate.

It is not uncommon in today's age to be faced with doing business with people who originate from a different context than our own. However, our contexts and the assumptions and beliefs contained in them do not have to necessarily line up with others' contexts, beliefs, and assumptions in order for us to operate in business successfully. Since I have already introduced the Lutheran church that I consulted with on a church growth strategy, allow me to introduce another example about our interaction that fits well within the context of this discussion. As a charismatic evangelical pastor, there are clear differences between my Lutheran clients' beliefs and my own beliefs surrounding matters like preaching styles, worship contexts, and the audiences that our respective churches attract. During one of our growth strategy meetings, I sat there across the conference room table listening to an explanation of beliefs that were much different from my own, and the wheels in my mind started turning. What should I say? It was then that I began asking myself, "Are our differences so strong that I cannot continue to work with this church?" "Will the differences in our religious practices impact our work as we seek to develop an effective church growth strategy?" "Do we even need to acknowledge these differences?"

You're probably wondering what the final decision was as I sat there asking myself all of these questions, right? Well, to me, the answers were clear, so it took me less than a minute to arrive at a conclusion: I could indeed help them come up with a strategy to grow. I came in as a strategist to help them develop a plan of how to grow; *with whom* they chose to grow was not my business! In this case, I was faced with my own ability to adapt on the spot. I had to examine my moral compass and what I thought to be right and wrong, consider the context in which I was operating, consider the orientation of the individuals I was working with, and make a mature decision on how to adapt my beliefs or approach without compromising my own core values in the process. If you will be an effective leader, you must learn to do this too, because this skill plays a key role in adaptability!

Leader Triad Side 3 | Adaptability
CATEGORY 3:

AUTHENTICITY

Authentic leadership is a particular approach to leadership in which a leader seeks to build legitimacy with followers through the development of open and honest – or authentic – relationships. Authentic leaders, who tend to be positive people, value the input of their followers and promote openness. They endeavor to lead in such a way that they engender trust and enthusiastic support from those whom they lead, primarily because they emphasize people over profits and ethics over economics.[39] According to Forbes, authentic leaders are self-aware, genuine, mission driven leaders who lead with their hearts and focus on results and the long-term.[40] Essentially, authenticity refers to a leader's ability to be real and true with him or herself and others. Younger people would define authenticity as "keeping it 100." Whatever you call it, leadership authenticity is an important part of adaptability. In fact, it is the trait of being authentic in and of itself that is an adaptation on traditional leadership styles.

When we expose ourselves as leaders to our followers, allowing them to peer into our lives to see not just who we are but why we are, a funny thing happens: people tend to be more willing to follow us and give us more of themselves for the good of the organization. This is no wonder, because in today's high-tech and low-touch society, many young people are looking for something or someone to connect with, whether that something is a purpose or a reason to live, or whether that someone is a friend, work associate, or even a leader. They spend most of their lives connecting with and through technology and social media. However, despite all of the extensive opportunities to "connect" that technology offers, as human beings, we are programmed to have relationships with real people. This is why when we allow people to look into our lives beyond the surface of what we represent and see that we are real people, they are inclined to be better followers!

It should be said that although being an authentic leader is a leadership style that is deliberately engaged for the sake of drawing more out of our followers, the relationships that authentic leaders develop with their followers are real and sincere relationships; this is what makes them "authentic." Leaders open their lives up to reveal who they are and what they believe to their followers, and they take the time out to learn about their followers and what they believe. Followers appreciate the fact that leaders actually care about them enough to trust them with knowing who they (the leaders) are beyond their titles, and they value the idea that their leaders see them as more than an employee number, a slot on an organizational chart, or a cog on a wheel. They are grateful that someone in the world has taken the time to see them as a person – to know their name, where they are from, what types of activities their children are engaged in, the welfare of their parents, the different extracurricular activities they are involved in outside of the job, and their emotional state. People appreciate the fact that someone else just cares, and when they see that their leaders are willing to interact with them on this level, they regard the relationship as special, and they reciprocate with an equal level of openness. The exchanges in this relationship between leader and follower become truthful and authentic interactions, and they develop a genuine connection with one another, because they have dared to expose themselves to one another through equivalent levels of transparency.

Because of the depth of the relationship, which has gone beyond the traditional surface-level leader-follower relationship, when the leader makes a request, the follower responds differently than he or she might respond to a leader that leads out of a more traditional style of leadership. In fact, research indicates that authentic leadership is positively related to workplace engagement, which is a follower's individual involvement, satisfaction, enthusiasm for work, and sense of personal commitment.[41] Followers who work under authentic leaders are more willing to push beyond their physical, emotional, and even financial comfort in order to execute what needs to be done. They will give 110 percent of their time, focus and energy to get things done, because this is about responding to a person with whom they are in a meaningful relationship, not just a boss! Considering this, the productivity potential of an organization can increase exponentially when authentic leader-follower relationships are engaged.

Because I am a pastor, my orientation always leads me in the direction of using biblical examples to help develop an understanding of a particular concept. I make no apologies for this. That said, I can think of no better example of what authenticity looks like in a leader than Jesus Christ. God chose to veil Himself of His divinity, become flesh and walk among men as Jesus Christ, the Son of Man, just so that we could go beyond surface knowledge of Him and know Him intimately. Because He was both fully God and fully man, when men saw Jesus, they saw God. In fact, Jesus said Himself, "Anyone who has seen Me has seen the Father."[42] God gave us the greatest possible glimpse into who He is and how He operates by sending His Son to walk among us – right in our midst! As a result, because we have seen Jesus (and because we today can read the accounts of those who both saw Him and walked with Him), we have seen God, and we can better understand who He is. Then, not only did man gain a deeper understanding of God through Jesus Christ, Christ is now able to understand man, because He became a man Himself. If God's model is not a prime example of what authenticity looks like in a leader, I don't know what is! He showed us at another level the place where the leader and follower meet and expose themselves to one another, and this exposure has led to more than 2,000 years of people being fully committed and passionately devoted to following the leadership of Jesus Christ!

Leader Triad Side 3 | Adaptability
SUMMARY & CONCLUSIONS

In summary, leaders must become skillful in answering the question, "How far am I willing to go to make shifts in my beliefs and behaviors in order to connect at a deeper level with others for the benefit of the organization?" Without answering this question, leaders are prone to miss out on opportunities to connect with others in ways that produce more favorable outcomes. They will remain locked into certain ways of doing things that are driven by their own cultural beliefs and assumptions without considering the cultural beliefs and assumptions of others, and this lack of flexibility in the way that they approach things will inevitably affect their business interactions and their leader-follower relationships. Ultimately, they will never be able to maximize their leadership efforts by drawing the most productivity possible out of their followers or by connecting with others in business at a level that will result in greater wins for their organization.

If You Know *Why* People Do what They Do, You Can Shift Them towards Doing Something Different!

Often, you might hear leaders sitting around and commiserating about how they have been unable to move their people to do a certain job, act a certain way, or complete a certain task. You might have even been one of them on more than a few occasions! Despite all of what they consider to be their best efforts, they have been unable to break the unwanted behaviors in their people and produce the desired behaviors in them that will get the leaders what they want. If I have the fortunate privilege to happen to be sitting in one of these sessions, after listening to these leaders take their turn at downing their followers, I will always insert a question into the dialogue for consideration: *Why* are your people behaving this way? My question is usually met with blank stares, as if to say, "Well, if we knew the answer to *that*, we wouldn't *be* in this mess of a situation!"

My point in asking the question is to help my fellow leaders to consider what is motivating the mentalities and behaviors of their followers. After all, we can all admit that judging and condemning our followers is quite unproductive. Wouldn't it be more beneficial to understand the feelings that are motivating the undesirable behaviors of our followers and then work to influence their feelings towards a more positive state designed to produce more desired behaviors? In other words, why don't we exercise our emotional intelligence to identify what the people are feeling and then adapt our own behaviors as leaders in such a way that we shift those feelings to those that will benefit the organization? Of course, this would mean that the leaders would have to be willing to be flexible and adaptable in their approaches with both individuals and groups within their organizations. This is the work of a leader – an effective leader, that is! If you are not working, I can guarantee that your people are not following, and you are not getting the results you desire out of them!

Lazy leaders make assumptions about why their people are acting and responding a certain way. They then act, based upon their assumptions, to motivate their leaders to do something different. However, assumptions can be wrong. Dead wrong. Thus, these types of leaders will find themselves trying strategy after strategy to move their people to produce desired outcomes, all to no avail. On the other hand, effective leaders do the work to try to understand why their people are doing what they are doing (i.e., what feelings are motivating their thoughts, words, and behaviors), and once they are armed with this information, they use their emotional intelligence to adapt their approaches to help their people feel something different – and consequently, produce something different!

"No" Doesn't Always Mean "No"
When an Adaptable Leader is in Charge!

I have learned some valuable leadership lessons over the years, but one, in particular, has continually left me feeling empowered like no other. Each time I see it in action, I cannot help but smile at the result. The lesson is this: people have a hard time saying "No" to an authentic, emotionally intelligent, adaptable leader. When they do say "No," if their leader is an adaptable, authentic, culturally aware and emotionally intelligent one, their answer does not remain "No" for long.

I teach my clients that effective leaders understand that "No means know"! Experience over decades of leadership has taught me that when people tell me "No," it is because I do not know them; we only have a surface-level leader-follower relationship that does not lead them to feel obligated in any way to extend themselves beyond their personal comforts to tell me "Yes." However, the more I know a person, the more difficult it is for that person to say "No" to me. After all, we share a transparent, authentic relationship in which we understand each other beyond a surface level and respect each others' needs. As a result, I can get them to push past every instinct that they have to say "No" and instead say "Yes"! Because they have developed a relationship with me as an adaptable leader, they are willing to give more of their time, more of their talent, and more of their resources than anyone else in the ministry. Even when they don't feel good about it, they do what is asked of them in ministry.

Mind you, the "Say 'Yes' when you want to say 'No'" response is reserved for me as their primary leader. I can send other leaders on my behalf to ask people to do things, and without a pause or a blink of an eye, the people will say, "Nope!" My leaders return to me, deflated and frustrated because they were unable to get anyone to agree to execute my requests. Then, I immediately pick up the phone, call the people, make the same, exact requests of them that I had my representatives make of them earlier, and without a pause, they say, "Okay, Pastor. Yes!" What is the difference between my representatives making the request and me making the request? Was it that I spent more time explaining the need for them to do what I requested? No. Was it that I was nicer when I made the request? No. Was it that I used a friendlier and less-aggressive tone? No. Was it that they knew that they would face some negative consequence or penalty if they said "No" to me? No. The differentiating factor between their response to me versus my delegates is that I continuously engage in the work of leadership by getting to know my people. Consequently, when I pick up the phone to ask them to do something, because we *know* each other – not just because I lead them – they are inclined to say "Yes," even when everything in them wants to cry out "Nooooo!"

If you are having a hard time moving your followers and getting them to say "Yes" to you, you do not have a "No" issue; you have a "know" issue. Take the time to learn more about them and what moves them. Tap into their belief systems and their internal values. Open yourself up to them and invite them to do the same with you. Then, adapt the way you approach them and interact with them based upon this new knowledge and level of relationship. You will find that it will make all the difference in the way that they respond to you when you make requests of them; they are less inclined to say "No" and more inclined to do whatever it takes to make your request happen, even if it means inconveniencing their own lives to do so. People say "No" to bosses, leaders, and figureheads who carry authority based upon their title. People say "Yes" to leaders who care about them, are transparent with them, and carry influence with them based upon relationship.

Adaptability Helps Leaders to Capitalize on Assets – Human Assets, that Is!

It is no secret that most non-profit organizations, and many for-profit businesses, for that matter, manage their day-to-day operations with a budget that is so tight, it often feels like they are grasping for air! These organizations do not have lots of money working for them, but they do have something that is just as important to getting things done: people and the energy that they bring! To lament your organization's lack of financial resources without maximizing your human resources, particularly volunteers, could prove to be a huge and costly mistake! In fact, if you as a leader can effectively maximize the time and energy that your people are willing to give, their contributions can make up a significant part of what you are lacking in your budgetary shortfalls!

The ability to maximize your people resources when you do not have money to use as a motivator takes some skill. It takes everything that we have discussed surrounding being an adaptable leader – and then some! To be effective in this endeavor, leaders must develop relationships, be willing to stroke people emotionally, and concede a little territory to followers in ways that make them think that they are winning in order for the leader and organization to ultimately win in the grand scheme of things.

One leadership adaptation that works well for me as a pastor is to always help my volunteer ministry partners to see that there is a deeper and more significant meaning behind the work that they are doing. It's more than just mindless, meaningless, trivial busywork! To maximize these volunteers, when I ask them to complete certain tasks or engage in ministry work, I carefully explain to them they are not only meeting the needs of the church that serves them, but they are meeting God's needs. I point them towards a greater eternal reality and help them to understand that the ultimate purpose behind all that we do is to build a strong ministry that is able to reach out and touch souls that are lost, to bring these souls to Christ, to build them up, train them in the things of God, and help them to continue to live their lives for Christ. Simply put, the work is always about the bottom line of evangelism and discipleship! When their time, energy, and resources are focused on these things, they are on-task with God's purpose for their lives. Even more, their engagement in ministry at this level means that anytime that they play any role in an evangelistic effort that results in someone coming to Christ, fruit abounds to their account. Who wouldn't want fruit to abound to their heavenly account? Empowered with this level of understanding, my volunteer partners work harder than ever, giving it everything they've got, and feeling good about it! Because of this, I get a lot more accomplished in ministry by leveraging their free labor. This is more than money could ever buy, even if we had a strong, healthy budget at our disposal!

Another by-product of my approach that motivates followers by pointing them towards a higher reality is that they are more willing to work together as a team, because evangelism and discipleship are more effective as community goals rather than individual ones. As leaders, it is our job to make people feel good about working together, get them excited about communal goals, and motivate them to engage in something that might not benefit them tangibly in the here and now but later in eternity. A great example of this principle at work in my own ministry is that of the Super Bowl service that I mentioned earlier. In order to motivate my fatigued and aggravated worship team, as I sat with them in my office, I intentionally pointed them towards the higher reality that they could not see with their natural eyes in their frustrated state: souls would be saved as a result of the sacrifices they were making in planning and rehearsal for the worship service. Thus, what they were doing was going to benefit someone else, and playing a part in causing others to benefit would help the volunteer partners in the long term. Though they had gotten little sleep and showed up the next morning for the worship service as tired as ever, they executed the Super Bowl production flawlessly – for the sake of someone else's potential salvation. It all paid off; ten souls came to Christ that morning! As they witnessed people making their way to the front of the church for salvation, these same weary members who were so worn out that they could barely stand sat in their seats and cried tears of joy at what God had done through their sacrificial hard work. In fact, to see the results of their sacrifices in action gave them so much renewed energy that no one went to sleep; for the rest of the day, we celebrated together and rejoiced about how great the outcome of the service was!

My approach to pulling all that I do out of my volunteer ministry partners is not magic; it is deliberate, intentional leadership that sees where my people need to be and adapts my approach to get them there so that I can have access to their time, energy, resources for the organization's benefit. You can do it too! Try to tap into the emotions of your people and teach them the benefits of collaborating with one another on tasks and projects. Teach them that when we all contribute, we all win. I won't mislead you by telling you that this will be an easy task; your people will likely give you some resistance every step of the way. However, in the end, everyone will rejoice, because the end results will have been well worth the sacrifice!

Committed and enthusiastic volunteer partners can fill in spaces and meet needs where money cannot, but only if you develop and maintain a relationship with them as an adaptable leader. For example, you might need to have some graphic design work done, which costs $1,200. Well, if you have a person in your organization who works as a graphic designer, and you are willing to engage your emotional intelligence, cultural awareness, and authentic leadership skills, you can adapt your behavior towards the designer so that he or she feels special, valued, cared for, appreciated, and a major part of fulfilling the organization's mission. Consequently, when you make the request for him or her to do the design work for the organization pro bono, it will be very difficult – next to impossible – to say "No" to you!

People assets can be some of the greatest assets that you have access to, especially when you have limited access to finances. Leadership adaptability can help you to capitalize on your people assets for all they are worth; and they are worth *a lot*! Adaptable leadership helps us to empower, engage, and experience the collaborative power that people have when they come together for the benefit of the organization.

PART 5:
THE FOLLOWER TRIAD

Building an Awareness of Who Might Work with You and How Far They Might Be Willing to Go to Successfully Execute a Task

Follower Triad Side 1:
Personal Influences

What known or hidden personal values, motivations, or feelings are present within me, and how do they affect my perceptions and interactions, skew my interpretation of the facts surrounding critical situations, and influence my decisions, actions, and reactions with others?

Follower Triad Side 2:
Followership Style

What level of support does this follower offer to me as a leader, and how does it affect his or her propensity to challenge my directives when asked to execute an organizational task?

Follower Triad Side 3:
Leader-Follower Relationship

How close is the relationship that I share with this follower, and how should I order my interactions, communications, and expectations with him/her based upon this level of closeness?

The 720° Snapshot

THE FOLLOWER TRIAD

PERSONAL

C.O.R.E.
S.T.A.R.C.H.
P.O.R.K.
S.H.O.E.S.

FOLLOWERSHIP STYLE

Partner
Implementer
Individualist
Resource

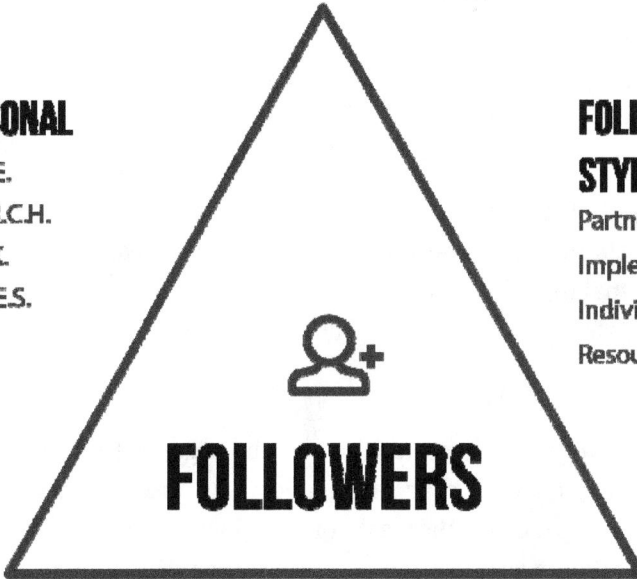

FOLLOWERS

LEADER-FOLLOWER RELATIONSHIP

Exchange Level
▶ Out-group
Stranger Phase
▶ In-group
Acquaintance Phase
Mature Partner Phase

FOLLOWER:

Someone who supports and is guided by another person or group and who does what others say to do.

The fourth and final triad of *Moody's 720° Leadership Decision-Making Model* is the Follower Triad. It is comprised of three sides, elements, or sets of considerations about which the leader should be aware when making decisions regarding a given task: Personal, Followership Style, and Leader-Follower Relationship.

When a leader is approaching a task within the organization, there will inevitably be people other than the leader who are responsible for executing various parts of the task or the task as a whole. These individuals are followers. Followers fall under the guidance and direction of the leader; they are under the leader's authority and are expected to "follow" the leader's orders. How the leader approaches the designation of the tasks at hand to the followers should not be random. Instead, the leader should make informed decisions about how to delegate the various aspects of the tasks to the followers based upon his or her awareness of certain key factors. Once these assessments are made, the leader can make a decision to strategically delegate all or part of the tasks to those followers who are in the best position to complete them and produce the leader's desired outcomes. Thus, it is critical for the leader to understand his or her followers, particularly each follower's style of following and how he or she works and interacts with the leader.

How a follower actually follows plays a large role in a leader's effectiveness! When we consider that a leader is graded solely on the ability to get things done and meet certain goals, and they use their followers to do the work to meet these goals, how good of a grade would the leader receive if the followers consistently failed to meet the goals? This is an important question to consider if leaders will operate with high levels of effectiveness. They cannot only be intimately aware of their organization and themselves; they must be fully aware of how and where their followers are too!

Without a keen awareness of how their followers follow, leaders will experience unnecessary frustration and disappointment. Why? Because they will desire one level of exchange with their followers and receive another undesired level of exchange, time and again. Followers' lack of ability to give their leaders what they want can leave leaders feeling rejected, frustrated, angry, and confused. They cannot figure out why, for the life of them, they continue to give clear, detailed directions to skilled, capable, and intelligent people and yet their followers repeatedly do not execute the tasks in the way that their leaders have prescribed! Say what you will, but being engaged in this type of continuous cycle that always starts with high expectations and always ends with a failure to produce results is enough to have any leader questioning whether he or she has the abilities to lead an organization.

What these leaders fail to consider is that, although they might *appear* to be so, the followers that they have to work with within the organization are not a monolithic group. They might all share the same level of educational attainment, they might all have been through the same developmental trainings, and they might all belong to the same professional organizations; however, there are subtle invisible differences beneath each of their surfaces that makes one perfectly suited to execute the leader's task to perfection and that makes another one perfectly inclined to sabotage it. The same differences make one follower eagerly responsive to the leader's direction and another follower dismissive, apathetic, and unresponsive to it.

Learning the differences between their followers helps leaders to manage their expectations so that what they anticipate receiving from their followers, they actually get. Their increased awareness surrounding how their followers operate cuts down on disappointment and frustration and increases levels of satisfaction and efficacy, all because they are empowered to delegate the right tasks to the right followers. When training leaders on how to effectively manage followers, I often reference the expectations we have of our pets, because we tend to have more accurate expectations of our furry pals than we do of our followers! For example, we do not expect our cats to fetch. No matter how many colorful, bouncy, squeaky balls we buy, our cats will never fetch. Thus, if we are in the mood to play a friendly game of fetch, we do not go wake up our cat Fluffy; we go wake up our energetic, enthusiastic dog Titan, because he is *always* eager to chase down and retrieve a good ball – for hours at a time! Whether our pets or our followers, the same principle holds true: expecting the wrong things from the wrong individuals will always result in wasted time, energy, and emotional resources.

Whether our pets or our followers, the same principle holds true: expecting the wrong things from the wrong individuals will always result in wasted time, energy, and emotional resources.

CHAPTER 13

FOLLOWER TRIAD SIDE 1: PERSONAL INFLUENCES

ASSESSMENT QUESTION:

What known or hidden personal values, motivations, or feelings are present within me, and how do they affect my perceptions and interactions, skew my interpretation of the facts surrounding critical situations, and influence my decisions, actions, and reactions with others?

In precisely the same ways that your awareness of yourself and your Personal Issues as a leader affects you in the Leader triad, your level of self-awareness and your Personal Issues affect you as a leader in the Follower triad. The impact of your emotions, psyche, education, exposure, training, and experiences has created your worldview – the lens through which you automatically interpret and respond to interactions with people and situations. Considering this, it is easy to understand how a leader's Personal Issues can also clearly affect how they deal with followers.

Understanding how your Personal Influences impact your expectations of, interactions with, and responses to your followers is critical if you will ever effectively maximize your abilities to lead others. In fact, this understanding is so vital that it deserves attention of its own. Thus, as with the Personal Influences introduced in the discussion of the Leader triad, I will dedicate a later chapter with focused attention on understanding these leadership influences and how they can either hurt or hinder your leadership effectiveness.

CHAPTER 14

FOLLOWER TRIAD SIDE 2: FOLLOWERSHIP STYLE

ASSESSMENT QUESTION:

What level of support does this follower offer to me as a leader, and how does it affect his or her propensity to challenge my directives when asked to execute an organizational task?

Throughout your tenure as the leader of your organization, you might have noticed that not all followers are the same. They do not share the same level of buy-in, commitment, enthusiasm, support of the organization, or dedication to the organization's mission and vision, among other things. Understanding this, it makes sense that because all followers are not the same, we should not relate to them in the same way. However, despite this seemingly common-sense understanding, we as leaders do it *every day*! The reality is that each and every follower under our sphere of leadership has a particular followership style, and the various dimensions that define an individual's followership style is measured by the degree of support that he or she gives to the leader.[43] Some give everything they have when they interact with their leaders, others give as little as possible, and still others fall somewhere in-between.

Only after a leader determines the degree of support that a follower is willing to give to him or her should the leader be willing to delegate a task to the individual. However, this task should be one that is commensurate with the follower's followership style. Leaders who assign organizational tasks only *after* they are empowered with knowledge of their followers' followership style experience fewer surprises in what their followers produce at the end of a given task. This is because their high level of awareness of their followers has equipped them to make an informed decision to give those with greater levels of support and commitment high-level tasks. Conversely, those who demonstrate a lower level of commitment receive lower-level tasks. Leaders' awareness of their followers also prepares them in advance for managing their own expectations of what they can expect their followers to agree to do and not agree to do. Again, those with a lower level of support and commitment for the organization and the leader will not even accept tasks that require too much of their time, energy, and resources. On the other hand, leaders know that they can ask followers who are fully supportive and highly committed to the organization to do just about anything. Regardless of what the cost may be for these followers in terms of time, resources, comfort, and convenience, the leader will more than likely get an easy and enthusiastic response of "Sure! I'll do whatever you need!" You might wonder, "Can being aware of a follower's followership style tell a leader all of this?" The answer is absolutely yes! Being aware of your followers at such a level is quite empowering!

Leaders should understand that a follower's followership style is not fixed or set in stone; it can be dynamic, not static. Once a leader assesses that a follower is operating at a lower level of support and commitment, he or she can create an individual development plan, based upon the relationship, to strategically move the follower from a lower-level followership style to a higher-level one. The ultimate goal is to move as many followers as possible to the highest and most supportive level of followership – from the outer circle of participation to the close, inner circle of core followership – because this will translate directly into the leader having increased influence with and increased access to the follower's discretionary resources. In the meantime, however, the leader will be careful to only assign what the follower can handle at his or her current level of followership, engaging each follower only at the level that he or she can handle.

There are four different types of followership style that followers can possess,[44] and they typically fall into the following four categories:

1) Partner
2) Implementer
3) Individualist
4) Resource

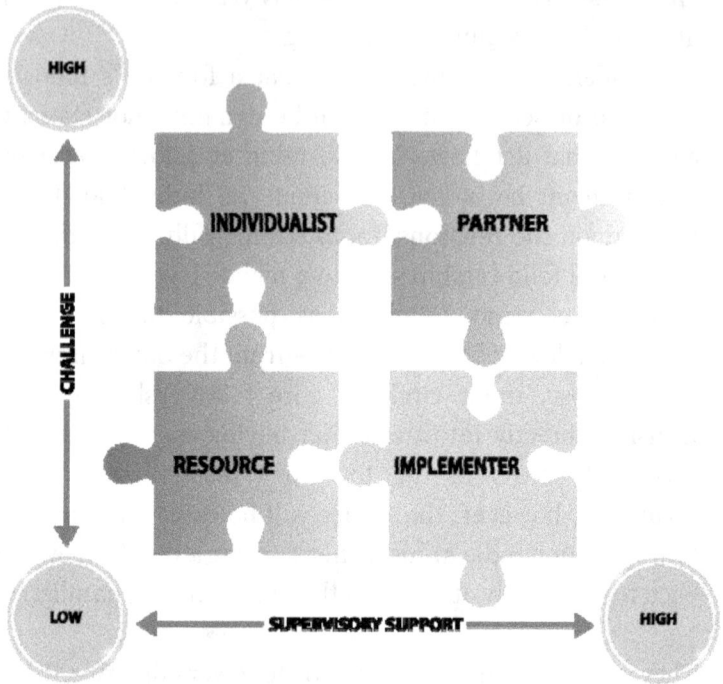

Figure 1. Styles of Followership

Follower Triad Side 2 | Followership Style
CATEGORY 1:

PARTNER

Partners are followers who are fully engaged with the leader and the organization, both emotionally and professionally. They possess a passion for the vision and the visionary leader of the organization, and they have fully bought in to all that the organization represents. For the Partner, it is not the leader's organization and vision; it is "our" organization, "our" vision, and therefore, ensuring that all of the necessary tasks are executed effectively becomes "our" responsibility for this follower. By definition, a Partner is an individual who joins with other individuals, or Partners, in an arrangement where gains, losses, risks, and rewards are shared among the Partners.[45] Thus, Partners consider themselves stakeholders whose own success is wrapped up in that of the organization, and this is reflected in their levels of participation, commitment, and aggression.

Partners vigorously support their leader and are willing to question their leader's behavior and policies.[46] Because of the level of buy-in and ownership that Partners feel for the organization, they do not mind asking tough questions and having tough dialogue about issues concerning the organization. They do not challenge the leader's ideas and decisions for the sake of questioning his or her capabilities or undermining his or her authority. Instead, they will easily challenge things within the organization in order to come up with the best possible strategy that will move things forward, make the vision a reality, and make the visionary happy. They have high respect and the utmost regard for their leader, and they position themselves as true assets that are at the leader's disposal to make things happen in the organization, even if it means giving of their resources, time, and energy, and even if it means inconveniencing themselves. Partners are on board, ready to think, and ready to work!

It is easy to tell followers who are Partners in the midst of a group of people sitting in a meeting. For example, as the leader is speaking during the meeting, the Partner's body language and behavior will be alert and attentive; they will be leaning forward, engaged, taking notes, asking questions, engaging in the dialogue, providing feedback to ideas, asking what-if's, and contributing lots of energy to the meeting. They feel that their presence is needed there so that they can have a voice in the direction of "their" organization, and they value being able to contribute whatever they can that can help the organization and its leader advance.

When followers who are Partners are engaged in a task, they are usually assertive and driven to get the job done, because they understand that the success of their organization depends on them getting the job done and getting it done right. Rather than simply execute the task detail by detail according to the instructions provided for them, Partners will critically think about what they are doing and why they are doing it all the way through the execution. If they come across something that does not make sense to do because it seems to contradict what the organization is trying to accomplish, rather than just do what they have been told to do, Partners will go to their leader and question the instructions. Partners do not operate like mindless robots who are simply trying to get a task done; because they are invested and committed to the organization, they tend to evaluate what has been asked of them in light of the overall vision of the organization and make judgment calls or critical decisions in the midst of the task. For example, they might question things like how a particular task fits into the overall plan of the vision, whether there is enough time to complete a particular task or not with excellence, how the completion of one tasks impacts or intersects with tasks that others are doing, or whether their limited time should be spent on this task versus spending it on something more time-sensitive. Partners are so committed to the success of the organization that they might even sometimes alter certain elements of the task in order to ultimately improve it and have even been known to invest high levels of their own personal time and resources in order to produce outcomes of the highest possible quality!

Clearly, followers who fall into the followership style of "Partner" are on the wish list of every organizational leader who desires to be successful, whether these followers are paid or volunteer. There is a misconception that the more you pay a person, the more invested and committed to the organization's success that person will be. What a myth! This level of followership has nothing to do with money; it has to do with the leader's ability to lead effectively and the follower's willingness to connect with the leader and his/her vision in such a way that it belongs to him/her. Once you can get followers to the Partner level of followership, their primary concern will be that of bringing the organization's vision to pass, because again, this is not *your* organization, it is *their* organization. Be careful to listen to the language that your followers use; when they begin to use pronouns that are inclusive rather than exclusive, this is a clear signal that you might have a bona fide Partner on your hands – every leader's dream!

Because Partners are such valuable assets to the organization, they should be used in a special capacity. Wise leaders bring their Partners close to them, strategically positioning them in the middle of any of their key initiatives and using them to lead any critical areas of the organization. In fact, I advise leaders to ensure that each and every task group has at least one Partner participating in it. Without the presence of a Partner in the group, the task is more inclined to fail; the group will not have a clear idea about how its task connects with the overall vision, so it will act blindly *"according to the instructions"* without stopping to consider whether what they are

> *The goal of Non-Partners is to say, "We got what you said to do done!" rather than "We completed something with excellence that will advance the organization!"*

doing will actually fulfill the organization's needs. In my experience, groups without the guidance and energy of a Partner will often do the minimal amount that is required to complete the task, and they will typically treat the task as a check-off item. Their goal is to say, "We got what you said to do done!" rather than "We completed something with excellence that will advance the organization!"

There is a difference between the work being and the work being done right. Non-Partners are more likely to just get the work done. Partners are going to do everything they can to ensure that the work is done right. This is a lesson that I learned through first-hand through trial and error. When I moved our organization into our current facility, we had quite a bit of renovation to do. I assembled my troops together, broke them into task groups, gave them their marching orders, and set them loose to execute my commands. It took all of one day to realize my error in not assigning at least one Partner to each of these task groups. Now, if you have any experience with painting a room, you know that you cannot simply walk into the room with a brush, a paint roller, and a can of paint and start painting! Instead, in order to do a good paint job, you will need to tape and float the walls to ensure that the areas where the wall panels connect are smooth and seamless. You will need to move the furniture out of the way and cover it and the floors with cloths or plastic to protect them from paint spatter. You will need to use painter's tape on the borders of the area where you will paint in order to ensure clean, neat lines... and *then* you begin to paint! Further, for the best paint job, you do not use just one coat of paint, you use two! My Non-Partners were those who tended to jump right in and start painting without doing any prep work first. When they finished, they had done a really shabby job (that actually had to be re-done), but they wanted to be appreciated for the fact that they "got it done!" On the other hand, my Partners were those who were patient and invested enough to take their time, painstakingly prep the room, do the best possible job on the painting, and produce a quality paint job. You've just got to *love* your Partners! If I had ensured that there was at least one Partner in the Non-Partner task groups, I know that the Non-Partner paint jobs would have come out differently. As soon as the Non-Partner group members began to cut corners and compromise the quality of the project, my Partner follower would have stepped in and said, "Oh no! We've got to do this with excellence! Our organization's reputation is at stake, so we have to represent quality!"

As critical thinkers, Partners also play a key role in helping Non-Partners make sense of the tasks that they are executing. Let's take another renovation project that I was a part of as an example. When you tell a group of Non-Partners to renovate a room by installing a hardwood floor and painting the walls, it would be a given by any logical person that these actions would be taken in a particular order, right? Well, it turns out that it depends on who you ask. Partners would agree with you, but if you ask a group of Non-Partners, the answer is "No." Remember: Non-Partners tend not to invest a lot of thought into what they are doing, because their only goal is to get it done so that they can finally get back to doing what they would rather be doing anyway. Partners would tell you that the last thing that you would do in the room is the hardwood floor. After all, you would not want to install the shiny new hardwood floor and then paint the room, because the paint might damage the floor. However, in one particular situation when I was a Partner (prior to my current position as leader), I had the unfortunate experience of witnessing a group of non-critical thinking

Non-Partners say, "Well, the guy with the paint is still on the way, and the floor is already here, so let's go ahead and install the floor! Our assignment is to get it done today, so we're gonna get it done today! I don't want to get into trouble!" Fortunately, the Partner that I was, I was available to help them think through how illogical the approach they were taking was, and they held off on installing the floor until the painting was completed... although they replied with a chorus of, "We can do it your way, but *you're* going to take the fall for this room not being done today!" The room missed the original deadline of being completed that day (it was completed the following day), but it was completed with excellence and without running the risky cost of damaging an expensive, new hardwood floor. Partners lead a group in thinking critically and in answering the tough questions.

Partners are going to be your "prime time" players in your organization. When you are seeking to develop your team, do not exclude them just because they have already achieved this followership level. Though they might already be highly committed, invested, gifted, and passionate, they still have to learn how you work, how your systems work, and how to continually think like the organization (vision, values, beliefs, etc.). Otherwise, because they tend to be thinkers, you run the risk of them making decisions that are based more upon what they have learned from their past organizational experiences rather than what you have placed in them as a follower in your current organization.

IMPLEMENTER

Implementers are followers who are dependable and who will contribute their efforts towards helping the organization reach its goals. However, unlike Partners who will critically think through and challenge their leaders decisions in an effort to ensure that the best possible outcomes are realized by the organization, Implementers will not; they will be hesitant to question any leadership decisions.[47] This is due to their level of commitment to the leader and the organization, which is halfhearted at best. Though a leader will be able to get a lot out of them, he or she must realize that these followers are not fully bought-in and must not treat them as such.

Although Implementers are not as fully vested with the leader and the organization as Partners, make no mistake about it: they are dedicated! Implementers want to help by doing what the leader needs done. Their key goal is to complete any tasks that their leader assigns to them – sometimes, even with enthusiasm – so that they can say that they did their part to support the organization. The main challenge with this group of followers, though, is that leaders cannot expect for them to critically think through a project or to consider how the project is connected to other projects or goals within the organization.

Another challenge that leaders will encounter when trying to mobilize Implementers, especially when organizing task groups, is that Implementers often tend to operate in a silo, as they prefer to work alone. This tendency is, in large part, due to their having a higher level of self-interest than one might encounter in a Partner. You see, Partners set aside their own self-interests for the good and advancement of the organization; once they have become fully bought-in to the vision, being a key player in the organization's goals literally becomes a major part of their identity. Implementers, on the other hand, hold back much more. They tend to protect themselves while helping the organization. Thus, while they are willing to "do things" and execute certain tasks, they are not willing to allow their lives and identities to become fully absorbed by the organization. Unlike Partners, they hold back a significant part of their lives for themselves. Wise leaders will not grow frustrated at the level of commitment and engagement that Implementers are willing to offer to the organization; they will accept what these followers are willing to give and maximize every drop of it.

Implementers might not be as ideal a group of followers as Partners, but they can be of great benefit to the organization! For example, if leaders call a meeting, Implementers will be there, because they are committed; they might even arrive early, because they tend to be dependable. During the meeting, Implementers can be observed taking notes, but there is a strong likelihood that the notes are only concerning things that directly pertain to them and their individual tasks; they want to be sure that whatever they are responsible for doing is done right. If the leader of the meeting is talking about anything that Implementers do not feel is directly relevant to them, they will quite possibly tune out. During the presentation of all of this "irrelevant information," they are prone to completely disengage. They might sit and stare at the leader with blank looks on their faces, busy themselves with checking their e-mails on their mobile devices, or perhaps doodle on a piece of paper until the leader starts to discuss "more important matters," that is, matters that contain their specific marching orders. Once the meeting reaches such a point and the specifics of the discussion apply to them, Implementers are known for asking a series of clarifying questions, like what the deadlines are for their part of the task, where the clear lines of demarcation between their part and another person's part lay, etc. I would not go so far as to say that these followers cannot be team players, but I can say that if they are working with a team, their primary concern is simply getting the parts that they are directly accountable for done. In fact, if they complete their part of the project, they will often not see the need to turn around and assist their team members with completing their part of the project. Instead, they will proudly say, "I did my part, and I am done!" leaving their teammates to struggle through the completion of their own.

One of the most critical mistakes that I see leaders make is that of trying to "force" Implementers to engage in critical thinking skills. I understand that they are only trying to get these followers' buy-in to catch up with their level of willingness to execute, but without some really intentional development, this is simply not going to happen. Implementers are much like robots: if you program them the right way, they will do exactly what you want exactly the way you want it done. However, if they run into an unexpected obstacle, that's it! Game over. When Implementers become engaged in a task, they generally work to complete the task according to their leader's specifications in a timely manner. This level of productivity will last as long as they do not encounter a hiccup, like not having all of the components necessary for them to execute their task. Rather than think through how to get the components, it is characteristic of an Implementer to simply freeze. They get stuck! You might walk into a room expecting to see them working diligently on a particular project and instead see them sitting in a chair doing something else. When you ask why they are no longer working on the project, they will reply, "*I didn't have all of the things that I needed to get it done.*" Rather than engaging in just a little bit of critical thought, the Implementer will simply choose to enter into a state of paralysis, not even considering the impact that not getting their part done will have on other goals within the organization. The only exception to this is when Implementers think that they might get into trouble for not completing their assignment. In these cases, they might be motivated to overcome the hurdle and get the project done, simply so that no one can ever say that they did not "do their part." These followers are called Implementers because they implement, or put things into action. However, I add a caveat to this that helps to describe them more accurately. I call them "Implementers under ideal circumstances," because when circumstances are not ideal and they run into even the smallest obstacle, all implementation comes to a stop!

I have one Partner – a very sharp, very intelligent one – who simply refuses to critically think. This person manages my inventory of speaking products and is responsible for ensuring that the organization maintains a certain number of CD's, a certain number cases, a certain amount of ink for the label printer, etc. However, let's say that I have a special event coming up during which I will be doing four times more speaking than I do in a typical month. Since my inventory manager is aware of this fact far in advance, I would expect extra CD's, cases, and ink to be ordered in order to accommodate the need for more products to be produced. However, it never fails that when such a scenario arises, the inventory manager comes up short; no projections were made, no planning was done, and no additional inventory was ordered. Yes, the standard amount of inventory was ordered, just like clockwork, and the person had the authority to order 30 of everything instead of 10 of everything. However, there was no critical consideration that went into the ordering, so when I walked in expecting to see my materials produced, I was met with the reply, "You preached more than you usually do, and we only order a certain amount of products per month, so we do not have any additional materials to produce your additional products." Now, I could easily grow frustrated with encounters like this. However, as a wise leader, I choose not to. Instead, I just make a mental note of the type of person that I am dealing with – an Implementer, not a critical thinker – and I adjust my approach. Rather than assume that the day will come when my Implementers will think through things, I have learned to ask the right questions and make the right critical thinking connections for them so that in the end, we all win!

The good news about Implementers is that they have great potential. In regards to followership style, they are just one level away from being Partners! Thus, I advise leaders to do all that they can to develop their Implementers into Partners. Be strategic about building their levels of buy-in and commitment; the more they are willing to give of themselves to the organization and become fully bought in, the more they will be inclined to consider how their actions affect the organization – their organization. People always give a little more, go the extra mile, and sacrifice a little more when they are doing something for themselves. If leaders can help Implementers develop a significant sense of ownership of the organization, they could very well be leading them on the straight path towards becoming a Partner. If leaders cannot help their Implementers make this critical transition, believe me, it is okay! Again, a leader can get a lot out of Implementers, as long as an expectation of critical thinking is not attached to anything assigned to them. Instead, leaders must critically think for them!

I recall explaining this concept to another leader and receiving the question, "If I have to do all of the thinking as a leader, what do I need the people for? Isn't that just too much to ask a leader to do?" My answer to this colleague was that if you are not willing to do the work of a leader, which is to critically think for the organization, you are not a leader at all – or, at least, not an effective one. Leaders critically think, engage people, project problems, and develop solutions. It's our job!

All leaders love people that they do not have to actively lead – the self-starters. It is a luxury to have people in the organization that operate at the level of Partner who feel like they also own the organization and who are willing to critically think through things, including the leader's decisions, in order to produce what is best for the organization. However, most of the time, a leader is only going to have a very limited number of true Partners as followers. For all of the other followers, the leader will have to critically think on their behalf! If you say that this is too much as a leader, you are essentially saying that you do not want to do the job of a leader! To be the most effective leader that you can be, you must accept reality: you will have talented people, available people, and people who critically think. It is very hard to find all three of these characteristics in one follower (and when you do, you have hit the jackpot, so keep them close!). Once you understand this, you will accept people for who they are, and while you do all you can to develop them into something greater, you will simply maximize those whom you have for what they are.

Follower Triad Side 2 | Followership Style
CATEGORY 3:

INDIVIDUALIST

As is suggested by their name, Individualists are followers who tend to seek things that are solely for their own good and will typically only engage in organizational tasks and projects that benefit them. Though they consider themselves to be an active part of the organization, they also make an intentional effort to maintain a high level of separation between themselves, the leader, and the organization. As negative as they can be, these followers also tend to be Type A personalities who are very strong, highly opinionated, self-motivated, accomplished, and often very successful in their careers because of their higher-than-average levels of drive and aggression. Many of them might have even been leaders in their previous workplaces, because Individualists also tend to be highly talented. Mind you, they have not climbed their way to the top of the ranks in their career because of their nice people skills; their abilities to move and motivate people are usually conspicuously absent. Instead, Individualists tend to rise to the top because they seek position and power, so they do whatever it takes to be the one in charge making the call. This, in large part, is why they have such a difficult time following the leader of their organization.

Individualists are followers who are also known for voicing their criticism of the organization and for withholding their support of the leader's decisions.[48] They are highly critical about ideas that do not originate with them, often speaking openly about their feelings of opposition to anyone who will listen. In fact, I call this group of followers "sneezers," because rather than keeping their critical opinions about the leader and the way that things are done to themselves, they spread them throughout the organization like a virus and can easily infect an entire group of people!

As with other follower types, Individualists have their own language that makes them easily distinguishable. For example, they are quick to globalize their own personal opinions by saying things like, "Everybody knows that...," "Nobody is going to want to...," or even "All smart leaders make sure that..." They are also well known for their trademark pessimism, being quick to shoot down their leader's ideas with the response, "That will never work!" Individualists love to speak, and the strength of their personality makes them they feel that their positions should always be heard – and believed – by others. In a meeting, Individualists are usually the first ones to speak out negatively about whatever idea is on the table, raining on any hope, excitement, or optimism that was previously present in the room. If they do not have an opportunity to verbally express their doubts about the leader's position and the way the organization is operating, they are happy to express these feelings through nonverbal cues that are intentionally designed to communicate their apparent disgust, disdain, and frustration. Whether spoken with words or without them, Individualists *will* ensure that they are heard!

A "grapevine," or an informal channel of business communication, exists in every organization. Grapevine communication is typically characterized as "water cooler talk" or "break room talk," because it is the level of random communication that followers engage in when they are talking about their superiors, what they do not like about the organization, what someone has heard concerning a move that their supervisors are planning to make, and other rumors, gripes, and complaints. By tapping into the grapevine, leaders get a real, true sense of what their followers think and feel, and it can also help them to become abreast of problems that need to be addressed. As you might imagine, just about any time leaders tap into the grapevine and discover that a problem is brewing in the organization, Individualists are not only a part of it; they are usually at the very root of it! Individualists tend to have very influential voices, so people look up to them in the organization and will listen to and disseminate what they say. In every sense of the word, they are leaders, though undocumented ones. However, despite the fact that they are not official leaders and might not have any type of official title, they have a voice and carry the strength to sway others in the organization. In fact, sometimes, when I am talking to other followers within my organization and I hear their positions and responses, I know that I am not talking to them directly; I am talking to whichever highly-influential Individualists that influenced them. Wise leaders should accept the fact that Individualists possess some real influence (which is equivalent to possessing power) and take the necessary actions to rein in this influence when it seems to get too far out of control.

It should be said that Individualists do not perceive themselves as negative people; they consider themselves to simply be blunt individuals who are bold and brave enough to express opinions about matters that other people will not. They consider those who will not speak up and voice their critiques, objections, and differences of opinion as followers who are afraid to speak their mind – as "Yes men." Of course, we know that this is not necessarily true, because those who fall into the Partner followership style will critically engage and challenge their leader, but their critiques of the leader's decisions are driven by a different motivation. Unlike Individualists, they will say to the leader, "I will try that, but first, have you considered this?" Partners offer critical thought, which is desirable and productive in an organization. Individualists offer criticism, which is undesirable and counterproductive in an organization.

When Individualists are placed on a task, especially with a group of other followers, watch out! Although they are provided with clear details and directions on how to execute a task, they are notorious for tossing the instructions and making changes to the project. Why? Because, of course, they feel that certain things that the leader has asked them to do are irrelevant and unnecessary and that to complete the task or project according to the leader's specifications makes no sense at all. Also, keep in mind that Individualists are not known for being quiet! Throughout the duration of a given task, they are constantly speaking negatively, draining emotional energy out of their team members and the environment. That is not to say that they will not get the job done; they will always ensure that they are known as finishers in order to maintain a "positive" public profile. Thus, they do not endeavor to complete a task because of its benefit to the leader or the organization; they seek to complete it because it is to their own benefit of being able to look good. For best results, I advise leaders to either not put Individualists on a team with others or to put them on a team comprised of followers who are stronger than them (i.e., comprised of several Partners that can counterbalance the effects of their vocal negativity).

Over the years, I have had many experiences with Individualists. As much of a thorn in my side as they can be, however, Individualists do not deserve to be thrown away any more than any other followership type. I am wise enough to recognize that they serve their purpose in the organization; I just have to keep them on a short rope. For example, I had one Individualist that seemed to be wreaking havoc on my organization, undermining everything that I was trying to do with my followers. He was a typical Individualist: highly influential, charismatic, and very articulate. Over time, he was able to develop his own following within my organization to the point that whenever I gave a directive to my followers, they would turn and look at him first to see if he approved! I recognized the power that this Individualist had developed within the walls of my organization, so rather than distance myself from him, I pulled him close – very close. My rationale for doing so was that if he was going to attack, I would rather see it coming from close range versus having him at a distance and being surprised by an attack from the back. Thus, I chose to keep him right there in my side pocket.

I kept my powerful Individualist close, because he was too powerful to be out there alone as a live wire. With him right beside me, I was able to keep close tabs on him and to probe and investigate what he thought and felt about the projects and initiatives that I was trying to implement within the organization. It was my strategy to hear, address, and defuse these issues with him in private before he could express his concerns in public. Before I would introduce something publicly to my followers, I would first run it by him, encouraging him to ask me the tough questions and to be critical with me so that, if necessary, we could take steps to refine the idea. Only after I went through this process with my powerful Individualist would I introduce the ideas to the rest of my followers, saying, "This is what we are going to do. I have already run it by Joe, and he had some insights and concerns that we have worked together to address. Now, we have a very well-defined idea that can bring us success if we implement it effectively!" Instantly, I cut off his corporate influence and silenced any potential grapevine fodder. By making the small strategic move of containing my powerful Individualist's critical tongue, making it sprout in my presence rather than in public, I was able to clip his wings and mitigate his potentially negative influence among my – and his – followers!

> *I kept my powerful individualist close, because he was too powerful to be out there alone as a live wire.*

Having an Individualist actively working within your organization is about as fun as having the flu. However, it is an unfortunate reality that you will have at least one of them (and if you are lucky, it will only be *one*) "following" you at any given time. If you will be an effective leader, you've got to learn to deal with the hand you are dealt, and this includes dealing with Individualists! I encourage you to do as I do and keep your friends close and your enemies closer. Draw them close and address their issues and complaints one on one so that you can have greater control of what is happening among the followers in your organization. If you push them away, I have learned that they will make even more noise and build even more influence anyway.

The logical question that any leader might ask concerning Individualists is, "Why not save myself the frustration and heartache and put Individualists out of my organization?" I explain that leaders do not seek to get rid of people; they seek to develop them. Consider the level of leadership and influence that your powerful Individualist has already managed to develop in the organization. This is a clear indication of leadership potential, if I have ever seen any. Individualists constantly demonstrate the ability to think and to stand on their own, which are critical qualities for a leader to have. Should you throw them away because they have some but not all of the qualities that they need to be an effective leader? If others had thought this way about many of us as leaders, we would not be in the leadership positions that we occupy today. Many of us did not look like leaders when others first identified us as leaders. In fact, many of our Individualists look more like leaders than we did before we were leaders in our current organizations.

Although they are usually immature, rebellious, and ignorant, organizational rebels, especially those whom others already follow, have already demonstrated that they possess leadership ability. If they are salvageable, they will only be salvaged by a leader who will take the time to mentor them one on one, teaching them how to think, what to say, what not to say, and what actions to take to lead in a more appropriate way. The leader must teach the Individualist to harness his or her influence and use it to lead other followers of the organization in the right direction (towards supporting the leader) versus the wrong direction (against supporting the leader). Who knows? You might have the workings of the greatest leader that your organization has ever seen, right in front of your very eyes!

RESOURCE

Resources are followers who look for the minimum amount of commitment necessary to be considered a part of the organization, because their passions lay outside of the organization.[49] This type of follower tends to be very reserved in the level of resources that they are willing to give over to the organization, reserving the bulk and most valuable portions of their time, talent (they can tend to be quite talented, but unwilling to use this talent for the organization's benefit), energy, and other discretionary resources to benefiting themselves and their lives alone. Thus, they are tremendously self-serving. Their issue is that they are so self-absorbed that life is all about them; they see everything with respect to how it will impact their goals, pleasure, progress, and ability to function freely and unrestricted. Since their lives are about being completely internally focused, they find it difficult to fully commit to something external, like an organization.

Followers who are considered to be Resources desire to be perceived by others as being an official part of the organization; everyone needs to feel a sense of belonging to *something*, and Resource followers are no different. However, Resources endeavor to only meet the minimum level of standards that are necessary to qualify as being a part of it, because they are only a part of the organization in the first place to satisfy their own selfish needs. Refusing to be absorbed into the deep core of things, they choose to maintain their position on the periphery where the pull and demands on their time, talents, and assets are not so strong and the expectations are not so high. The outer edge of organizational commitment is the Resource's comfort zone.

Because they are so intentional about maintaining low levels of engagement, it is easy to differentiate Resources from more committed followers by the language they use. They are characterized by saying things like, "Exactly how many hours do I have to give in order to keep my job?" "What are the bottom line tasks that I need to complete in order to maintain my membership in the organization?" "Exactly what specific things do I have to do, and by when does it have to be done in order to avoid risking the loss of my position?" Resources will give their leaders very low levels of task completion. Leaders should not expect them to give any discretionary effort towards their assigned tasks, as they are only committed to doing what is required. Their goal is not to say, "Here is my completed project! I did the best I could! Isn't it great?" Instead, they will only contribute as much effort as it takes to be able to say, "Here you go. I got it done exactly according to the instructions." As a result, Resources will complete the chart that the leader has assigned to them, but it will be a plain Jane product that is black and white with no "pop" or visual appeal. Contrast this with, let's say, a Partner who is given the same project. A Partner will likely produce a chart that has been blown up to poster size, mounted on a board, glossy and full of color, with a specialized design scheme that makes it so visually appealing that people say "Wow" when they see it! Unlike Partners, Resources do not offer an effort to make things excellent for their leaders; they only offer basic levels of completion.

It is also easy to distinguish Resources from other followership types by observing them in the setting of a meeting – that is, if you can get them to actually come to a meeting. Resources are the followers who will always ask for a change in protocol by requesting to be Skype'd, video conferenced, or patched in to a meeting via conference call. Often, they will skip the meeting altogether, asking for the meeting notes to be e-mailed to them or to have only critical action items pertaining to them sent to them via a text message. Resources are always pressing for the leader and the organization to make serving in the organization more convenient for them. Though they would not willingly admit to it, meetings are an intrusion into their lives, upon which their focuses are centered. Thus, they always have a good reason (to them, at least) for either not physically attending a meeting or not attend the meeting at all.

When engaged in a task or project, Resource followers are constantly questioning the extent of energy, effort, and resources that are *really* necessary to get things done. They will ask, "Does it need to be like this? I don't understand why we have to do it like this. Why can't we just do A, B, C, and be done?" Resources look for shortcuts that will minimize how much of their time, talent, energy, and resources must be used to accomplish the task. Remember: their goal is to reserve as much of these resources as they can to use for their own lives!

I advise leaders to never give Resource followers any project that will be shown to the public or that will be publicly consumed in any way. Leaders should only present their best to the public, and "best" is not something that they can expect to get from a Resource. Instead, leaders should only assign minimal tasks that represent only a small part of a larger, whole project. In doing so, leaders make full use of as much as their Resource followers are willing to give them, while helping to advance the larger goals of the organization. Also, because Resources can be highly talented, leaders should not make the mistake of allowing a Resource to lead a project. They are too filled with negativity, criticism, and self-centeredness to effectively lead others in the organization. Though they might get the task done with the group, the leader will have a big mess to clean up in the end, as the Resource's attitude might have contaminated the other followers in the group. Now, the leader must engage in the work of decontaminating the followers and restoring them to health – and this is more trouble than it is worth. For best results, keep Resources away from leading groups altogether. In fact, leaders should keep Resources from anyone valuable in the organization, including fresh, new people who could also potentially become contaminated by their negative attitudes. If new people, who represent energy, enthusiasm, and optimism, encounter Resource followers, they are sure to suck the life out of them, so keep them far apart!

When discussing Resource followers, one of the inevitable questions that arise is that of what to do with these individuals. Boot them out of the organization, or let them be, while the leader constantly runs around decontaminating those within the organization that the Resources have infected? I offer a solution to dealing with Resources that involves engaging one of two approaches. The first option is to surround them with strong Partners that will either change them or squeeze them out of the organization. When Resources get around strong Partners, who are vocal and highly-supportive of the organization, they will be the minority in both number and attitude. Because their interests are the health, productivity, and success of the organization, Partners will get Resources in line any time they begin spewing their negativity into the atmosphere. They will squash negativity as soon as Resources even *think* about expressing rebellious opinions in opposition to their leader! Strong Partners will passionately explain to resources why their approach is harmful to the organization, and they will stand up to the resources, challenging them to keep their mouths closed and change their attitude, or get out! If the Resources are truly interested in being a part of the organization, the Partners help them to understand that it will not be on negative terms – only positive. After interacting at this level with strong Partners for a while, Resources will inevitably either make the decision to get on board and truly commit to being a part of the organization, or they will say "Farewell" and be on their way to another organization that allows them be the "free, independent thinkers" that they pride themselves on being.

The second option for dealing with Resources is to simply allow them to "hang themselves"; rather than the leader disqualifying them for inclusion in the organization, they disqualify themselves. To accomplish this, I establish guidelines for being a part of a group or the organization, and I lay them out for all of my followers to clearly see in black and white. Then, I instruct them that if they abide by the stated guidelines, they can remain a part of the group or organization. If they violate the guidelines, the group or organization will no longer consider the follower an official part of the team. I assemble these guidelines with the full knowledge that my Resource followers are not going to meet them; they will require far too high a level of commitment than they are willing to offer. For example, one of the guidelines might be that individuals must be able to attend at least two out of three meetings in person each month. Predictably, my Resources violate the standards that I have laid out, and in doing so, they disqualify themselves from participation in the group or organization.

I have had to sit down entire groups of people – important people with key roles – in my organization, because their level of commitment was not where I needed it to be. They were neither meeting, nor

241

performing, nor practicing, and they were blatantly violating every guideline that I laid out before them. Some of the followers, upset by my decision responded with cries like, "But I *called* to let everyone know why I was not going to be at the meetings!" and "But I had something else *really* important to do, and it was at the same time as the meetings!" Because they were Resources, however, I realized that it was simply beyond their ability to understand why these excuses were not acceptable to me as a leader. It was clear that they did not have enough time to do what I needed them to do, so I decided to make them inactive and move the organization on around them. It was nothing personal. It was doing what is necessary to maintain the quality, integrity, excellence, and productivity of the organization – and this is what leaders do!

When leaders implement this practice in their own organizations, I caution them to only implement standards with consequences that they are willing to act upon. I encourage them to think carefully through things, asking themselves, "How far am I willing to go?" "Who am I willing to lose?" "Is my organization going to be able to function effectively if I set this person up to hang himself and he violates the standards? Can I afford to lose him and still maintain my operations at an acceptable level?" For best results, be sure to have a back-up plan when engaging this method. Especially where Resources are involved, you stand to lose more than a few people!

Follower Triad Side 2 | Followership Style
SUMMARY & CONCLUSIONS

In summary, leaders must become skillful in answering the question posed by the Followership side of the Follower Pyramid, "What level of support does this follower offer to me as a leader, and how does it affect his or her propensity to challenge my directives when asked to execute an organizational task?" Without answering this critical question, leaders will experience the unnecessary frustration that comes along with expecting one thing from followers and getting yet another.

When leaders are aware of each individual's followership style, they become empowered to allocate assignments to their followers based upon their levels of commitment, quality, and ability to adhere to leadership directives. For example, the most important tasks will go to the Partners at the most committed end of the followership spectrum, because they will critically think through the task as they execute it, are highly vested and will go over and above the call of duty to produce the best possible product. The least important tasks will go to the Partners at the least committed end of the leadership spectrum, because they will only do what is required of them and absolutely nothing more.

Followership Styles Are Not Forever Static: They Can Be Changed

Leaders who seem to have organizations that are predominantly filled with followers that fall into undesirable followership styles need not despair. There is hope for a more committed, more supportive followership base. That's the good news. The bad news is that you will never see this new and improved followership base until you are ready to put in some real work into developing your followers into what you need them to be in order to advance your organization. Consider that when Jesus was recruiting His team of disciples, when He came upon them, He said to them, "Follow Me, and I will *make* you fishers of men."[50] Jesus knew something that we all must learn if we will be effective leaders: good followers are not born, they are *made*. Your followers will be as committed and supportive as you train them and mentor them to be. This development process, however, is not fueled by wishful thinking; it is fueled by a lot of time, energy, and effort on the leader's part.

Believe it or not, Resources can be developed into Individualists, Individualists can be developed into Implementers, and Implementers can be developed into Partners. Think of it like a conveyor belt upon which each of your followers sits. With each new level of intentional development by their leader, they advance closer and closer to becoming a Partner. Considering this, leaders should never consider throwing anyone away who does not appear to be a Partner. Partners do not just happen by accident; followers do not just wake up one morning and say, "Hey! I feel like being a fully vested, totally committed Partner today! It's time to take my followership to the next level and be all-in!" As nice as this would be, this is not something that will ever happen in the real world. Instead, leaders must roll up their sleeves, clear away some time in their already-strapped schedules, put their strategic thinking caps on, and go down into the training and development trenches. What will result, after some time (not overnight), is a base of followers that is well-equipped to execute and bring the organization's vision to pass. However, leaders should remember that one size developmental strategy does not fit all. They should be careful to strategically plot out an individual plan to increase the level of personal investment of each follower.

Leaders might be surprised to learn that as prized as Partners are in the follower base of an organization, not all who seem to be Partners are actually Partners. Those whom you think are Partners *might* just be exhibiting Partner traits and giving Partner-level input while being neither fully vested nor highly committed in their heart to the leader or the organization. They are simply in the relationship to get out of it what they want and need.

> *Those whom you think are Partners might just be exhibiting Partner traits and giving Partner-level input while being neither fully vested nor highly committed in their heart to the leader or the organization.*

Is this a bad thing? Not really. The relationship is mutually beneficial; they are getting what they need, and the organization is getting what it needs. The important thing is to set the rate of exchange so that everyone's needs are met at the same level; the organization should be getting as much from the follower as the follower is getting from the organization.

How Can a Follower *Really* Be Transformed Into a Partner? A Glimpse into My Personal Strategic Approach

I used to have a key leader who played a very instrumental role in every aspect of my organization. He was a major Partner and a major contributor, and I leaned upon him heavily to get things done. Eventually, the time came for him to move on to bigger and better things, and when the time came for him to say his goodbyes to the team, we were saddened; we knew that his absence would create a major void in our followership base. In fact, as I assessed all of the areas of the organization in which he played a major role, I realized that it would take several new people to fill the roles he played in these areas. Unfortunately, there was no one who was prepared to step into his shoes to bring to the table the high level of support, commitment, influence, and partnership that he once brought.

I decided that I needed to develop another set of leaders to fill the void, and I got to work, developing a strategy immediately. I gathered a group of seven men together who stood out to me because they showed some level of energy, potential, and ability to solve problems. They also displayed some other raw makings of a leader in that they seemed talented, dedicated, hard working, and they seemed to have a general passion about the organization and life. All together, the final group that I chose consisted of three Implementers, two Individualists, and two Resources. I met with them every Monday evening, talking to them about different aspects of leadership, helping them to find their significance in the organization, expressing my appreciation for the great things that they were already doing, and providing constructive feedback about how to become more effective.

In addition to our corporate meetings together, I had "break out meetings" with each level of followership. I met with my two Resources over lunch once a week. At these lunches, we would discuss the vision of the organization, discuss the corporate meeting that we recently had with the other members of the group, and I would encourage them to voice their criticism and thoughts about what the organization was currently doing. Once they shared with me their criticisms and concerns, I used some of the time to explain why I was making the decisions that I was making as the leader, and I helped them to see the rationale of them in light of the goals and direction of the organization. In doing so, I was strategically pointing them in the direction that I wanted them to go for the next meeting. Once we all convened as a group again, I would mention the issues raised by my Resources, and I would ensure that the issues were addressed. Again, as I previously explained, I was able to clip their wings so that they could not fly publicly! By first hearing and addressing their issues and criticisms in private, I was able to proactively present these same issues and criticisms in public – but with my personal, strategic spin that assured everyone that I had already discussed and resolved the issues with those who held them. Now, even if one of my Resources reared up in the meeting to voice the concern, the other members of the group would immediately shut him down, saying, "We've already addressed that, so let's just move on!" My strategic approach stole the power from the Resources while giving the other members of the group confidence in my ability to act proactively against potential threats to the organization.

One might wonder whether or not my Resources could possibly feel disempowered by my strategy. Might they feel like they are not given a fair chance to publicly present their critiques and issues with my leadership? Allow me to put you at ease by telling you that the answer is "No!" In fact, my two Resource followers have shared with me on more than a couple of occasions that they look forward to the individual time that they get a chance to share with me each week. It makes them feel like they are an important part of the organization and that they are really contributing to what the organization is doing. They also explain that the time they share with me makes them feel like they can be heard, that it helps them to understand me better as their leader and that they are learning a lot through our interactions.

Every other week, I would also meet with the two Individualists over coffee, breakfast, or lunch and enjoy the same level of interaction. They were two levels removed from the Partner follower stage, so they did not require as intensive interaction as my Resource followers needed. I only had to meet with my three Implementers once a week, because they were the closest to becoming Partners already. With each group, I worked systematically to allow them to voice their concerns, after which I took the time to explain why I was doing what I was doing and why I was making the decisions that I was making. After only a few short months, I began to see changes in each of the seven men that I was meeting with and mentoring. Today, one hundred percent of them are contributing more of their time, their talents, their energy, and their financial resources. In fact, they began to see themselves as their own exclusive little group. Just as Jesus pulled the disciples closer in order to work with them, I have managed to pull my followers close to me to work with them, and the results that are produced are priceless.

Although I used this follower development strategy in my non-profit setting, it can easily be adapted to a corporate for-profit setting. Leaders of any organization can put together a leadership development program for which they identify a few key people within the organization to participate. They can set up area meetings with several smaller groups of followers and even go a step further to have individual lunches with the followers in each of the smaller groups. Ultimately, whatever the details of their strategy, their goal is the same: to develop the mindsets and goals of their followers so that they form a stronger follower base that will provide a higher level of support and commitment for the leader and the organization.

CHAPTER 15

FOLLOWER TRIAD SIDE 3: LEADER-FOLLOWER RELATIONSHIP

ASSESSMENT QUESTION:

How close is the relationship that I share with this follower, and how should I order my interactions, communications, and expectations with him/her based upon this level of closeness?

If you have varying levels of relationship with your followers, you are no different from any other organizational leader. You might share a closer relationship with some of your followers while experiencing a more distant relationship with others. If you have been paying close attention to the relational dynamics that you experience while interacting with and leading these differing groups, you might have picked up on a trend between these two groups: they provide two different levels of contribution to the organization. Thus, it is essential for you as a leader to be aware of the level of relationship that you share with each and every follower with whom you interact. Your level of relationship will determine the amount of access that the individual will allow you to have to his or her resources and will also determine the level of support that you can expect to receive from him or her as a follower.

Leader-Member Exchange (LMX) leadership theory explains the premise that the level of relationship that exists between the leader and the follower directly affects the level of contribution that the follower provides to the organization, with the "Exchange Level" representing the level of interaction between the leader and the follower. [51] In scientific language, researchers would say that the level of relationship is positively correlated with the level of discretionary effort that a follower will willingly contribute. However, practically speaking, it simply means that the deeper and more involved a relationship that a follower has with a leader, the more effort the follower will make in getting things done for that leader. Those followers to whom you are the closest are the ones whom you can ask to do more. These are the followers who will accept the request and complete the task to the best of their abilities, even if it means being inconvenienced on their part!

I recall a clear instance of this principle in action. I was out of town participating in a conference, and on the last night of the conference, I was the speaker, so I asked someone to drive my wife down to join me. The faithful supporter that she is, my wife gladly agreed to come; she was coming down for the afternoon and returning home the same night, so she would not have to make any special arrangements for the children. However, once she had arrived and supported me in that special way that only a wife can, I did not want to put her back on the road, riding three hours to get back home; I wanted to keep her right there by my side that evening. The only problem was that she had not arranged for anyone to stay overnight with the children and to care for her the next day. After I asked her to stay, she immediately picked up the phone and began calling people upon whom we typically rely to help watch our children, but she could get no one to step in for her. I could see the look of disappointment creeping over her face with each "No" she received. With no other options, she would not be able to stay in town with me; she would have to go back home. As we sat enjoying dinner, she finally said, "Babe, I'm going to have to go back home tonight. Nobody can watch the kids for us." Immediately, I picked up the phone, called one of the young ladies who had just given my wife a definitive "No" back, and asked her to watch the kids for me. Her reply was an instant, "Sure, Dr. Moody. I'll do it. I'll head over there right now!"

The young lady who gave my wife a clear "No" but gave me an enthusiastic "Yes" did not agree to watch our children because she loves children so much and really values the opportunity to babysit, especially at such a late notice. She said "Yes" because of the relationship that I have with her; she is one of my close followers, and we share a level of relationship as leader-follower that she and my wife simply do not share. In fact, when I picked up the phone to call her, I knew without a doubt that she would agree to help us out if I asked her.

In fact, I can ask any of my close followers to do things that they simply would not do if someone else asked them, and even though they have no real desire to sacrifice whatever it is that I am requesting, they agree to do it. It happens in my organization all of the time. One of my lower-level leaders will ask for contributions of time, energy, or finances, and the people will say "No." I will come right behind the leader five minutes later and ask for the exact same things, and the people will say, "Sure!" It is my close relationship with them that allows me to push them past their comfort zone... even when they *can't stand* it!

In every organization, there exists an "in-group" and an "out-group." The in-group is characterized by closeness to the leader, while the out-group is characterized by having a more distant relationship from the leader. Within these respective exchange levels are phases that differentiate the stages of relationship through which followers navigate as they move from the out-group to the in-group.

Followers who fall in the out-group are at the periphery of the relationship circle, in contrast to followers who fall in the in-group and are closer to the leader at the core of the relationship circle. Out-group followers tend to be your typical worker bees in the organization: they come in on time, get their job done according to the specifications given them by their leader (and not an ounce of effort more), and leave on time. They are checkmark employees who treat their job like what it is: a place where you go to do exactly what you are told and are given money for doing so. To this end, they ensure that they set up their tasks and to-do lists and complete them systematically and efficiently. They do not do these things because they find a great sense of passion, enjoyment, or fulfillment in them; they do them because these are the functions that they must complete in order to get their paychecks.

Most often, out-group followers are not engaged at all with the other people in the organization like their co-workers or their bosses. This is because they tend to see themselves as being completely separate from "the machine" of the organization. Be it far from them to feel a sense of ownership or self-interest in the organization and its success. Instead, when they refer to the organization, they tend to say things like, "Do you all allow people to..." or "You guys' organization is..." Rarely, if ever, will you hear them use possessive pronouns like "I," "Me," or "My." In their mind, the organization belongs to "Them," or "You," not to "Me." The follower him or herself is just there to help the organization out and "collect a check," not to build relationships or a social life.

It is important for leaders to identify followers who fall into this out-group category of Leader-Follower Relationship Exchange, lest the leader put too much of a stake in them. As leaders gain a better understanding of where an out-group person follower's interests lay, they will not expect high levels of energy and effort from them. They can reasonably shift their expectations downward, recognizing that they will only get baseline effort from their out-group. Savvy leaders will also assign out-group followers to tasks that require no real efforts to produce quality or excellence. They are good for simply completing tasks – getting things done.

Any time new followers join or enter an organization, they fall into the out-group category of the Leader-Follower Exchange Level. Some will soon begin to draw closer to the leader and eventually become a part of the in-group, while others will make a conscious effort to maintain their distance from the leader and stay a part of the out-group. Out-group followers make such a choice for a variety of reasons that are as different as the individuals themselves. Perhaps they have a fear of getting too close to the leader because they think that doing so might make them a bigger target for their work being under close scrutiny. Perhaps they are intimidated by their leaders, and the thought of ever engaging them one-on-one really scares them. Perhaps they do not like their leaders and simply want nothing to do with them other than to receive clear directions of what is required so that they can execute each step of the tasks on their checklists and then go home. Or, perhaps they are not interested in having any social interaction with their leaders, because they believe in keeping business as "strictly business." There are a number of reasons that out-group followers are inclined to remain in the out-group. Only through the intentional efforts of the leader will they break away from the edge of the relationship circle and allow themselves to be drawn closer towards the core of the relationship circle where the leader resides.

On the other hand, followers who are a part of the in-group tend to spend more time with their leader and enjoy a deeper level of relational intimacy (not physically, but emotionally and psychologically) than a leader would share with the average member of the organization. For example, a leader who has followers at a higher exchange level might know these followers' names, their children's names, family stories, events and activities in which their children are involved, and challenges that the followers might be having outside of the organization. However, not only does the leader know such things about followers at this level, but the followers also know similar things about their leader's life. Thus, this relationship is deemed an exchange, because it involves the act of giving one thing in return for another.[52] In this case, what is exchanged is intimacy, or access to the more personal inner workings of one another's lives. This intimacy breeds a level of mutual commitment and support that is higher than what might be expected of a follower that is not as close, and it ultimately results in the follower's increased willingness to give more and do more for the leader.

Because of the high level of care that they have for the leader, those in the in-group are intrinsically motivated to execute with as much excellence as they are capable of producing for their leader. When in-group followers are assigned an organizational task, they do not treat their assignment as a simple checklist item in which they exert only the base-level effort required to complete it. Instead, because of their relationship with their leader, the assignment means more to them. Thus, they will go above and beyond the call of duty and look for every way possible to make the end product the best that it can be. Because they know that what they produce will affect the leader and the organization, they do not aim to do a good job; they aim to do a great job!

In-group followers offer a level of discretionary effort that cannot be demanded of a follower; it must be willingly yielded by each individual. I often like to use the parallel that leadership is about making love, not about sexual assault. Although they both involve the same physical act of sexual intercourse, one is characterized by forced intimacy between two people who are emotionally distant from one another, while the other is characterized by two people with mutually-yielded intimacy and who share emotional closeness. When a leader tries to force a follower to produce a quality outcome through the exercise of his or her power, authority, organizational weight, or ability to threaten the follower with serious consequences, the follower might yield and offer a little more effort in completing the task. This would be akin to the sexual assault scenario in which the follower is literally forced to offer the discretionary effort necessary to execute the task. In contrast, when a leader shares a higher level of intimacy in the relationship with the follower, the follower will willingly yield the higher levels of discretionary effort that are necessary in order to do a great job. These followers will not only complete the task, but they will feel good about it both during the performance and after the execution of the task. Feeling good about what you are doing for another person really matters!

The relational phases that characterize the level of relationship that might exist between a leader and a follower within an organization typically fall into the following categories:

1) Out-group Stranger Phase
2) In-group Acquaintance phase
3) In-group Mature Partner Phase

OUT-GROUP: STRANGER PHASE

The Stranger phase is the initial stage that a follower navigates through when coming aboard an organization. Because they are brand new, they are strangers to both the organization and their leader, and they relate to their leader at a level of relationship that is relatively shallow. This relational phase is characterized by rule-based and position-based interactions.[53] Rule-based interactions are those between the leader and follower that are based upon clearly-stated guidelines and stipulations. These guidelines dictate for the follower when and how interactions are to occur with the leader as well as the types of responses that are appropriate in these dealings. For example, these guidelines might include when meetings are held with the leader, when, where, and how to report to the leader, how formal the reporting process needs to be, how often the leader will call the follower into the manager's office for updates and accountability, when departmental and organization-wide meetings are held with the leader, etc. Rather than operating out of anything remotely close to an interpersonal relationship with their leader, followers in the Stranger phase of relationship with their organizational leader will only interact with their leader "by the book."

Position-based interactions are those between the leader and follower that are based upon where the follower fits within the organization. These interactions are guided by varying levels of power, authority, and title, so as a follower's position changes, so do the types of privileged interactions that are considered appropriate between the follower and his or her new leader. With each promotion, followers are typically granted greater levels of access and opportunities to associate with higher-level superiors within the organization, whether these superiors are their team leaders, managers, area supervisors, or even the CEO. For example, when followers receive a promotion, it is commonplace for them to feel the confidence and comfort to speak to superiors with whom they have not engaged previously, because the distance between them and the leader in the organization's hierarchy was too great. The follower's promotion to a higher position shortens the gap between the follower's position and the leader's position, resulting in the follower feeling a greater sense of ease when approaching the superior leader. In addition to being allowed to address higher-ranking leaders in the organization, gaining a higher position allows followers to use certain facilities and have greater access to areas that are off-limits to lower-level followers. In the military, an example of this might be the officer's club. When soldiers are promoted to a higher rank of officer, they now have the opportunity to mingle and socialize with officers that were previously not accessible to them in settings that they were restricted from entering. In a non-profit organization, this might be a VIP suite that only organizational leaders are allowed to access. When a follower is promoted to a leader within the organization, instantly, the dynamics of the interaction change, because they can now access places and address people that would have previously been inappropriate to engage. Followers in the Stranger phase of relationship with their leader would not dare to step over the boundaries of their position to address a higher-ranking leader in the organization, because according to the rules – and in their own eyes – to do so would be inappropriate.

Because followers in the Stranger phase operate according to their understanding of rules and position, they are mindful of the parameters of interaction. They usually will not approach their managers' office unless they are asked to do so; the notion of ever stopping by to simply say "Hi" is completely out of the question. Followers in the Stranger phase of relationship tend to see their immediate manager or leader as a distant overseer or overlord whose primary purpose is to delegate tasks, reinforce deadlines, and review their work. Thus, their interactions that they have with their leaders are like stranger meeting stranger; they are totally black and white with very few gray areas, and they are based solely upon function and task – nothing else.

How Stranger phase interactions play out between leader and follower are pretty standard across the board, although there might be some variance between organizational contexts. For example, in a church setting, it might look like a congregant not feeling comfortable in addressing the pastor; God forbid that the congregant would *ever* dare to knock on his office door! Instead, congregants who are still in the Stranger phase will view the pastor as an authority figure to be related to at arms-length rather than a person to be related to in a close-up and personal way. In light of this, the follower learns to deal with the rules (written or unwritten in this case) that govern the interaction in order to stay in a safe place and ensure that their dealings with the leader remain appropriate.

Another example of a context in which Stranger phase interactions play out between leader and follower is that of the military, a highly rule-oriented environment. The military calls the rules that govern the interactions between followers and leaders "military courtesies" and consider them a means of showing respect to officers or NCO's (non-commissioned officer) of superior rank and a reflection on one's own level of self-discipline. For instance, when a soldier talks to an NCO or officer of superior rank, the soldier should stand at attention until ordered otherwise. A soldier must always walk on the left of an officer or NCO of superior rank. When entering or exiting a vehicle, the soldier with the lesser rank (the junior soldier) is the first to enter, and the senior in rank is the first to exit. Also, when a soldier is outdoors and approached by an officer or NCO, the soldier is to greet the higher-ranking officer by saying, "Good morning, Sergeant," for example. When soldiers report to officers of superior rank, they are to approach the officer, remain about two steps from him or her, stand at attention, and salute, always being sure to use sir or ma'am to signal politeness and respect.[54] These, among many other rule-based and position-based guidelines, govern the interaction of those in the U.S. military, which, being under the U.S. Department of Defense, is the largest employer in the world![55]

Someone looking from the outside in might think that having such a highly-structured environment is not practical or that it might not allow for the freedom of thought and self expression. However, in this context, that's not a bad thing. Some organizations, like the military, actually function more effectively through such stringently-defined Stranger phase level relationship dynamics. Think about it. These hard lines between soldier and superior keep people confined to their rank and in their place. No, they do not allow for a lot of critical thinking or free expression when it comes to tasks, because during times of war, there is not a lot of room for such things. In the midst of battle, a soldier cannot afford to engage in a dialogue with the leader, asking, "But what if I die?" or "What if I do what you said and I don't make it back?" Instead, they have maintained such a level of respect for the officers who lead them that they charge in full speed ahead as soon as they are given an order; they do not question the commands given to them. Thus, in this case, operating at an arms-length Stranger phase level of relationship helps the military to operate more effectively.

It should be noted, however, that despite the highly-structured system that guides interactions between soldiers and their superiors and that reinforces Stranger phase levels of relationship, the military also operates according to a peculiar dynamic that we do not see in most highly rule-oriented environments. The military environment is more mechanistic and mechanical in nature than most other organizations, and this allows it to operate with great levels of efficiency. However, while mechanics are good for achieving efficiency, human beings are programmed with a relational nature; we are not emotionless, mechanical robots. Even within such a mechanistic, rule-oriented organization, a platoon of soldiers along with their officers is comprised of men and women who have formed an allegiance so deep that they would never leave one another behind on the battlefield and a bond so close that they would give their lives for one another. Thus, even within a mechanistic organization that stringently reinforces Stranger phase relationship dynamics, there are relational elements. There are a myriad sub-groups of people throughout the organization that have formed relationships that function well outside of rule and position-based guidelines and that far exceed the Stranger phase level of relationship interaction.

While Stranger phase interactions might really work well for the military, I would dare to say that for most organizations, it would be a better option to try to strategically develop followers at the Stranger phase level into members of the in-group. The distance of out-group dynamics helps to maintain a high level of respect, while the closeness of in-group dynamics helps to maintain a level of relationship. Ultimately, it's a balancing act that leaders will need to perfect based upon the varying needs of their organizations. However, research shows that closeness and relationship will produce more follower energy, effort, and excellence than distance and authority will.

Follower Triad Side 3 | Leader-Follower Relationship
CATEGORY 2:

IN-GROUP: ACQUAINTANCE PHASE

The Acquaintance phase is the second phase that a follower navigates as a member of an organization. In this phase, while the follower is no longer on the outskirts of the organization operating at arms-reach and basing interactions according to rules and position, he or she is also not a completely sold-out Partner of the organization upon which the leader can rely without reservation. During this phase of the leader-follower relationship, the leader is getting to know the follower, and the follower is becoming more acquainted with the leader.

This phase of leader-follower relationship interaction is characterized by an increase in information sharing, a growth in resource contribution, and boundary testing. [56] With information sharing, followers get first-hand intimate information from their leaders, have the opportunity to hear their leaders share the sentiments of their heart concerning certain issues, learn about organizational issues that are going on, and engage in close, intimate dialogue with their leader. In this phase, this type of communication might occur at a special assembly attended by only a certain group of followers, in an executive lounge that is restricted to others, at a special lunch meeting to which only a select group of people have been invited, or any other corporate setting. Those who are recipients of the information feel privileged to be there hearing their leader talk about such close and intimate things, even though it is the entire group that is being entrusted with this level of sharing rather than just the individual follower him or herself.

Growth in resource contribution occurs in this phase because as a function of being closer to the leader, the follower's contribution of resources to the organization is expected to increase. Simply put, to whom much closer access is given, a greater level of contribution is required. This expectation is not in place to serve as a fee for the privilege of being closer to the leader; it is an expectation based upon the rate of exchange that occurs in the leader-follower relationship at this level. In the in-group Acquaintance phase, the follower receives more privileges from the leader or organization, like privileged access, privileged information, privileged treatment, etc. In exchange for these privileges, the follower is expected to reciprocate by giving back to the leader and organization more of his or her resources, whether energy, effort, excellence, or in the case of some religious organizations, finances.

Boundary testing in the Acquaintance phase involves the trial and error efforts of the leader to test or evaluate exactly how much can be required of the follower. Leaders test the boundaries in a very slow and deliberate manner by asking the follower to do one thing, then another thing, and then another, each time increasing the level of resources required to execute the task. Though each assignment is a genuine assignment, it is also a test of the boundaries that the follower has set in order to restrict the leader's access to his or her resources. Because it is a test, when the leader sees that the task is easily accepted by the follower and executed with a high degree of quality, a request for the follower to complete another more demanding task is made. If the follower performs at the same capacity and with the same level of quality, another even more demanding task request is made. This process of boundary testing continues until the leader senses some resistance from the follower. In this case, leaders know that they have reached a follower's boundaries, so they pull back a little. At the end of the boundary testing process, leaders will have a clear idea of what they can and cannot ask their followers to do, say, and contribute in this new level relationship.

Because the Acquaintance phase represents a new level of relationship between the leader and the follower that is markedly different from the level of interaction that they shared when the follower was in the out-group, the process of getting acclimated to being a part of the in-group is prone to leave a Partner feeling a bit anxious and unsure in the beginning. After all, though the followers are in the same old organization, the in-group represents a level of interaction that is new to them, so they are unsure of what to expect. They tend to simultaneously feel privileged yet nervous, and excited yet concerned, because they do not know how to interact with their new leader yet – and the last thing that they want to do is mess up by interacting inappropriately! For example, when the leader says something during a meeting that causes eyebrows to raise, is he or she joking or not? When the leader asks for an update, does he or she want a lot of details or just the bottom line? Does the leader have a short fuse? What makes the leader angry, and how is this anger expressed? What makes the leader happy? What will the leader tolerate and not tolerate? Followers who are new to this level of relationship with their leader have a million questions about their leader, because they simply do not know him or her. Over time, as they grow more comfortable and learn the ropes about how to interact with the leader, things function much more smoothly for them.

On this level of interaction, leaders constantly emphasize to their followers that it is a privilege for them to be able to engage in this level of relationship with their leader. Doing so is an intentional effort on the part of the leader to make the followers feel like they are truly different and set apart from many others in the organization. Initially, the leader does not test the boundaries of their followers; the first order is for the leader to open up his or her life to them so that they can see that their leader is a real person and that it is safe to have a relationship with him or her. After the leader makes him or herself a little vulnerable, the followers' response is generally one that makes them feel like they, too, can open up in this environment with their leader. Only after this sense of safety and comfort with the leader is established among the followers should the leader begin to slowly implement the process of boundary testing. To engage in boundary testing prior to creating a safe environment would be premature, for such an environment is necessary in order to be able to ask followers to give more and do more. If the leader makes the ask before the followers feel safe and comfortable, instead of the followers being willing to accept the tasks and their accompanying demands, the leader will have to reduce his or her demands in order to accommodate only what the followers are willing to do.

It is important for leaders to engage in the processes that accompany the Acquaintance phase of the leader-follower relationship in order to make a proper assessment of where each follower is and to what level the follower can be engaged to complete organizational tasks. For example, if leaders do not make such assessments, they could potentially mistake followers who are in the Acquaintance phase of relationship for followers who are in the Mature Partner phase of relationship and accidentally share either too much information or information that is too sensitive. In doing so, the leader would be disclosing information to Acquaintance phase followers that should be reserved for Mature Partner followers. This information could potentially overwhelm the acquaintance follower to the point that he or she actually pushes back against the leader, having no desire to be in relationship with the leader at such a close level.

This actually happened to me in my organization! When I became the new leader of my ministry, I was handed the reins from the previous leader who had already established a leadership team for the organization, so when I inherited the organization, I also inherited the leadership team. One day, I found out that one of the leaders was leaving the ministry and that everyone else, including all of the Elders, already knew about it. Concerned about the matter, I called a meeting with the leaders and their wives so that I could get to the bottom of things. After I expressed my concern about all of them knowing that someone in such an important position was leaving and no one feeling that they needed to share the news with me, their leader, I was surprised at the response. One of their wives explained that the reason that no one told me was because "We don't roll like *that!*" In other words, she was telling me that although I felt close to them as their leader, they did not share the same level of relationship closeness with me. I thought that we were at a Mature Partner phase of relationship, and I had been relating to them based upon this assumption, even sharing very sensitive information about the ministry with them. This was the level of relationship they'd shared with our previous leader and with me when I was at their level of leadership, and since I had been promoted and the reins of leadership had been handed over to me, I just assumed that we would continue to share the same level of relationship closeness. However, in reality, with me in the new position as leader of the organization, the dynamics had changed without my recognizing it; we were now only at the Acquaintance phase of relationship. The whole time that I was thinking that we were a tightly-knit group and in this thing together, they had been keeping their distance from me and had no desire to be in a close relationship with me! Upon this realization, I was shocked and disappointed at the same time. Needless to say, my eyes were opened, and I released the entire leadership team so that I could eventually build my own.

Follower Triad Side 3 | Leader-Follower Relationship
CATEGORY 3:

IN-GROUP: MATURE PARTNER PHASE

The Mature Partner phase is the third phase that a follower navigates as a member of an organization. In this phase, the follower engages in the closest possible relationship with the leader, and the leader and follower share a mutual trust and respect for one another.[57]

It is important for leaders to understand how to discern when Acquaintance phase followers are ready to be considered Mature Partners. Time, testing, and talking sum up the mechanisms that leaders can use to move people from Acquaintance phase followers to Mature Partners. During this time of strategic development, there should be a lot of dialogue between the leader and follower, consistent monitoring of this dialogue, a great deal of time spent together, an increase in responsibilities designated by the leader to the follower, constant strategizing about how to bring ideas to manifestation, and any other activities that help to develop the Acquaintance phase Partner into a Mature Partner.

After a period of testing the boundaries in the Acquaintance phase, leaders should be able to effectively gauge the follower's level of maturity. For example, if leaders are considering the option of beginning to relate to Acquaintance phase followers as Mature Partners, test the waters first. In a meeting with these followers, give them a little bit of very sensitive information, so sensitive to the point that it could even be inflammatory or offensive. Then, the leader should just sit back and watch their reactions, both verbal and non-verbal, and listen to their responses. Based upon these observations, the leader will have a good idea of who is ready to be moved to the next level and be considered a Mature Partner and who is not.

Once followers matriculate to the phase of Mature Partner, leaders are able to continue to share top-level, sensitive, and confidential information with them; because of their high level of maturity, leaders can share the intricacies of what is happening behind the scenes of the organization with them – the good, the bad, and the ugly – without fear of offending, intimidating, or overwhelming them and without concern that they will judge the leader or the organization. Then, not only do leaders speak more in-depth to their Mature Partners, but they are more apt to listen to the feedback and critiques of Partners who operate at this level. Greater confidence can be placed into what Mature Partners say, because they have demonstrated that they can be trusted and that they mean well for both the leader and the organization. However, those who have demonstrated that they cannot handle such sensitive information, like Acquaintance phase followers, should not be made privy to such information. Instead, leaders should share only surface level information about what is happening in the organization; anything deeper, like the leader's worries and concerns about a future project might be too much for Acquaintance phase followers to handle.

Mature Partners are those who have demonstrated consistency in caring about the organization and the leader's well being over time. However, they do not just say that they care; they show that they care through generous and sacrificial contributions of their time, talents, and financial resources. They are also very intentional about making the organization better, making open demonstrations of support for their leader, monitoring what is happening by always keeping a finger on the pulse of important areas of the organization, providing honest feedback about the workings of the organization, and helping to oversee and drive initiatives. In a nutshell, the mark of a Mature Partner is that they mean well and monitor!

Of course, Mature Partners are the ideal type of followers within an organization, because they are a source of strength, support, and productivity for the leader. Because of this, my clients often desire to know how long it typically takes for a person to reach the Mature Partner phase. I wish that I could give a blanket answer to this question, but I cannot. The reality is that each follower is so distinctively different that there is no rule of thumb or set period of time in which a leader can expect for a follower to reach this point. Each individual has life experiences, agendas, schemas, a worldview, etc. that affect the rate at which they move from an outsider to a Mature Partner in the in-group. Those who have had good relationships in life and who have learned to trust people more easily tend to reach the Mature Partner phase more quickly. Those who have dealt with a lot of hurt and pain throughout life and who are emotionally scarred and wounded tend to take a great deal longer to reach the Mature Partner phase. The emotional health of the

Those who have had good relationships in life and who have learned to trust people more easily tend to reach the Mature Partner phase more quickly.

Those who have dealt with a lot of hurt and pain throughout life and who are emotionally scarred and wounded tend to take a great deal longer to reach the Mature Partner phase.

The emotional health of the individual really helps to determine the rate of development into a Mature Partner.

individual really helps to determine the rate of development into a Mature Partner.

When an organization is comprised of a large number of Mature Partners, it operates as a visibly cohesive organization with a tightly-knit core of people who are engaged and energetic about bringing the organization's overall goals to pass. They speak in dialog that is loaded with possessive pronouns that signal their ownership, investment, and buy-in to the organization. Most importantly, they operate under their leader as a productive, well-oiled machine with tasks being brought to a point of completion with high levels of efficiency and excellence.

Follower Triad Side 3 | Leader-Follower Relationship
SUMMARY & CONCLUSIONS

In summary, leaders must become skillful in answering the question posed by the Leader-Follower Relationship side of the Follower Pyramid, "How close is the relationship that I share with this follower, and how should I order my interactions, communications, and expectations with him/her based upon this level of closeness?" Without answering this critical question, leaders will not be empowered to identify followers from whom they can command higher levels of discretionary effort versus those from whom they cannot draw such efforts. Relational closeness determines the difference between the two.

Also, without learning to skillfully answer this question, leaders will assume that any follower within the organization is fair game for being asked to perform certain tasks, and they will expect any followers who accept tasks from them to "give it all they've got"! They will also not make the mistake of attributing the basic, no-frills outcomes produced by some of their followers to merely a lack of capacity to complete something with quality and excellence. After all, many followers possess exceptionally strong capacities, but this does not necessarily mean that they will be willing to exert their full capacity to complete an assigned task for their leader. Instead, leaders will understand that the level of relationship that they share with their followers plays a significant role in the quality of work that their followers will produce for them when assigned a given task. Again, the degree of closeness in the relationship will determine exactly how much of him or herself is directly related to how much energy and effort a follower is willing to give when assigned a task.

Only informed leaders who are empowered with an understanding of Leader-Follower Exchange Levels will know to anticipate higher levels of task energy from in-group followers than with out-group followers. Being armed with this expectation in advance will save the leader lots of frustration and disappointment. When they assign tasks to in-group followers, they will foresee the completion of the tasks with quality and excellence. When they assign tasks to out-group followers, they will foresee the tasks being simply completed. Understanding

Leader-Follower Exchange Levels takes the surprise out of the level of effort that followers will offer and the level of quality that followers will produce for their leaders!

The Most Successful Leaders Want Their Followers to "*Feel* This Thing"!

Leaders can only produce the best outcomes for their organization when they have in-group Mature Partners with whom they can connect internally – followers that can *feel* the relationship that exists between them. When followers reach this deep and intimate level of relationship in which they are literally emotionally connected to their leader, the sky is the limit for what they are willing to produce! They know that their leader is not only connected to them but to their families as well. In a manner of speaking, these leaders become even more than a leader or a boss; they become almost like an extended family member or a like a close, genuine friend upon which followers can depend while they are at work in the organization. They know that their leaders have their back! Having such a relationship as they work in an organization can have a significant and positive impact on a follower's motivation.

Studies show that financial incentives are not the be all end all determinant of whether people are satisfied with their jobs. For example, according to the *Harvard Business Review*, money does not buy the engagement of workers. In fact, it reports that "Intrinsic motivation is also a stronger predictor of job performance than extrinsic motivation – so it is feasible to expect higher financial rewards to inhibit not only intrinsic motivation, but also job performance.[58] *Inc. Magazine* supports this notion, reporting, "Employees work for a paycheck (otherwise they would do volunteer work), but they want to work for more than a paycheck: to work with and for people they respect and admire – and with and for people who respect and admire them... A true sense of connection is personal. That's why exceptional bosses show they see and appreciate the person, not just the worker."[59]

It is actually no wonder that people respond so favorably to a leader when that leader shows a sense of care and concern for them. It makes followers feel like they belong to or are a part of something. By nature, human beings are social creatures. We are not genetically programmed to live isolated lives apart from one another; we are programmed to live in communities among others who will help to care for us, protect us, and ensure our best interests. From a sociological evolutionary standpoint, our forefathers understood that their chances of survival increased if they stayed amongst the safety of the group and were lessened if they strayed off from the group to live on their own. They learned then what we know now: there are benefits to staying in a group, and just as those learned behaviors assured their longevity, in a way, they have also assured our longevity today. When people feel like they are a part of something bigger, and that this larger entity cares about them, this belonging has a subconscious effect on them. It makes them feel safe, it gives them a sense of identity, and it provides for them a sense of living for a purpose that exists outside of them. This sense of identity and belonging is what makes them give more.

When leaders are able to make their followers feel special, cared, for, seen, known, appreciated, and like they belong, their followers will do their absolute best to produce and perform at the highest standard possible. A leader's care goes a long way in gaining the commitment, support, and effort of followers – even more than money!

Is There a Way to Develop Your Out-Group Followers Into In-Group Partners? You Bet There Is!

Let's say that you have a few in-group Mature Partners, but your organization is really hurting for more, and you need to get not one, but several new Partners on board quickly! Well, "quickly" is relative, but you can accomplish this pretty effectively. The goal here is to identify those in the out-group whom you perceive have some potential to become in-group Mature Partners, given the right level of investment on your part. Once you identify these individuals, you can objectively classify them and set goals on how to reach them in order to develop them into in-group Partners that will yield greater levels of output.

I know that this process works because I have successfully engaged it myself on a number of occasions. For example, at one point, I realized that there was a group of women who were an out-group in my ministry. Because of the nature of what I do, working with volunteers rather than a big staff of paid employees to get things done, my organization thrives off of the quality and excellence offered by in-group mature in-group Partners. Thus, the more Partners I can develop, the better, because not much in my organization could get done without them.

I invited these women to be a part of a class that was just for them, which I called "Renovate." This made them feel special – like their own little group that was receiving personalized attention and grooming from their leader. I would text them once a day with motivational words and meet with them once a week about topics that were strategically designed to help them become greater individuals and equip them to be greater assets in the ministry. In just weeks, the results of the strategy began to manifest. The women shared that they felt closer to me as their leader, they expressed that the organization felt much warmer and more comfortable to them, they started volunteering at the church a lot more, and they gave significantly more of their time, energy, and finances – marks of Mature Partnership for my organization. In turn, I gave them greater levels of responsibility and higher levels of visibility in the organization, which made them feel even more special and important to the organization!

With a clear strategy and a small investment of my time and energy, I was able to draw these women away from the periphery of the relationship circle toward me as their leader in the center of the circle. All they needed was for me to show that I cared enough about them to bring them close, and since their development into in-group Mature Partners, I and my organization have received an immeasurable payoff of their support, energy, and quality execution!

I encourage leaders to make the development of in-group Partners a regular part of what they do as leaders in their organizations; it should be an intentional priority. In fact, I would go so far as to recommend that leaders develop a system in which they target groups of out-group followers and strategically engage them in a process that is designed to transform them into in-group Mature Partners. The more of an investment you make into these systematic efforts to develop Partners, the more of a return they will realize in their organization's level of excellence and effectiveness!

The Solution for the Leader Who Says "But I Don't Have *Time* to Develop My Out-Group Followers Into In-Group Partners!"

Each leader should have systems or mechanisms in place that are designed to make out-group followers feel like they are close to their leader. These groups are especially important for those who have not been invited to participate in a special group with the leader and for those who have not had the privileged opportunity to be developed by their leader face-to-face. When leaders effectively deploy lower-level leaders to interact with the followers, these leaders should be intentional about saying and doing things to make the people feel close to the leader, even though they might not have any direct interaction with him or her.

For example, in a meeting, if a follower has a special request, my deployed leader might say, "That's a really good idea, Jan. I will run it by Dr. Moody and ask him what his thoughts are. He really appreciated it last month when you thought so thoroughly through the details of the project and caught that important aspect that we missed. We were talking about how you really saved us on that one! After I talk to him about your idea, I'll get back with you." Just that easily, my deployed leader has made one of my followers feel much closer to me! Without my even having to engage the follower personally, I and the organization will reap the benefits of the person eventually becoming a mature in-group Partner!

The deployment of leaders or representatives in my stead is called creating "pseudo touches" in the organization. Ideally, it would be great if the organization's leader or CEO could always come down to where the worker bees are, walk among them, engage in some small talk, smile, and make the people feel like individual persons who are special, valued, cared for, appreciated, and seen. However, for most organizations, this simply is not practical. As a leader, followers might not be able to touch the CEO, but they can touch their manager, who can touch the regional supervisor, who can touch the vice president, who can touch the CEO. Thus, by touching the manager that is connected to the CEO through only a few degrees of separation, followers feel like they are touching the CEO him or herself! Again, this only works if the manager is a reflection of the organization's chief leader and only if the manager is intentional about making the followers feel like they have been heard and touched by the leadership.

Another mechanism that leaders might consider to accomplish this same purpose is the development of small groups that are led by representatives that have been hand-picked to represent the leader. Especially in volunteer organizations, leaders must become masterful at leading a large group of followers that is comprised of a number of smaller groups. Each small group should have its own special identity and feeling, and each should be led by a representative that will strategically connect the members of the group to the organization's leader through doing and saying the right things. When executed successfully, small groups can make a large organization feel small and can make followers who have never had a personal conversation with their leader feel as close to the leader as those who sit around the conference table with him or her every day. As a result, the follower becomes an instrumental part of the in-group, and the leader has yet another person to mobilize who is willing to give it all he's got when assigned a task! Remember: Any time a follower can be developed into an in-group Mature Partner, regardless of what mechanism is used to accomplish this end, the organization benefits in "priceless" ways that even money cannot buy! Thus, the investment of time and energy to transform a Partner from the out-group to the in-group is always well worth it!

The 720° Snapshot

PART 6:
THIS IS PERSONAL

How YOU Impact Your Leadership Decisions and Actions

Embracing Your Reality:
Who You Are is Who You Are In AND Out of the Office!

Who you are as a person is who you are as a leader, so the personal issues you deal with day to day also affect your leadership behavior.

Leader & Follower Triads Side 1:
Personal Influences

What level of support does this follower offer to me as a leader, and how does it affect his or her propensity to challenge my directives when asked to execute an organizational task?

Ready for the Workout:
The Exercise of Digging Up & Dealing with Your Personal Issues

How strengthening your S.H.O.E.S., C.O.R.E., and A.B.D.O.M.I.N.A.L.S. and minimizing the P.O.R.K., S.T.A.R.C.H., and F.A.T. can lead to leadership health and longevity!

The 720° Snapshot

CHAPTER 16

EMBRACING YOUR REALITY:

Who You Are is Who You Are – In AND Out of the Office!

If you will ever be the highly-productive and super-effective leader that you envision yourself becoming, it is critical that you understand this important tenet of leadership: who you are as an individual is who you are as a leader. Accept this and remember it daily as you lead your organization! It is not unusual for me to run into a leader and begin having a casual conversation about leadership and organizations, and in the midst of our dialogue, hearing the leader say, "Yeah, that's what I'm like in my *personal* life, but when I'm leading my organization, I'm a *completely* different person!" As the other guy is saying this, I cannot help but respond by giving him my characteristic tight-lipped Moody smile, accompanied by a raise of the eyebrows and a few slow, subtle nods of the head. These nods are not for the sake of communicating, "I agree"; rather, they are my way of communicating, "Yeah, this guy is completely unaware of how who he is bleeds through in his leadership style!"

In these moments, I am processing whether or not I should attempt to dispel this leader's myth about how who he is "in his personal life" has no impact on how he is as a leader. Should I continue to let him function in ignorance, or should I attempt to engage in an uphill battle that is designed to bring him into reality? Because I know that by virtue of reading this book, you are seeking fundamental truths that will empower you to become a more effective leader, I will gladly share the reality of the matter with you: who you are as a person *is indeed* who you are as a leader, and it is *impossible* to separate your office as a leader from the internal workings of how you are as person – the innermost true *you,* including all of your issues!

Each of us walks around life wearing a pair of invisible glasses with lenses that have been custom-tailored for us over time. If you actually wear glasses, you know that your prescription was specifically developed for you and that no one else's vision prescription is going to be exactly the same as yours. Based upon the individual, some people's lenses will be thicker, some thinner, some wider, some narrower, some reflective, some with a singular function, some with bifocal function, some with hues that change with the amount of light in the environment, and others with special tints on the lens that come in varying colors. Each person's lenses are as unique as the individual him or herself, and they ultimately determine the way the wearer sees the world.

Not only is this true with actual prescription lenses in the glasses that we wear, but it is true for the figurative lenses that each of us wear as we walk around experiencing life on a daily basis. Rather than going to an eye doctor in a spiffy white lab coat to get these lenses developed, however, life itself has helped us to develop them over time. The DNA with which we were born, the way we were raised and socialized, our culture, our education, our exposure, the influence of our family and friends, our romantic relationships, the music we listen to and the movies and television shows we have watched, the places we have traveled, our religious training and experience, our careers, and many other things about life have created these lenses through which we view and interpret the world; they have birthed issues within us that have defined and continuously refine our prescription lenses as we go throughout life. Because no two people's lives will ever be exactly the same, the lenses that their lives customize for them will be dramatically different; thus, because their personal issues are different, each person will view life differently than the next.

With actual prescription glasses, everything that we see is filtered through the lenses, and based upon the image that comes through the lenses, we are able to mentally interpret what we see. If the lenses are dirty and scratched, we might see an image and interpret it as a massive gray mountain off in the distance, marvel at its majesty, and want to take a picture. If the lenses are clean and sharp, we might see that the image is actually a massive gray elephant moving in our direction – and run! If these same lenses have a dark brown tint, the elephant might appear to be dark brown instead of gray, so you will think a large dark brown elephant is approaching. In the natural world, what we see all depends upon the lenses through which we are seeing it. These lenses determine whether we see things accurately or inaccurately, whether we see things clearly or unclearly, whether we understand what we are seeing or misunderstand what we are seeing, and even the color and beauty of things. Lenses matter.

If your vision is so good that it does not require you to wear any type of prescription lenses, good for you! The way you see the natural world is affected only by the built-in lenses that God gave you when He created your eyes. However, although you are fortunate enough to not have to wear artificial lenses, there's no getting away from wearing our figurative lenses. Regardless of age, ethnicity, class, or gender, everyone wears these, and there's no getting away from them or taking them off! Just like our natural lenses, our figurative lenses, which represent our personal issues, color the way in which we see and interpret the world. When we interact with the world and encounter different images and experiences, depending upon what type of lenses we are wearing, we are all prone to interpret them differently, and consequently, respond differently. Some of us have developed lenses throughout life that tend to make us see the good in people and situations and always remain hopeful and optimistic. Others of us have developed lenses throughout life that tend to make us see the bad in people and situations and that always cause us to be jaded and pessimistic. Some of us have lenses that cause us to interpret interactions with people as pure and innocent, causing us to feel at peace and respond with trust; others of us have lenses that cause us to interpret the same interactions with people as disingenuous and motive-driven, causing us to feel anxious and respond with suspicion. Again, just like our natural lenses shape what we see and how we respond to people, places, and things that we encounter in life, so do our figurative lenses shape the way we view and interact with the world!

Now, allow me to take your understanding of these figurative lenses a step further: because everything that we experience in life is filtered and interpreted through lenses that have been custom-shaped by our personal issues and that can never be removed, we will see things the way that only we can see them regardless of the environment or context. Whether we are seeing things from the title of parent, friend, teacher, mentor, church member, and yes, even from the title of organizational leader, *everything* that we encounter when wearing each of these hats will be filtered through our unique worldview. This is why the leaders that I encounter who say that they are one way in their personal lives but completely different people when they lead their organizations are mistaken. The reality is that you are who you are, wherever you are, at all times because of your worldview!

Considering the truth of this tenet, here is another reality that I challenge you to accept on your way to becoming a more effective leader: you are not the totally objective leader that you think you are. You are a great deal more subjective than you realize! Just in case you are not clear about the difference between what it means to be objective versus subjective, one who is objective is not influenced by personal feelings, interpretations, or prejudices and he or she is unbiased, basing interpretations and responses on facts.[60] On the other hand, one who is subjective operates out of that which belongs to and proceeds from his or her own mind and not out of the nature of the object being considered. In essence, subjective people allow their emotions, prejudices, etc. to influence how they interpret and respond to the world.[61]

I know, I know. You really think that despite what I say, you are objective. *Really* objective. Like, more objective than 99 percent of the people out there, because you are *so* intentional and disciplined about being objective that you have even mastered the ability to be objective about your objectivity! You are not alone. People like to be able to boast that even though they hold their own personal feelings and opinions about things, they are mature enough, unbiased enough, and impartial enough to detach themselves from what they think and feel on a personal level and deal with a situation based solely upon facts and principles. They feel like the ability to solemnly swear that they are objective makes people take them more seriously, have greater confidence in their leadership, and not question their decisions and methods. Good try, but decades of leadership experience, research, and training at the doctoral level have taught me that this is simply not true!

No matter what you might think, it is not possible for anyone to be totally objective, because each of us is impacted, both consciously and subconsciously, by our own internal dialogue... our personal issues... our worldview. Have you ever empowered someone in your organization to make certain decisions on your behalf and been completely disappointed? You had trained, mentored, and personally worked with this individual, even allowing them to stay in close proximity to you, observing your every decision, assessing the process you used to arrive at your decisions, and charting every move. You had trained the person in all of the scientific aspects of leadership from a matter-of-fact standpoint, including what you want and why and how you want it. However, when it came time for this person to think like you and make the calls that you would have made in a particular situation, they got it all wrong, making decisions that you *never* would have made!

How could this be, considering that you had personally groomed and prepared them to think and process exactly as you do so that in your absence, they could think like you would think? Why couldn't your mentee echo the same decisions that you would have made? Simple. When you are faced with making a crucial decision, you think like *you* – not like someone else. When the person you trained was faced with making a crucial decision, they actually did take into account each and every thing that you imparted during the training season; and yet they arrived at a completely different decision. Even with all of the facts present before them, there were subtle differences between the ways in which the two of you process things. This further illuminates the reality that each of us operates with a measure of subjectivity!

This is nothing new. I could lock ten people in a room, train them all with the exact same training, go through the same role play scenarios, and take them through all of the same critical thinking processes with the hopes that they would all end up thinking the same way about a particular topic. However, when the rubber meets the road and it's time to make a decision, as much as they are intentional about putting to use all that they learned from me, each of them will very likely end up making a different decision. Why? Because our worldviews are our worldviews, and our minds operate the way that they operate because they are impacted by our worldview. This makes us who we are, and we cannot *help* but to be the way we are!

Even if we try not to, despite our best intentional efforts, we cannot help but see the world the way that we see it! As a leader, you have a choice between two options. Option A calls for you to fight this understanding and continue to try to convince yourself that you are as objective as you think you are. If you choose this option, also realize that you will continue to manifest the same leadership results that you have been realizing up until now. Option B calls for you to accept this understanding, appreciate it for what it is, remain aware of it in your leadership efforts, and compensate for it in the way that you lead your organization. I recommend that you select the latter option; your effectiveness as a leader will increase all the more for it!

CHAPTER 17

LEADER & FOLLOWER TRIADS SIDE 1: PERSONAL ISSUES

ASSESSMENT QUESTION:

What known or hidden personal values, motivations, or feelings are present within me, and how do they affect my perceptions and interactions, skew my interpretation of the facts surrounding critical situations, and influence my decisions, actions, and reactions with others?

You might recall that during our examinations of the Leader Triad and the Follower Triad, the discussion of the first side of each of these triads, Personal Issues, was postponed for a later time. Because of the significant impact that they have on becoming an effective leader, I felt that they deserved some dedicated time and attention, and I did not want the focus on them to get lost in the overall presentation of the interpersonal dynamics that affect one's relationships in the organization. Personal issues really *are* that important, and they merit a deeper dive because of the essential function that they play in our level of effectiveness as leaders.

Whereas the other dynamics that we have discussed up to this point are interpersonal, this discussion about your personal dynamics is just that – personal. These dynamics differ from the others that we have discussed, because they cause us to take a long hard look at ourselves, including what moves us, what drives us, and what inside of us causes us to think, act, and react the way we do to certain people and situations. While the dynamics that we have previously examined have heightened our awareness of various intersecting elements that contribute to the direction of the decisions that we make, nothing is more important than having a heightened awareness of ourselves, including our personal issues.

This examination of the internal workings that directly impact your leadership will require several things on your part, including courage, honesty, transparency, and perhaps most of all, understanding. Most importantly, keep in mind as we go along that we are not here to beat you up for who and how you are. Instead, we are here to understand who you are and accept that reality. It is our goal to increase your awareness of who the real "you" is and learn how to mitigate the personal issues that decrease your effectiveness as a leader. Further, we aim to help you capitalize on the personal issues that increase your effectiveness as a leader. If you are ready for this significant leg of the journey, let's go!

THE LEADER TRIAD

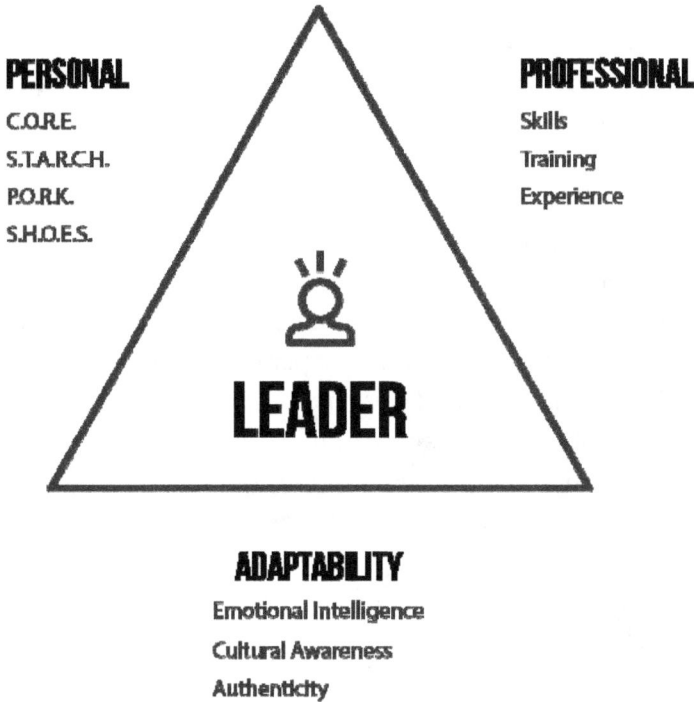

PERSONAL

C.O.R.E.
S.T.A.R.C.H.
P.O.R.K.
S.H.O.E.S.

PROFESSIONAL

Skills
Training
Experience

LEADER

ADAPTABILITY

Emotional Intelligence
Cultural Awareness
Authenticity

Personal Issue Awareness & the Leader Triad

As we learned in our discussion of the Leader Triad, authenticity is critical in order for you to lead an organization effectively. However, one of the key characteristics that precede the ability to be authentic is that of being aware of your personal issues, whether good, bad, or ugly. I use the phrase "good, bad, or ugly" quite deliberately. All personal issues are not bad and harmful; some are more neutral, and others simply deal with our biases and individual preferences, like preferring blondes over brunettes or preferring a cold office environment to a warmer one. When most people hear the term "issues," they immediately think in terms of negative internal characteristics that a person possesses that can cause others some level of harm. While the term does traditionally lean towards having a negative connotation, for the sake of our discussion, an issue merely refers to the internal traits and tendencies that affect how we act, interact, and respond to the world – and yes, they can be good, bad, *very* ugly, or just plain neutral!

You must first be aware how you are prone feel, think and behave given particular situations in order to be able to deal with them with the type of transparency that it takes to be an authentic leader. When we are courageous enough to dig out, uncover, and examine our personal issues, as uncomfortable as this process is, it empowers us in unspeakable ways – ways that those who choose to remain ignorant of these internal workings will never experience. You see, when you operate with the awareness that you tend to think and feel a certain way about certain people or things in certain situations, you can take pre-emptive action to minimize the impact of these personal issues, preventing them from completely overwhelming the decisions or actions that you take about the situation. However, if you choose to remain ignorant of your personal issues, you will be ill-equipped to minimize their impact on the decisions that you make or actions that you take.

If you are not aware of your personal issues, you cannot manage them. In fact, you will make certain decisions and engage in certain actions without a full comprehension of why you did things the way you did. You'll just know that for some reason, they *felt* right to you. Someone might ask you, "Why did you choose to react that way to the situation? Why did you opt to do things the way you did?" Rather than have an immediate response that is based upon the fact that you thought things through and intentionally took into consideration your personal issues and other impacting factors before choosing to react, you have to pause and think about it. You will end up saying to yourself, "That is *actually* a good question! Why *did* I choose to react that way to the situation? What was I really *thinking*?" When you remain unaware of your personal issues, you can be assured that they are always behind the scenes, driving you to places that you probably would not be going if you were making fully-informed decisions about how to act for yourself!

When we endeavor to be fully aware of the issues and biases that move and drive us, we can proactively factor them into the decision-making equation, resulting in a well-calculated determination of how we will respond to a matter. Our response deliberately seeks to identify and eliminate the influence of as much interference as possible by these issues and biases. In essence, although it is impossible to be totally objective, an awareness and acknowledgement of our personal issues helps us to function as close to objectivity as is possible. On the other hand, when we remain ignorant of the issues and biases that move and drive us, while we like to think that we have made an objective decision about something, we are operating with a gross misunderstanding. In reality, this ignorance of our personal issues and biases means that we are no longer in control of our own actions and reactions. Our *issues* are!

> *In reality, this ignorance of our personal issues and biases means that we are no longer in control of our own actions and reactions. Our issues are!*

Are you getting the idea of how empowered you become as a leader when you are willing to identify and deal with your personal issues head-on? When you are empowered with an awareness of your personal issues and biases, you operate with a level of clarity that most others do not exercise, and this gives you a wonderful competitive advantage as an organizational leader! For example, let's say that you are about to go into a business meeting in which you are meeting with a husband and wife team that are interested in partnering with you on a business or organizational deal. If the partnership goes through, it could be of great benefit to everyone involved; you just need to have this meeting to close the deal.

As soon as the couple walks in, you realize that you don't like the wife; you don't know why, you just don't. As you reach out to shake her hand, you look her in the eyes and smile, but you are not getting a good vibe from her. Your instinct is to immediately come up with an excuse for the couple for why this partnership is not going to work. Your feelings are screaming, "Don't do business with her!" However, as you take your seat at the conference table, your awareness of your personal issues kicks in.

Instantly, you realize that this lady looks exactly like your third grade teacher, who always seemed to talk down to you and who never defended you when the other kids made fun of you. When you told your parents about it, she was not forthcoming with the truth; she said the kids were not actually making fun of you and that she did everything possible to boost your confidence in the classroom. You felt betrayed by her, and this caused you to develop distrust for her and anyone who remotely resembled her. Further, you recall that when you started your first business, the first customer that failed to pay the balance of a large invoice, almost causing you to have to shut your doors, was a business lady whose voice sounded very familiar to the one sitting across the conference room table from you. Finally, your mind reminds you that your mother and father once owned a business as you were growing up; your dad complained to you that your mother had become so absorbed in the business that she never paid attention to him anymore. When they divorced, he blamed it solely on the business, which she happened to walk away from the marriage with in its entirety being the shrewd business woman that she was.

As you sit at the table allowing yourself to actively identify the personal issues that are driving the feelings that you are having about this lady, you realize that the issue is not her. After all, she is a nice enough lady. She is very pleasant, attractive, classy and professional. She has been smiling ever since she entered the room, and just from the small talk that you have heard so far, you can tell that she is a humble woman. Understanding this, here is where you have the following quick conversation with yourself: "This lady has done absolutely nothing to cause me to think and feel the way that I am thinking and feeling about her. The reason I am feeling this way is because of my own personal issues of the past. She does not represent the past, and I will not make her pay for the mistakes from the past that others have made. I will not allow my personal issues to drive my behavior or to get in the way of doing what is best for my organization, which is developing the partnership. Thus, I choose to move forward with the deal!" In this case, because you allowed yourself to become intentionally aware of your personal issues, you were able to make a clear-minded decision that was as objective as it is possible. You were able to answer the "Why?" behind what you are feeling because you had the ability to identify and deal with your issues head-on, and this ultimately benefited your organization.

Now, imagine that you were completely unaware of your issues and how they impact the way you think and feel. When the couple walked in, all you would be sure of is that you did not like the woman – at all. In fact, you could not bear the idea of working in such close proximity with this woman in the partnership; the thought of it made your stomach turn, and you literally felt sick. The funny thing is that you don't know why! You don't even take a couple of moments to ask yourself, "Why am I feeling this way about this woman? Why is it that I just met her and yet I can't stand her?" All you know at this point is that you have to go with your gut, and your gut says that this is a no-brainer: the deal is off! Unfortunately, in calling off the deal, you have also deprived your organization of some very lucrative profits and what would have been increased expansion and exposure; however, for you, this is not the important thing. For you, the important thing is that you were "true to your gut." Never mind the fact that your "gut" is just your issues that have resurfaced and influenced you to the point that they completely destroyed the biggest deal that your organization has been presented with in almost a decade. You have no other potential offers on the table that could offer the same benefits. But who's counting?

An understanding of your personal issues helps you to wade through the fluff and get to the bottom line in order to make the best decisions for your organization. It allows you to dismiss anything that is not directly relevant to the decision at hand, including your personal issues, and focus only on the critical facts that are necessary to make the best decision possible. It allows you to filter out as many personal issues as is feasible in an attempt to make the most objective decision that one can make. These benefits in and of themselves offer great benefit to organizational leaders and no doubt increase their leadership effectiveness.

THE FOLLOWER TRIAD

PERSONAL

C.O.R.E.
S.T.A.R.C.H.
P.O.R.K.
S.H.O.E.S.

FOLLOWERSHIP STYLE

Partner
Implementer
Individualist
Resource

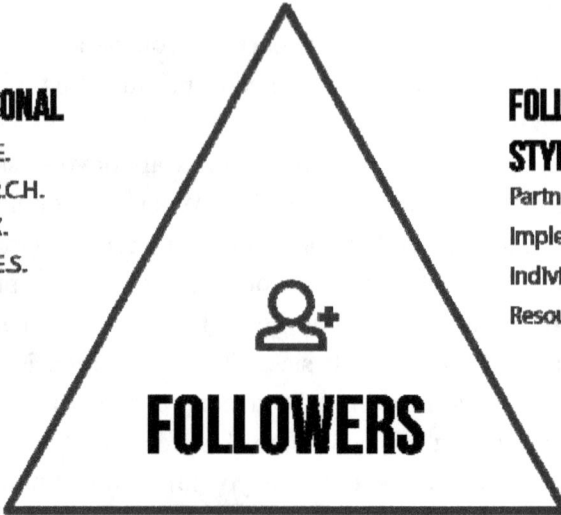

FOLLOWERS

LEADER-FOLLOWER RELATIONSHIP

Exchange Level
▶ Out-group
Stranger Phase
▶ In-group
Acquaintance Phase
Mature Partner Phase

Personal Issue Awareness & the Follower Triad

Another equally important benefit of understanding your personal issues is that it helps you to understand your thoughts, actions, and reactions as a leader as you relate to your followers. If you are like me, you can frustrate yourself with the ways in which you behave sometimes. For example, there are times when I am in a meeting and I see someone looking at me in a way that agitates me, because I consider the person's expression and body language to be disrespectful to me as a leader. Because of my training, though, I can always identify why the person's expression and body language has set me on edge and frustrated me. Of course, the "why" always has to do with my personal issues. When I arrive at such moments, I have to turn on the intentionality and self-control, reminding myself that I am probably feeling disrespected because of my issues. When I am feeling disrespected, it takes everything in me to keep from shouting, "You will *not* relate to me like that!" Sometimes I address it with the individual in the meeting (if I determine that the behavior has surpassed being about my personal issues and is about being blatantly disrespectful), and other times, I simply chalk it up to me being extra sensitive to the individual's behavior towards me, and I just leave it alone.

The funny thing is, I can ask my wife or another leader who was in the meeting about the incident afterwards, and neither of them interpreted the individual's expression and body language as disrespectful. Needless to say, I am never surprised at these different interpretations. I see, experience, and interact with the world through my eyes, and they do the same through their own eyes. That's the way that issues work: we all have our own customized set of them through which we view the world!

> *That's the way that issues work: we all have our customized set of them through which we view the world!*

Being aware of your personal issues as a leader can help you understand why you can make good decisions but have bad feelings about them, why certain people in the organization irk you and others do not, why you tend to be harder on some people and more understanding with others, why you might find yourself talking down to and nearly abusive towards some type of people rather than others, and even why you prefer to select a certain type of person to be a leader rather than others. This awareness helps you to be clear on why you feel what you feel and can help you to keep your feelings in perspective so that you can deal with each individual on his or her own merits rather than out of your emotions. It also helps you to pull back from having issue-driven interactions with your followers, allowing you to focus only on what is relevant to the person's job performance. Essentially, being aware helps you to put the feelings and the gut checks to the side in order to make better holistic judgments.

Another big benefit to being self-aware when dealing with followers is that is keeps you as a leader from developing a homogeneous organization in which everyone has to look and think just like you; it helps you to develop a more diverse organization! Let's face it: most of us like ourselves and the way that we operate in an organization – a lot. When you mix this with the fact that you are a leader, which probably means that you have more of a driven, assertive personality that tends to get things done, who *wouldn't* want to have an organization full of people just like you? Right? Here's something else that we have to face: we are all biased. We don't like to admit it much, but we tend to have preferences for people of certain races, classes, educational backgrounds, social standing, etc. They just *appeal* to us... and they are usually very similar to us, too!

When you combine the fact that we like ourselves and that we are incredibly biased, the result is played out in how we pick people for our organization: we pick people that are like us! The figurative lenses that we wear help us pick these types of people right out of a crowd as keenly as an eagle can spot a fish three miles away! This is especially true in the selection of leaders that we choose from among the followers in our organizations. Granted, it is reasonable that you, as a leader, will want some similarities to exist between you and the followers

> *We pick people like us! The figurative lenses that we wear help us pick these types of people right out of a crowd as keenly as an eagle can spot a fish three miles away!*

that you select for next-tier leadership. However, as the world is becoming increasingly more diverse, diversity in leadership becomes all the more beneficial to your organization. For example, a diverse follower base and next-tier leadership team can offer broader perspectives to addressing the challenges you face, and the differences that exist amongst the team can offer a variety of approaches to addressing an issue, which can lead to making a more comprehensive assessment and producing a more carefully thought-out outcome. As the Bible says, there is both wisdom and safety in a multitude of counsel.[62] Wise, effective leaders neither make decisions in a vacuum, nor do they only desire to entertain perspectives that are the same as their own!

> *As the Bible says, there is both wisdom and safety in a multitude of counsel. Wise, effective leaders neither make decisions in a vacuum, nor do they only desire to entertain perspectives that are the same as their own!*

Understandably, it takes setting aside personal issues and dispensing with internal biases in order to build such diversity into an organization. Choosing members and leaders of your organization based upon their merits and abilities to contribute to achieving the organization's mission and goals should be the determining factor of whether or not they are selected to join the team, not how much they satisfy your bias as a leader by being just like you. It is an unfortunate reality that many leaders judge books by their covers, and when the book covers do not look like their own, they discount what they have to offer and/or completely overlook them.

If you will be an effective leader who builds a diverse organization, you must realize that if a person does not look like you as a leader, the lack of resemblance does not make the individual any less intelligent or capable of getting the job done.

If you will be an effective leader who builds a diverse organization, you must realize that if a person does not look like you as a leader, the lack of resemblance does not make the individual any less intelligent or capable of getting the job done. Toss those biases aside, evaluate the individual based upon his or her merits, and if the qualifications are met, give it a chance! Dare to add some diversity to your organization of "Mini-me's"! However, a word of caution: when you deal with people who are not like you – you know, the diverse crowd – be careful of how you interact with them. Our natural tendency is to deal with people who are more like us with more fairness and understanding and to deal with people who are less like us in a more partial and unsympathetic way. In other words, we tend to beat them up a little more without realizing it. Always be mindful to make an extra effort to be aware of your personal issues when dealing with the diverse followers in the organization! Your effectiveness as a leader will depend on it.

When leaders build organizations based upon their own biases that are filled with people that look and act like them, the singularity of thought that pervades the organization will inevitably produce a culture of comfort for everyone… but it will also produce an organization that is driven by and that operates completely off of bias! You might wonder, "Why is singularity of thought a bad thing? Isn't it preferred for everyone in the organization to be on one accord?" To answer this, I refer to Ira Chaleff's work on *The Courageous Follower*[63], which asserts that followers within the organization must be courageous and that they have an ethical obligation to speak to offer questions, insights, and on some level, challenges to their leaders' decisions and ideas. These challenges are not made to minimize the leader's capacity to lead the organization; they are made for the purpose of enhancing existing plans and ideas. Again, when a leader builds a homogeneous organization, there will not be many challengers to his or her ideas, because everyone thinks alike. As a result of the uniformity of thought in the organization, plans and ideas never get a good "working over" based upon diverse and varying perspectives, which is necessary to refine and produce the best plans and ideas possible. What good is a think tank session when everyone thinks alike? What good is a strategy session when everyone strategizes the same way? From this perspective, singularity of thought is not a good thing. You need some diversity!

Personally, I welcome a diverse follower base and the challenges that these individuals launch against my plans and ideas – the courageous ones, anyway. In my organization, I have a saying: "Ideas are meant to be developed, not protected." By this, I am referencing the fact that most of us protect ideas,

> *Ideas are meant to be developed, not protected.*

particularly the ones that originate with us. Because we are the ones that developed the idea, we have a hard time differentiating or creating space between ourselves as the originators of the concepts and the concepts themselves. Consequently, we interpret any challenge to our idea as a challenge – or an attack – against us directly. This is simply not so! As an effective leader, it will be up to you to not only cast off your biases and build the most diverse organization possible but to take full advantage of the thoughts, perspectives, exposure, and experiences of the diverse follower base around you by asking them to challenge the things that come out of your mind. After all, what good is it to set aside your biases and build a diverse organization if you are not going to make full use of the diversity that surrounds you? Encourage your followers to realize that the challenge process is one that is designed to refine, develop, and strengthen the idea. In order to accomplish this, the idea must be broken down, torn apart, argued against, and reassembled with other well thought-out components that could easily come from several different followers on the team. Do not take this process personally! In the end, when you put your ideas on the table and allow them to be developed by your team of diverse, critical thinkers, the idea will come out stronger and more efficient, and this will benefit the entire organization – and you as its leader.

Full disclosure: as clear as I am on this point now, I had to learn the lesson myself the hard way! When I began as a student in my doctoral program, I was not accustomed to having my ideas publicly challenged. As the top leader of my organization, what I said was pretty much accepted without contest or dispute. However, when I started attending my graduate classes, right there in the middle of class, people would openly say things like, "I would disagree with you, Charles." This not being familiar to me, I would sit there thinking, *Wow! How could you put me out there in front of the professor? Why did you come out against me in class, and yet after class, you always want to go have coffee with me? You are NOT my friend!* Of course, looking back on those days as a newbie in a graduate program, I can see that I was definitely not mature; my hurt feelings were a clear indication of this fact. Nonetheless, I did not stop. Every time the other students challenged my positions or ideas, they made me go back to the books to develop them further and further. Their challenges made me strengthen my arguments until they became razor sharp! For this, I could neither be mad nor resentful – only grateful for how they helped to make me a more astute and intelligent student.

My peers were not the only ones from whom I had to learn to accept open criticism; challenges that I received from my instructors made their critiques look like compliments! I had submitted a paper to one of my academic mentors, very proud of the work that I had done. The child of an educator who was determined to excel academically, I typically emerge as one of the sharpest students in any scholastic environment. As it turns out, the academic mentor to whom I had submitted my paper didn't think so. He wrote: *Dear Charles, I can appreciate some of your thoughts. I would have hoped by now that you would have developed your Lilliputian way of thinking.* Talk about an ego buster! In using the term "Lilliputian," he was referring to the novel *Gulliver's Travels*. The Lilliputians were a colony of people who were very small, so the use of Lilliputian in the context of my writing meant "small and trivial." In my academic mentor's estimation, I was very small minded, and his comments were meant as an encouragement for me to broaden my perspective; just because I believe something does not mean that the world actually operates that way. Needless to say, I took his painfully honest critique to heart and used his comments to enlarge my worldview, learning more and more over time how priceless a broadened perspective about the world can actually be, *especially* for a leader!

Ultimately, my point here is that when others challenge your ideas, it only makes your ideas better, and the execution of better ideas makes you a better leader. Thus, challenges can be your best friend! However, you will never create a follower base within your organization that has the capacity to challenge your ideas if you allow your personal biases to guide your hiring and selection decisions, because biases tend to favor people who think just like us. Instead, go for diverse! Go for different! Go for building a team that will help to develop you – and your ideas – for the better!

Don't Fear what You Might Find when You Dig up Your Issues!

Whether you are dealing with personal issues from the standpoint of better understanding yourself as the leader of the organization (the Leader Triad) or better understanding yourself in relation to your followers (the Follower Triad), the message is the same: do not be afraid to bring the personal issues and biases that dwell in your subconscious to conscious awareness! Whatever you do, do not bury your head in the sand like ostriches, who supposedly bury their heads in the sand when they feel scared or threatened by a potential predator. The premise, which experts have actually debunked as a myth, is that the ostriches engage in this behavior believing that if they cannot see their predators, their predators cannot see them. Although the accuracy of the phrase

Do not be afraid to bring the personal issues and biases that dwell in your subconscious to conscious awareness!

is questionable when it comes to the ostrich, the phrase "bury your head in the sand" itself has evolved to suggest that one "ignores unpleasant realities." Your personal issues are unpleasant realities that should not be ignored!

The prospect of bringing to the forefront knowledge of your personal issues and biases should not depress, dishearten, or discourage you, regardless of how unattractive they might be. To take this position would be the equivalent of saying, "I don't want to know which things about me are hindering my leadership effectiveness and which are making me effective." If you have the ability to isolate the elements of your personal issues that are doing the most damage, as well as those that are contributing to your effectiveness, why not do it? Without taking the time to identify these elements, any unknown element could be the one to make or break your success as a leader. Thus, every leader should want to know the personal issues in their lives that impact their leadership in order to increase the probability of becoming – and remaining – an effective, successful leader!

CHAPTER 18

READY FOR THE WORKOUT:

The Exercise of Digging Up & Dealing with
Your Personal Issues

Each of the elements contained in *Moody's 720° Leadership Decision-Making Model* plays an important role in helping leaders to become more aware of the factors that they should take into consideration when making an organizational decision or approaching a task. Raising your level of awareness of how the various elements surrounding tasks, issues, yourself as a leader and followers will also serve to raise your level of effectiveness as a leader, because you will be able to make decisions that are as fully-informed as possible about how to proceed – and we all know that fully-informed decisions beat out decisions made out of ignorance or in the absence of vital information any day! Thus, the comprehensive 720 degree perspective that *Moody's 720° Leadership Decision-Making Model* offers grants you as a leader the opportunity to bring to the forefront and factor in everything that might stand to influence the outcome of your decision, consequently minimizing your chances of making a wrong decision.

To understand the value of being empowered to make a fully-informed decision, let's consider the *only* being capable of making the right decisions 100 percent of the time: God! The reason that God is a perfect decision maker who always makes the right decisions without fail is because He knows everything; He is omniscient, or all knowing, and nothing escapes Him. In His omniscience, He knows all things at all times, past, present, and future. Thus, when God makes a decision, there is nothing that is hidden from Him. No information will ever be obscured at the time He is making a decision and then pop up as a surprise at a later time to suggest that He should have decided differently. Instead, He is fully aware of all of the knowledge and facts surrounding the decision to be made at the time He makes the decision.

Now, we know that God is God, and we are flawed human beings. Although we will never come anywhere close to being omniscient and empowered to make the right decisions 100 percent of the time, we can at least do the most that we can do by trying to be as fully-informed and aware of all of the facts as possible when it is time to make a decision or approach a task. Developing this ability will grant you as a leader a higher probability of making better decisions. *Moody's 720° Leadership Decision-Making Model* systematically helps to uncover all of the unknowns and expose every dynamic that is active and at play in the situation. In a nutshell, *Moody's 720° Leadership Decision-Making Model* empowers you to approach decision making with your eyes wide open with everything laid bare on the table before you!

I introduce this understanding to you because despite the significance of all of the other dynamics that this Model helps to uncover, the most impactful dynamics of all that it helps to uncover are your personal issues. Then, not only are these issues the most impactful, but they are the most challenging dynamics that leaders are faced with as they are learning to approach decision making as a 720° leader. Let's be realistic: no one *really* wants to do the work of digging up their personal issues. Very few of us want to actively deal with our personal issues unless we are gluttons for punishment! It's easier for us to admit that we have personal issues (without specifying exactly what they are and where they came from), try to suppress them when they rear their ugly heads, and do all we can to keep our leadership esteem and confidence in order to keep the organization moving.

Just like working out in the natural, digging up and dealing with personal issues can be an intense, tiresome, tedious drag, but it is necessary to engage in this self-reflective workout for the sake of your leadership health, endurance, and longevity. Nothing about the process of self-examination to get to the root of your personal issues will be comfortable or easy. On the contrary, it will be challenging, and it will *definitely* not feel good! Simply put, it will be a *real* workout! However, if you dare to strap on your shoes for the journey, do the work to strengthen your core, and discipline yourself to avoid the S.T.A.R.C.H. and the P.O.R.K., I guarantee that before long, you will start to see the results reflected in your leadership health that you have been desiring for years!

There are various types of personal issues and biases that affect your interpretations, decisions, actions, and reactions as a leader, and they typically fall into two groups, each featuring two categories.

The first group consists of issues of awareness that you should carefully consider and seek to *strengthen* while on your workout journey. They include the following:

1) S.H.O.E.S.
2) C.O.R.E.
3) A.B.D.O.M.I.N.A.L.S.

The second group consists of things that you should *avoid* in order to develop optimal leadership health. They include the following:

4) P.O.R.K.
5) S.T.A.R.C.H. (and F.A.T.)

S.H.O.E.S.

Everyone wears shoes. We wear them for a number of reasons that include both fashion and functionality, and most of us have more pairs of them than any person could every wear out in a lifetime. Most of us choose our shoes based upon how they well they will match our outfit, how tall or short they will make us appear, how polished or casual of an appearance they will give us when we wear them as part of our well-assembled ensembles, and most importantly, what statement they will make about us in general. Athletes choose their shoes based upon different reasons, including how fast they will make them, how much they will improve their jump game, how much traction they will provide as they run, how light they are, and of course, how cool and athletic they will make them look. However, whatever the type of shoe, what most people fail to realize is that shoes are actually *tools* – important ones!

When we do not invest in the right pair of these essential tools, we are likely to cause injury to our feet, and this could potentially lead to pain, discomfort, and even more severe maladies of the foot in the future. In light of this, choosing the proper shoes is a necessary step in developing and maintaining a healthy walking technique. They provide the support and protection that we need in order to prevent injuries. This is especially important, because every single movement that your feet make as you walk has a direct effect on other parts of your body! For example, if you wear shoes that do not provide your feet with good arch and heel support, your shoes will prevent the range of motion that your feet need in order to fully support your body. Consequently, because your feet are not able to function properly, other parts of your body must compensate for where they fall short. Then, when your body is forced to overcompensate, the inevitable outcome will be pain and discomfort in your lower back, hips, knees, heels, and ankles. Ultimately, if these minor injuries go unaddressed, they can lead to major injuries in other parts of the body.[64] Who *knew* that shoes could be so important?

As important of a role as the shoes that we wear on our feet play for the support of our physical bodies, our psycho-emotional S.H.O.E.S. are equally as important for the support of our lives. Our S.H.O.E.S. represent the mentalities and operating assumptions that we "wear" as we travel throughout life. As they relate to leadership, our S.H.O.E.S. help to shape our thinking process. Like physical shoes, our psycho-emotional S.H.O.E.S. keep us covered as we move in and out of situations, and they provide a basis of support for the different activities – mental activities – in which we engage. Just as we wear different types of shoes when engaging in different activities, we put on different S.H.O.E.S. for different situations. For example, we put on one set of S.H.O.E.S. for marriage, as we have our own personal set of beliefs, assumptions, and though processes when it comes to interacting in marital relationships. Then, we put on another set of S.H.O.E.S. when it comes to business, because we govern our business and organizational lives according to a different set of beliefs, assumptions, and thought processes. Thus, you see, we switch our psycho-emotional S.H.O.E.S. on and off to fit the task in the same way that we switch our physical shoes! One shoe does not fit all situations!

It is as necessary to invest in the right set of S.H.O.E.S. as it is to invest in physical shoes; without the right pair of these mentalities and operating assumptions, we stand to cause great harm and injury to whatever context we are operating in, whether business, marriage, leadership, or any other context. Even more, when we approach situations in these contexts wearing the wrong S.H.O.E.S., even greater future harm can result beyond that which is immediately seen. However, when walking into a situation using the right pair of S.H.O.E.S. that offer just the right amount support and protection that we need, we will be able to walk through it in a healthy way. Having the right S.H.O.E.S. on when we approach a situation also ensures that other areas of our lives will not have to compensate for any missteps we make. Remember: every movement that we make as we walk in both our shoes and our S.H.O.E.S. has a direct effect on other parts of the body! When we live our lives with the right set of S.H.O.E.S., or mentalities and operating assumptions, we avoid doing long-term damage to other areas of our lives!

Your S.H.O.E.S. represent the external factors that influence how you interpret behaviors and make decisions as a leader.

I'm sure that by now, you are wondering, *What does the acronym S.H.O.E.S. stand for?* Your S.H.O.E.S. represent the external factors that influence how you interpret behaviors and make decisions as a leader. S.H.O.E.S. represent five key influential areas that help to mold the mentalities and assumptions that comprise a leader's thinking processes:

S – Sociological factors
H – History
O – Opportunities or Oppositions
E – Experiences (professional)
S – Spiritual influence

S. *Sociological Factors*

Sociological factors are influences in your upbringing that have played a vital role in creating the filters through which you view life. They can include issues like your socioeconomic status, social influences, education, and family life, among other aspects of your background. These are the very experiences that made us who we are today, having branded upon us certain ways of thinking, certain beliefs about what should and should not be, and certain ways of interpreting people and experiences that we encounter in the world. Consequently, they have a heavy influence upon the way we see and what we expect in our interactions in life. Most of all, these factors are protective.

It is important for you to have a conscious awareness of the sociological factors of your past and the role that these factors have played in shaping and molding the way that you interpret people and situations. Without such a strong awareness, you could easily be quick to label people and experiences that possess sociological sensibilities that are similar to yours as positive and those that differ from yours as negative. This is a problem, because when you view others who were raised differently than you as negative, you can tend to relate to them in an unkind, biased, condescending, or judgmental way without even realizing it! As an aware leader, you must be willing to question the impact that the sociological factors of your past have shaped the way that you view the world and set them aside when they have no real bearing on the situation at hand.

For example, if you were raised by parents who loved to travel internationally, and you traveled around the world learning about different languages and cultures as you grew up – a high socioeconomic status lifestyle – this would have definitely shaped the way that you see people and interpret experiences. When you encounter someone who has never traveled outside of the country and who does not know any language other than English, you might be prone to look down up on the person for being "underexposed" and so "uneducated." However, is this really a fair assessment? Might the sociological factors associated with your upbringing be clouding your perception? Could it be that the person is simply among the *majority* of Americans that do not have a passport and that have never traveled outside of the country?[65] Is it a crime to *not* be one of the 15 to 20 percent of Americans that are bilingual?[66] Could it be that this person has a 1500 SAT score and is a whiz in science, technology and math, but that as a person of a lower socioeconomic status, he or she simply has not been blessed with the opportunities to travel and learn new cultures like you? Awareness of how factors in our sociological background affect our perception of things is a key factor in making better assessments as a leader.

H. *History*

Your history refers to the influence that your personal past, or your historical experiences, have on the way you make decisions today. Each of the situations and circumstances that you have encountered prior to now has had some effect on the way you think, what you believe, and what you expect to occur in life. This happens beyond your awareness, because the impact is made on your subconscious. However, though the impact of your history impacts your subconscious mind, the effects of it play out in your conscious day-to-day activities.

Wise leaders understand that they are never making decisions about matters of today without the intervening influence of what has remained with them from matters of yesterday – things that have happened in their historical past. Since this is not an impact or influence that we can avoid, it is one about which we must be aware. Negative historical experiences will tend to turn our perceptions more negative about current experiences that feature similar contexts or characters, and the opposite is also true. As you, a leader, approach situations and experiences throughout life, before you arrive at a final assessment about them, be sure to question not whether, but *how*, any of your past similar experiences – positive or negative – are impacting your perception or assessment of the current situation.

Wise leaders understand that they are never making decisions about matters of today without the intervening influence of what has remained with them from matters of yesterday.

O. *Opportunities or Oppositions*

Opportunities or oppositions refer to the two types of perceptions that can shape your mental and emotional approach to challenges as a leader. Whether you choose to see a challenge as an opportunity or to see it as an opposition will have a direct impact on the success of your endeavors. Scientifically speaking, the brain of a leader reacts differently depending upon whether he or she views situations positively or negatively.

When you view challenges positively (i.e., as opportunities), your brain provides you with the right amount of energy and focus necessary to execute the task. This type of emotional response leads to successful outcomes. Conversely, when you view challenges negatively (i.e., as oppositions), the part of your brain that deals with such matters becomes irritated. Not only does it not provide you with the energy that you need to address the situation, but it does the opposite, even negatively affecting your sleep cycles, appetite, social connectedness, motivation, and drive.

> *When you view challenges positively (i.e., as opportunities), your brain provides you with the right amount of energy and focus necessary to execute the task.*

When you approach challenges and find yourself already emotionally drained before you even begin to address them, there is a strong likelihood that you are viewing the challenge as an opposition rather than as an opportunity. The good news is that you can re-program your mind and turn around your perception of the situation! With a bit of intentionality, you can trigger your mind to switch from seeing things negatively to seeing things positively, and consequently, your brain will instantly empower you with the energy and focus that you need to overcome it!

E. *Experiences (Professional)*

Experiences of a professional nature refer to incidents and encounters that you have had in the past in serving as a professional leader in some capacity. As with other encounters of the past, each and every one of the experiences that you have had has helped to influence who you are as a leader today. More specifically, these experiences have a direct impact on your decision-making processes to the extent that when you approach a situation in your organization, you take into account, both consciously and subconsciously, what decisions you made about similar situations in the past. If these decision-making processes have worked in your professional past, you affirm the effectiveness of these processes and engage them in current situations. If the decision-making processes have not produced favorable outcomes in your professional past, you are more likely to take a different approach in current situations.

While positive past leadership experiences can lock you into a linear decision-making approach, negative past leadership experiences can make you more reluctant to address organizational and personal problems in an assertive manner. Further, other past leadership experiences can lead to your developing a myopic approach to problem solving; you have used a particular approach over and over again throughout your tenure as a leader, and it has seemed to work, so you dare not change it. As a leader, be carful not to make decisions out of an "auto-pilot" setting. Instead, you must ultimately take the time to assess not only how you are feeling about a situation but why you are selecting your current approach to dealing with it. Ask yourself how your decision-making approach is being affected by your professional leadership encounters of the past. Once you do, you might find yourself choosing to engage a different decision-making process altogether for the situation!

S. *Spiritual Influence*

Spiritual influence refers to the impact that your spiritual development has on you as a leader. To be clear, when I refer to spiritual development, I am referring to Christian growth that comes as a result of studying the Bible, listening to biblically-sound preaching and teaching, and maintaining an intimate connection and communion with God through prayer. That said, levels of spiritual development can be as varied as leaders themselves, so we cannot assume that anytime leaders refer to "spiritual development" that they are discussing it from the same vantage point. Some leaders engage in more extensive spiritual development, while other leaders take a shallower dive into spirituality.

If your spiritual development has included a reasonable amount of studying the Bible, training classes, having experiences and encounters with God, and allowing your spirituality to become a significant part of who you are, this will no-doubt affect the way that you lead your organization. In fact, it will automatically set up for you an ethical framework that is sure to guide your leadership decisions. Because of your level of spiritual development, there are simply some decisions that you cannot make with a clear conscience; you know that doing so would violate your core value system, which is grounded in your spiritual beliefs. However, if your spiritual development has not been as extensive and you have very little knowledge of spiritual principles, you are prone to have fewer parameters governing which decisions that you will and will not make.

Leader & Follower Triads | Personal Issues
CATEGORY 2:

C.O.R.E.

If you have ever enjoyed the painful yet profitable privilege of working out with a professional physical trainer, you have undoubtedly been advised about how important your body's core is to your overall physical functioning. Most people mistakenly think that their core is simply their abdominal muscles, but your body's core is comprised of much more than this. However, your core is actually your entire body, minus your head, arms, and legs and includes your back, sides, pelvic, buttock, and abdominal muscles as well as your hips and spine.[67] This essential part of your anatomy protects the organs, keeps your body stable and balanced, and it is assumed to originate and play a role in just about every bodily movement that you make. In fact, many experts draw parallels between our body's core and the trunk of a tree, because it represents a sturdy central link between our upper and lower body, and because it needs to be strong, yet flexible, because every move we make ripples upward and downward through our core.[68]

Any good personal trainer will lead clients in doing exercises that are designed to strengthen their core. A strong core helps us to have good posture, stabilize ourselves so that we can move in any direction, maintain our balance and reduce our risk of falling, help us to engage in sports like biking, basketball, and swimming, help us to bend, twist, and lift, and even supports us in activities like sex. Oftentimes, when people are having lower back pain, a common remedy prescribed by doctors (in conjunction with other treatments) is to develop their core. [69] Just about every move we make and action we undertake requires the use of our core, and the stronger and more powerful it is, the better we function!

As important as our core muscles are, many of them exist below the surface of the body – under the muscles that we can actually see just under the skin – so they are actually not visible to us. Even when athletes have engaged in intense strength training over time to produce a strong core, our eyes still cannot visibly see the well-developed muscles that comprise their core... but that does not mean that these muscles are not there or that they are not making a critical impact on the way that the athletes function. Unfortunately, because we cannot see these muscles, they tend to receive a lot less attention when it comes to developing our bodies; even when we are able to muster up enough energy to get to the gym, we tend to work on and develop the muscles whose size and definition we can actually see.[70] Think about it: when we go frolicking on the beach in our swimwear, no one is looking at our core muscles; they are looking at our abs, our biceps, our triceps, our quads, our pecks, and more than likely, our *gluteus maximus* – *not* our core! Despite the fact that people cannot cast admiring glares on our core, it still remains a part of our anatomy that forms the basis of every move we make. Thus, we have to give it some special attention, strengthening and developing it for our own well-being. If we do a good job, though people will never be able to see our nicely-developed core visibly, they will be able to make out the fact that we have a strong, powerful core by observing the way we walk, sit, stand, and move.

Now that you have a better understanding of the significance of your body's C.O.R.E., you will be more readily understand the value of your C.O.R.E. as it relates to your personal issues in the Leader Triad and the Follower Triad. C.O.R.E. is an acronym that stands for "Center of Relationships with Everyone." In the same way that your physical core is the center that controls all of the activities of your body, your psycho-emotional C.O.R.E. is the center that influences all of the activities of your mind, serving as the foundation of all of your beliefs. Each plays a critical role – one in how you move and the other in how you perceive.

Your psycho-emotional C.O.R.E. supports your psycho-emotional functions, including your personal vantage point, perspectives, ideologies, and biases; everything that you think and feel about people, places, things, and situations is filtered through it. Again, like your physical core, the structures behind your psycho-emotional C.O.R.E. are invisible to the naked eye. Even as you begin to engage in developing your C.O.R.E., no one, including you will actually be able to see the development. However, if they observe you closely and listen to how you react to, respond to, and interact with your followers, they will be able to make out the fact that you have a strong, powerful C.O.R.E. working behind the scenes!

If you are anything like me, the more you learn, the more questions you tend to have. Hence, by this point, you undoubtedly have many more questions about your C.O.R.E. Perhaps you are asking, *What exactly is it about your C.O.R.E. that is working behind the scenes? Precisely which muscles comprise your psycho-emotional C.O.R.E.? What are the C.O.R.E. equivalents to the muscle groups like the abdominals, pelvic muscles, back muscles, and sides that make up your physical core?* There are clear answers to these questions, and they start by understanding the secondary meaning of C.O.R.E. at its underlying, conceptual level.

The strength of your CORE can either improve the quality of your leadership or lower the degree of your effectiveness. At its conceptual level, CORE deals with:

C – Central themes
O – Ought to be's
R – Recurring issues
E – Expectations

C. *Central Themes*

Central themes are your central or key personal issues that affect what you think about, feel, and believe, and how you perceive people, places, things, and situations. Typically emotionally charged in a negative way, they might either stem from concerns that you developed during childhood or from life events in which you experienced major hurts and disappointments.

> *If you are operating with negative central themes behind the scenes, you will subconsciously filter anything and everything through those themes.*

Central themes can bleed into, or negatively affect, every area of your life. If you are operating with negative central themes behind the scenes, you will subconsciously filter anything and everything through those themes. Regardless of how harmless or innocuous the person, place, thing, or situation might be, you will find a way to tie it to the negativity associated with your central themes and cast a negative shadow of perception over it.

O. *Ought to Be's*

Ought to be's are your position on how things should work in life, and they determine in large part how you react and respond to the actions and beliefs of those with whom you interact. These subjective sets of standards and expectations about how people, organizations, or the world should and should not behave and what should and should not happen are biases that develop over time and are reinforced by our mentors, training, and personal experiences.

If people act in accordance with your ought to be's, your response tends to be more favorable and positive; if they act in ways that do not align with your ought to be's your response is less favorable and negative. In fact, when people violate your ought to be's, this can cause shockwaves in your interpersonal interactions with them. You might grow very angry with them, your ability to trust them might be greatly diminished, or you might even choose to terminate the relationship with them altogether.

R. *Recurring Issues*

Recurring issues are cyclical incidents, typically negative affiliations and outcomes, which seem to follow you everywhere you go, despite the fact that you make changes in your environment. These troublesome patterns emerge over time as you interact with others; though the cast of characters tends to change from place to place, your experiences and outcomes always seem to be the same. The one constant that is present each time you experience the same unpleasant types of experiences and outcomes is *you*; you are the common denominator in each undesirable episode, and thus, the probable cause of the constantly recurring issues!

The one constant that is present each time you experience the same unpleasant types of experiences and outcomes is you!

When you are willing to deal with your recurring issues, you can alter or adjust your behavior so that you no longer contribute to producing undesired outcomes in your life. In a manner of speaking, you identify your role amongst all others in the cast of characters, and you take a stand, saying, "I refuse to play this role! Instead, I choose to play another one who acts and reacts in a completely different way!" When you do not actively confront and address your role in producing undesired outcomes, you will continue producing these same outcomes time after time and context after context. Though you might not realize it, your role in the cast of characters is a recurring one, and you have played the role so frequently that you have become expert at it; it has become comfortable to you, and to choose a different role to play will feel awkward. However, if you will ever become an effective leader, you must make the grand leap out of playing the role that is most comfortable to you and into the role that produces results for you as an organizational leader!

E. *Expectations*

Expectations are the underlying assumptions that you have about people, places, and things. As a leader, your expectations most likely center on matters relating to business and organizations, including how the people and systems within them should operate and how issues within them should be resolved. The expectations that you have about the world are shaped by a number of factors, including your training, your mentoring, and your own personal experiences.

Despite the fact that we all possess our own expectations of how things *should* happen, the truth of the matter is that things do not always have to operate according to our expectations in order to be "right." Our expectations are often built upon our own subjectivities; sometimes, the world will operate in such a way that agrees with them, and sometimes not. The important thing is to remain aware of your assumptions and expectations and to constantly remind yourself of the need to be flexible enough to consider that doing things according to your expectations is not the only way! When reality happens in ways that defy their expectations, good leaders neither cry about the fact that their expectations have been disappointed, nor do they try to *force* the context into a box that will satisfy their personal expectations. Instead, they accept the reality with which they are faced, they tap into their leadership flexibility, and they deal with it!

A.B.D.O.M.I.N.A.L.S.

I might not personally know what it feels like to have a six-pack, and I'm not ashamed to admit it! After all, I know that chances are, you don't know how it feels either, so I'm in good company! However, I do understand the importance of having strong abdominal muscles, and I dare say that such an understanding is a great deal more important than being able to take off my shirt at the beach and have people admire the well-defined washboard that is my stomach, right? While the abdominal muscles are technically a part of the many muscles that make up your core, they play such a significant role in our physical functioning that they deserve some special attention of their own. For example, our abdominal muscles house the area where most of the absorption and digestion of our food occur, which means that it protects one of the most critical areas of our bodies – the area that ensures that we receive the nourishment we need to keep going. This important set of muscles also assists us with the breathing process and serves as protection for our inner organs. Finally, our abdominal muscles play a vital role in moving us forward, as they initiate the movement of our trunk in a forward motion.[71] Thus, without our abdominal muscles, we can neither walk ahead nor move forward in life – literally!

A.B.D.O.M.I.N.A.L.S. is an acronym that stands for:

A – All
B – Beliefs that
D – Dominate
O – Our
M – Mental
I – Images
N – Need to be

A – Adjusted to
L – Line up with
S – Scripture

Just like your physical abdominals, your psycho-emotional A.B.D.O.M.I.N.A.L.S. deserve special attention because of the significant role that they play in your life as a leader. Physically, our abdominals house the area where most of our digestion and absorption of food occurs; psycho-emotionally, your A.B.D.O.M.I.N.A.L.S. represent the area of your life where your ideas, suppositions, thoughts, and beliefs are broken down, only to be converted into mental images that can be absorbed into your psyche. This determines your actions and behaviors, which move you forward. Our A.B.D.O.M.I.N.A.L.S. also help us to breathe because they represent the presence of the Spirit in our lives, which is our very breath.

When you are a leader with weak A.B.D.O.M.I.N.A.L.S., the beliefs that dominate your mental images (and consequently, your actions) are subjective and worldly. You won't move ahead very far with these, and you also won't have the breath that you need to sustain you along the way. However, when you take the time to develop and strengthen you're A.B.D.O.M.I.N.A.L.S., the beliefs that dominate your mental images (and actions) are spiritual, because you are intentional about always filtering them through the Scriptures – the Bible. For example, when a thought pops into your head, rather than just accept it, believe it, and run with that belief, you filter it through what the Bible says. Does the Bible agree with this belief? Does it support the position of this idea? If not, you must toss it out... let it go! Doing so will help to ensure that you move far ahead on our journey with godly character and spiritual integrity in addition to strengthening your credibility and effectiveness as a leader. Strengthening your abdominals in this way will also

> *When you are a leader with weak A.B.D.O.M.I.N.A.L.S., the beliefs that dominate your mental images (and consequently, your actions) are subjective and worldly.*

ensure that you advance with the breath that you need – the very breath of God, which is the Spirit of God that permeates your life – to sustain you throughout your journey of becoming a more effective and successful leader who is functioning with optimal leadership health.

Leader & Follower Triads | Personal Issues
CATEGORY 4:

P.O.R.K.

Most of the people I know enjoy a good baby back rib every now and then. Seasoned and smoked just the right way, that pork can thrust your happiness level all the way up to cloud nine as you chomp away on its hot, tender, succulent goodness while tangy, delicious barbecue sauce – and pork grease – slide slowly down your fingers! No worries... just before it threatens to drip onto your favorite shirt, you quickly lap it up in the nick of time. That's part of the fun of it all, right? Well, considering that pork ribs – and pork sausage, and pulled pork, and pork chops, and *bacon*, and... you get the point – are so darn good, why do they have to be *so bad* for us?

I recall walking into my doctor's office for a routine exam and having all of the necessary tests done that might be ordered for a man of my age. I can also remember hearing my doctor's advice: lose some weight, and for goodness sake, lay off the pork! Now, being from Texas, where the official state food is barbecue by de facto, you can imagine my dismay at hearing my doctor advise me to lower my consumption of one of the few foods that bring me so much joy! Oh, noooooo! Nonetheless, I understood the necessity of cutting back for the sake of my health.

Once I had received my marching orders from my doctor, I chose to do some investigation of my own about what advertisers have so masterfully branded across the media as "the other white meat." What I found stopped me in my tracks. Most of us know that the Hebrews were forbidden by God Himself from eating pork, and the reason for this prohibition is most often tied to health concerns. Some writers consider the pig to be "nature's garbage disposal." It has a very simple digestive system, and it has no sweat glands to rid the body of internal toxins. Thus, the health problems that pork causes begin with the "unclean" nature of the animal itself![72]

However, beyond this, what *specific* health concerns make it a wise choice to refrain from ordering that full rack of spare ribs the next time you go to your favorite barbecue joint? I uncovered lots of specifics in my research. For example, did you know that pork consumption has a strong epidemiological association with liver disease (maybe even more so than alcohol itself), liver damage, and multiple sclerosis?[73] Pork can also pose health risks like infection, viruses, vomiting, abdominal cramps, and diarrhea, especially when it is not handled safely or cooked correctly. In addition to viral diseases, pork consumption is linked to roundworm infestation (from undercooked pork), heart disease risk (because pork is high in saturated fat and causes your "bad" cholesterol levels to rise), bladder cancer risk (especially if you eat well-done or burnt pork often), and more![74] Add to this the pounds that we tend to stack on (which lead to obesity and a reduction in life span) after we down handfuls of bacon at breakfast and finish off our day with a couple of fried pork chops cooked to a perfect golden crisp, and we've got a huge health problem on our hands! Our love of pork is literally *killing* us!

P.O.R.K. is an acronym that stands for:

P – People
O – Occurrences and
R – Reactions (that are)
K – Killing you

As dangerous as natural pork is to our level of functioning as healthy human beings, our psychological P.O.R.K. is doing just as much damage to our leadership lives! I know, I know. You think you're fine just like I thought I was fine before my doctor told me that pork was killing me. It takes an outside expert to offer you such advice for your own good, and in this case, I play the role of the outside expert to you: lay off the P.O.R.K.! If you don't, it will shorten your leadership lifespan and ensure that you do not live as high a quality of

> *Lay off the P.O.R.K.! If you don't, it will shorten your leadership lifespan and ensure that you do not live the highest possible quality of life as a leader!*

life as a leader as you could if you were functioning without the effects of your P.O.R.K. holding you back. Abolishing your P.O.R.K. can do nothing but improve your leadership health and make you more productive and effective in the long run.

Your P.O.R.K. refers to people like relatives, co-workers, friends, and even romantic relationships that you actually enjoy and the unnecessary "drama" that they bring into your life as a result of your reactions to the occurrences that take place when you interact with one another. These relationships are certifiably *downright toxic* for you! Toxic relationships produce stress, and prolonged stress produces the perpetual release of hormones. Over time, these hormones damage your tissues and harm your internal organs and also result in many other problems like heart and vascular problems, gastrointestinal problems, headaches, skin conditions, genitourinary tract problems, pain and inflammation, and lung and breathing problems[75]... all caused by the deadly emotions that stem from *toxic relationships*! Needless to say, you've got to get this P.O.R.K. out of your life once and for all!

The Bible says it best in Hebrews 12:1: *"Therefore we also, since we are surrounded by so great a cloud of witnesses, let us lay aside every weight, and the sin which so easily ensnares us, and let us run with endurance the race that is set before us."* P.O.R.K. is a weight and a snare that keeps you from reaching higher heights and fulfilling your leadership potential, so it needs to be laid aside! Your ability to identify relationships with people who represent the P.O.R.K. in your life is critical to your survival. As a leader, identifying your P.O.R.K. is the first step in ridding yourself of toxic relations or reactions that systematically destroy your health and inhibit your future as a leader.

> *Your ability to identify relationships with people who represent the P.O.R.K. in your life is critical to your survival.*

Without getting this P.O.R.K. out of your life, neither you nor your leadership success stands a chance! Once the P.O.R.K. is finally gone and out of your system as a leader, you will be in optimal leadership condition, able to run with endurance the race that is set before you – full steam ahead!

Leader & Follower Triads | Personal Issues
CATEGORY 5:

S.T.A.R.C.H. AND F.A.T.

Starches make us feel good. They're usually nice and warm, can be either sweet or savory, and they are the key ingredients of what we often refer to as "comfort food," because they make us feel nice, full, and, well... comforted. Oh yeah, and they can also make us fat, can cause diabetes, and stimulate our appetite so that we will overeat and be all kinds of uncomfortable, too. Any time you are endeavoring to get healthy and lose a few extra pounds, whether you talk to your doctor or to your personal trainer, their professional advice will usually entail instructions to lay off the carbohydrates, or "carbs." However, they do not tell you to lay off the carbs altogether, because there are two types: starchy and non-starchy. Starchy carbohydrates are found in foods like potatoes and whole grains and also include corn and peas. Non-starchy carbohydrates are found in other fruits and vegetables. They will tell you that for the best results on your journey to better health, focus on filling your diet with non-starchy carbs while limiting your consumption of the starchy ones.

Most of us love starchy foods because they give quick bursts of energy for the body. We love the rush of good feelings that a hot, fluffy stack of pancakes, a chewy toasted bagel, or a hot glazed donut give us – and yes, they are all starchy carbs, along with that moist, dense pound cake, those creamy mashed potatoes, that perfect al-dente pasta, and that savory white rice and gravy that we love so much. However, while our affections run high for these delicacies that simultaneously provide us not only with culinary pleasure but with a "food high," the energy that these foods provide for us are short-lived. While their non-starchy counterparts provide us with slowly-released energy that is able to sustain us for long periods of time to make it throughout the day, starchy foods give us only quick bursts of energy, or food highs, but they drop us off depleted of energy just as quickly. As soon as their quick energy burns off, we find ourselves completely depleted of energy, sluggish, mentally unmotivated, and unproductive. Therefore, for both increased well-being and maximum levels of productivity in our lives, we should limit the amount of starchy foods that we consume on a daily basis. After all, you can't get much done in life if you allow starches to deplete your energy resources!

S.T.A.R.C.H. is an acronym that stands for:

S – Situations that are
T – Tangible that
A – Attack your
R – Resources
C – Causing
H – Havoc

In the same ways that dietary starches drain our physical energy resources, our S.T.A.R.C.H. represents issues that can drain our psycho-emotional resources, whether mental or emotional, and our physical resources, whether physical, financial, or otherwise. Consequently, S.T.A.R.C.H. keeps us from fully functioning as a leader by depleting the levels of energy that are necessary for our leadership productivity.

S.T.A.R.C.H. keeps us from fully functioning as a leader by depleting the levels of energy that are necessary for our leadership productivity.

What's more, starches can also lead to another undesired consequence: body fat. We already understand that starch provides energy for our bodily functions. However, when our physical starch intake exceeds the amount that your body is able to burn off as energy, this starch turns into fat! The same thing occurs to S.T.A.R.C.H. in regards to leadership; when we have an overabundance of S.T.A.R.C.H. in our lives, we become F.A.T.

F.A.T. is an acronym that stands for:

F – Frustrated
A – Apathetic, and
T – Tired

F.A.T. leaders become easily frustrated about the simplest of matters, apathetic or dispirited in their approaches to tasks and individuals, and mentally tired. In fact, they become so negative concerning organizational matters that it depletes them of the mental energy necessary to assertively address different concerns. This occurs to the detriment of the organization; not only do the people not fully have the energy and focus of their leader, but the organization can become stagnant because of the leader's lack of energy, drive, and mental aggression. No one wants a F.A.T. leader, so lay off the S.T.A.R.C.H.!

If you look carefully, you can find S.T.A.R.C.H. throughout your leadership life. Some of these **S**ituations that are **T**angible that **A**ttack your **R**esources **C**ausing **H**avoc are easier to identify, while others are more difficult. For example, I have discovered over time that pop-up interruptions throughout the day are one source of S.T.A.R.C.H. in my life as a leader; I enjoy them, but they simply are not good for me, because they drain my sources and end up leaving me F.A.T. When my office door is open, people who are walking by will stick their head in just to say "Hello." This turns into talking and joking for two hours, and though these times are

> *When we have an overabundance of S.T.A.R.C.H. in our lives, we become F.A.T.: Frustrated, Apathetic, and Tired!*

enjoyable, I find myself rushing and trying to play catch-up at the end of the day to get my major work done before it's time to go home. In the worst case scenarios, I have to stay longer at work to complete certain tasks, and this makes me feel even worse! After these "fun times" have robbed me of my time and energy resources that I should have been using to complete the projects on my desk, I can do nothing but sit there feeling frustrated, apathetic, and tired – F.A.T.! Over time, I have managed to find a solution that has helped to eliminate this source of S.T.A.R.C.H. and F.A.T. from my life: I simply work with my door closed!

Ultimately, the necessity of restricting the levels of S.T.A.R.C.H. in your life, which can also lead to becoming F.A.T., is to limit the things that can slow you down, put unhealthy weight on you, and make you less productive as a leader. Good leaders know when they are in their best mental, physical, and emotional condition, so they work hard to remain in this condition at critical times during the life of their organization. On your road to becoming a more effective and successful leader, you should also put in the work to stay in the most productive physical and mental condition possible. When the leader is operating in optimal leadership health, so will the organization!

Leader & Follower Triads | Personal Issues
SUMMARY & CONCLUSIONS

In summary, leaders must become skillful in answering the question posed by the Personal Issues side of the Leader and Follower Triads, "What known or hidden personal values, motivations, or feelings are present within me, and how do they affect my perceptions and interactions, skew my interpretation of the facts surrounding critical situations, and influence my decisions, actions, and reactions when dealing with others?" Without answering this critical question, you as a leader will be subject to the influence of personal issues that are acting upon you beyond your awareness or recognition. When you neither have awareness nor recognition of these influences, you have no control over them and the impact that they have on your life. Thus, in order to ensure that you maintain as much control as possible over your thoughts, behaviors, and outcomes as a leader, seek to become intimately aware of your issues and the way that they tend to influence the way that you perceive and interact with the world.

The Personal Issues Leadership Workout
Is One that *Never* Ends!

Normally, when we say that we are going to start to work out and eat right, many of us have an end goal – an exit strategy. That pre-defined endpoint could be determined in a number of ways. For example, you might say that you are going to work out until you lose 50 pounds. Once you have successfully lost the weight, you give yourself the unspoken option to retire your running shoes and relax a little on the diet. In other instances, you might say that you are going to work out until you look just the way you want in your bathing suit, because summer is on the way. Once you look in the mirror and see all of the bumps and curves finally falling into the right places, the workout and eating plan are tossed out of the window. You might even say that you are going to work out from now until your wedding day. Once you say "I do," you never set foot into a gym again. In fact, you start stuffing anything into your mouth that isn't nailed down, because you're so blissfully happy!

While it's not the best idea in the world, you possess the freedom of having an exit strategy from your physical workout and dietary well-being. Yes, giving up your disciplines will affect you over time, but the likelihood is that although you might not end up moving along as healthily as you could be, you would still be moving. However, if you will become and maintain your status as an effective and successful leader,

> *Effective leaders never create exit strategies for themselves.*

you never have an exit-strategy; you're in it for the life of your leadership! From paying close attention to your S.H.O.E.S., to strengthening your C.O.R.E. and A.B.D.O.M.I.N.A.L.S., and from eliminating the S.T.A.R.C.H. in your diet to avoiding all of the F.A.T. it produces, your workout and well-being journey has to be about more than doing what you have to do to accomplish a certain end goal! In your case, you are on a journey to become a stronger, more effective leader, and there is no place called "there" when it comes to reaching for such a state. Good leaders are always engaged in the process of continuous improvement, and this process includes constant engagement in selecting the right S.H.O.E.S., strengthening your C.O.R.E. and A.B.D.O.M.I.N.A.L.S., and avoiding the S.T.A.R.C.H. and eliminating the F.AT. It never ends!

Good leaders are always engaged in the process of continuous improvement, and this process includes constant engagement in selecting the right S.H.O.E.S., strengthening your C.O.R.E. and A.B.D.O.M.I.N.A.L.S., and avoiding the S.T.A.R.C.H. and eliminating the F.AT. It never ends!

If You Fall off of the "Workout Wagon," Try and Try Again until You Succeed!

Adopting a new exercise and dietary routine is never easy. I'll just go ahead and say it: it is *so hard*! You will want to quit, you will fall off the wagon, and at some point, you will say, "Awwww... to heck with it all! Who needs all of this intentionality? It's such hard work to remember and to try to employ it all! And it hurts, too!" Don't feel bad when you reach this point; it's natural. Many leaders stronger than you have fallen off the wagon and abandoned their efforts as they worked towards optimal leadership health. However, even though you *should not* feel bad when you fall off of the workout wagon, you *should* feel bad when you do not get back up. Nothing worth having comes without a struggle, and you've got to meet your struggle head on if you desire to be a more effective, successful leader.

Each time you fall off the wagon, promise yourself that you will get back on! Each time you fail to be aware of how your S.H.O.E.S. are affecting your current perspective about an issue or challenge, the very next time, get back on the wagon by being intentional about assessing how your **S**ociological factors, **H**istory, **O**pportunities or Oppositions, **E**xperiences (professional) and **S**piritual influence are affecting the way you see things.

Each time you fail to take into consideration how your C.O.R.E. is affecting your relationship, the very next time you are dealing with people, get back on the wagon by allowing your **C**entral Themes, **O**ught to be's, **R**ecurring issues, and **E**xpectations to come to the forefront of your mind so that you can be keenly aware of how these personal issues are affecting the relationship between you and the other person.

Each time you find yourself operating with viewpoints, beliefs, or ideas outside of Scripture because you have not taken the time to strengthen you're A.B.D.O.M.I.N.A.L.S., the next time you are faced with an issue, simply ensure that **A**ll **B**eliefs that **D**ominate **O**ur **M**ental **I**mages **N**eed to be **A**djusted to **L**ine up with **S**cripture.

Whenever you realize that you are involved in a particular context in which you are encountering P.O.R.K. and have allowed it to persist rather than eliminating it, the very next time you are faced with **P**eople,

Occurrences, and **R**eactions that are **K**illing you, immediately usher it out of your life!

If you have found yourself consuming too much S.T.A.R.C.H., and especially if you find yourself getting F.A.T., rather than kick yourself, the very next time you are presented with **S**ituations that are **T**angible that **A**ttack your **R**esources **C**ausing **H**avoc, turn and run away from them, or else they will continue to make you **F**rustrated, **A**pathetic, and **T**ired. No one can eliminate these energy-robbing elements out of your life but you!

Getting into Optimal Leadership Fitness Will Change Your *Life*!

Do you have any family members, friends, or co-workers who have ever changed their eating, became more physically fit, and were totally transformed into new people? Sure, by getting healthier, they reduced their risk for heart disease, stroke, cancer, diabetes, and other medical maladies that affect unhealthy people. They undoubtedly looked a lot healthier with less excess weight, leaner muscle tone, and clearer skin, not to mention the fact that they looked better and more comfortable in their clothes. However, those are just the physical benefits; there are also widespread psycho-emotional benefits to losing weight and becoming healthier and stronger. If they are like many people, they no doubt underwent positive mental changes through their transformation, which made them appear to be happier, more confident, more secure people who had higher self-esteem and body image. Ultimately, all of these gains combined lead to an increased quality of life, both physically and mentally, which people would rarely trade for anything! They have done the work, and this new

> *Guarantee:*
> *If you constantly take heed to your S.H.O.E.S., C.O.R.E., and A.B.D.O.M.I.N.A.L.S., and you avoid the P.O.R.K., S.T.A.R.C.H., and F.A.T., you will see positive results!*

life, with which they are enjoying immense levels of satisfaction, is their reward.

In the same fashion, when you put in work as a leader who is embarking on a journey to reach optimum leadership fitness, you will also have your reward. It's a law of nature – cause and effect. If you consistently do the things that are required for you to become stronger and healthier, you *will* become stronger and healthier! Thus, if you are constantly taking heed to the S.H.O.E.S. that you are wearing, strengthening your C.O.R.E. and you're A.B.D.O.M.I.N.A.L.S., and avoiding the P.O.R.K., S.T.A.R.C.H., and F.A.T., I guarantee that you will see results that will literally transform your leadership lifestyle! With increased strength, health, and well-being, you will experience greater happiness, confidence, security, esteem, and self-image as a leader. When you reach this point, do not attempt to minimize it; celebrate it! It will be your well-deserved reward for putting in the work!

However, be cautioned: people will want to know how you did it! How did you go from being an *okay* leader to being an *exceptional* leader? Why do you look so happy? Why doesn't leadership seem to be so burdensome for you? How do you seem to have such a strong grasp on and influence with the people in your organization? Why aren't you dragging yourself through your organization looking frustrated, exhausted, and downright dreadful? Why do you seem to be able to make the hard decisions so quickly and still have the outcomes come out just right? Leader, you *will* have to give an answer for your leadership effectiveness! When the time comes, simply smile, stick your chest out, and say, "I've been *working out!*"

PART 7:
TAKING A CLEAR SNAPSHOT OF THE SITUATION

How to Practically Engage Moody's 720° Decision-Making Model to Achieve More Effective Leadership Results

---

Putting Moody's 720° Decision-Making Model into Practice

Leaders should consider each assessment question within the Tetra-triad in order to make more effective leadership decisions.

The 720° Snapshot: Developing a Clear Picture of the Organizational Dynamics at Play Using Moody's 720° 12-Minute Processing Snapshot Worksheet

How to enter into the decision-making moment and develop a clear snapshot of how each Tetra-triad dynamic influences the leader's decision – in only 12 minutes.

Ready to Launch:
Committing Yourself to Leadership Effectiveness the 720° Decision-Making Model Way!

Make a commitment to continually utilize Moody's 720° Decision-making Model when making leadership decisions and watch yourself realize more effective leadership results!

The 720° Snapshot

CHAPTER 19

PUTTING MOODY'S 720° DECISION-MAKING MODEL INTO PRACTICE

By now, you undoubtedly have some questions – lots of them – swimming around in your head. If so, you are not alone! In fact, if you have read each of the preceding chapters and do not have a range of questions running through your head, you missed a critical part of understanding *Moody's 720° Leadership Decision-Making Model*. After all, each of triads in the 720° model of leadership is designed to provide you, as a leader, with an assessment question, which, when answered, will help to guide your decisions regarding tasks and assignments in the organization. When approached with a high level of careful consideration, the outcomes of your assessment of these questions will position you on the right path to making the best possible decisions for your organization, resulting in greater levels of leadership effectiveness.

Each of the questions offered by the triads for you, as a leader, to assess is equally important – no one question is more essential than another in influencing the best possible decision that stands to be made for a particular organizational task, goal, or situation. As a recap, the questions asked by each one of the triads include:

THE TASK TRIAD

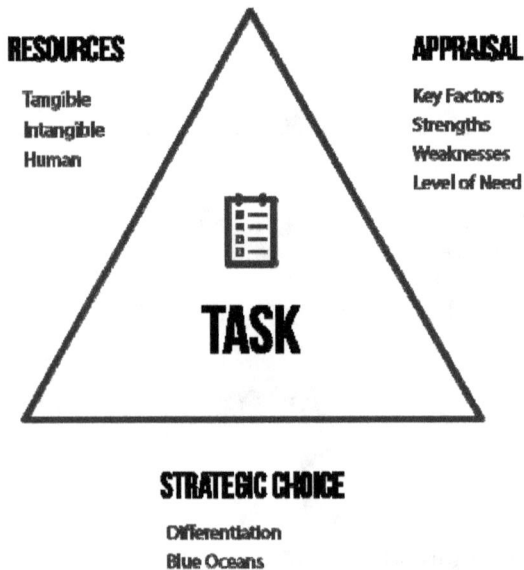

RESOURCES

Tangible
Intangible
Human

APPRAISAL

Key Factors
Strengths
Weaknesses
Level of Need

TASK

STRATEGIC CHOICE

Differentiation
Blue Oceans

1	Organizational Resources	*What do I have to work with to execute my task?*
2	Appraisal	*Do we have the capacity to execute the task?*
3	Strategic Choices	*How can I gain an advantage over my competitors in the market or create a new market altogether?*

THE ISSUE TRIAD

EXTERNAL ENVIRONMENT

Market Trends
Technology
Demographics
Porter's 5 Forces
➤ Competitors
➤ Suppliers
➤ Potential Entrants
➤ Substitutes
➤ Buyers

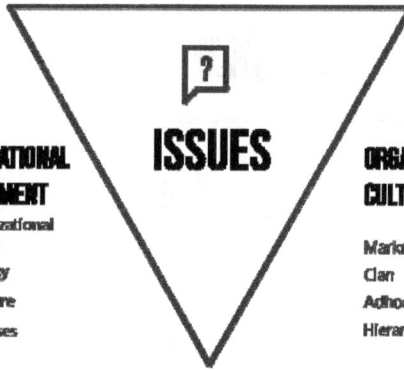

ORGANIZATIONAL ENVIRONMENT

➤ Organizational Design
➤ Strategy
➤ Structure
➤ Processes
➤ People
➤ Rewards

ISSUES

ORGANIZATIONAL CULTURE

Market
Clan
Adhocracy
Hierarchy

1	Organizational Environment	*Are we internally positioned and prepared as an organization to do what we are seeking to do?*
2	External Environment	*What forces or considerations outside of my organization affect my cost and ability to do what I do inside of my organization – and my ability to continue doing it in the future?*
3	Organizational Culture	*What are the structure and style of this organization's culture, and am I working with it or against it as I implement change?*

THE LEADER TRIAD

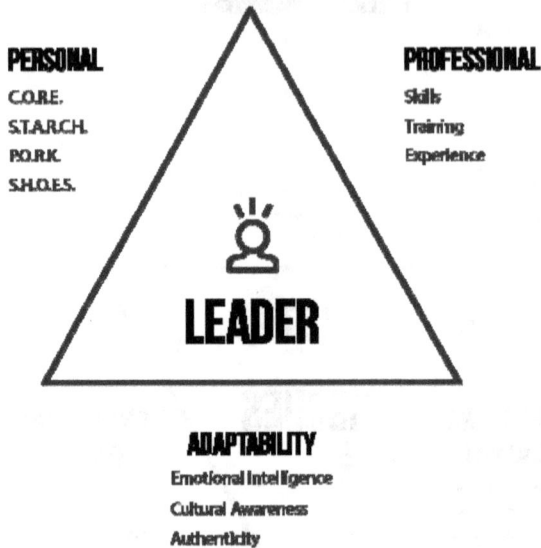

PERSONAL
C.O.R.E.
S.T.A.R.C.H.
P.O.R.K.
S.H.O.E.S.

PROFESSIONAL
Skills
Training
Experience

LEADER

ADAPTABILITY
Emotional Intelligence
Cultural Awareness
Authenticity

1	Personal Influences	*What known or hidden personal values, motivations, or feelings are present within me, and how do they affect my perceptions and interactions, skew my interpretation of the facts surrounding critical situations, and influence my decisions, actions, and reactions when dealing with others?*
2	Professional Expertise	*What are my professional capacities and limitations, and how can they be leveraged or compensated for, respectively, in order to increase my leadership effectiveness?*
3	Adaptability	*How far am I willing to go to make shifts in my beliefs and behaviors in order to connect at a deeper level with others for the benefit of the organization?*

THE FOLLOWER TRIAD

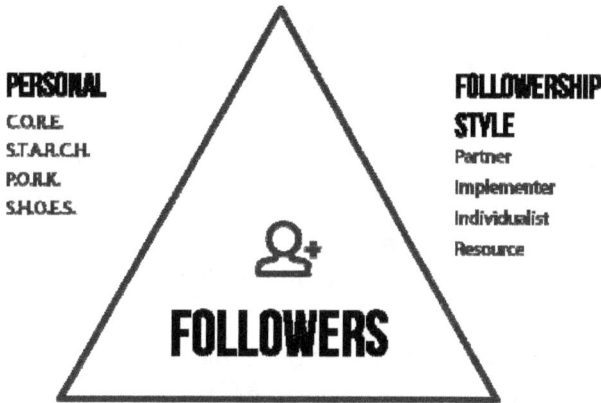

PERSONAL
C.O.R.E.
S.T.A.R.C.H.
P.O.R.K.
S.H.O.E.S.

FOLLOWERSHIP STYLE
Partner
Implementer
Individualist
Resource

FOLLOWERS

LEADER-FOLLOWER RELATIONSHIP
Exchange Level
▸ Out-group
Stranger Phase
▸ In-group
Acquaintance Phase
Mature Partner Phase

1	Personal Influences	*What known or hidden personal values, motivations, or feelings are present within me, and how do they affect my perceptions and interactions, skew my interpretation of the facts surrounding critical situations, and influence my decisions, actions, and reactions when dealing with others?*
2	Followership Style	*What level of support does this follower offer to me as a leader, and how does it affect his or her propensity to challenge my directives when asked to execute an organizational task?*
3	Leader-Follower Relationship	*How close is the relationship that I share with this follower, and how should I order my interactions, communications, and expectations with him/her based upon this level of closeness?*

Although there are a total of 12 questions for the leader to ask when making a leadership decision, for all intents and purposes, each of these layers of assessment all combine together to represent one comprehensive, overall question that leaders ask themselves throughout the day every day that they wear the title as "leader" of the organization. The question: what is the best decision to make in this case in order to realize the best possible outcomes for my organization?

While you might understand the objective of each layer of assessment that each one of the triads offers, perhaps you are not completely clear on how to practically engage them at the moment an organizational decision has to be made. Think about it: leaders probably make no fewer than 20 critical decisions per day regarding the tasks, goals, and situations in their organizations. When you are sitting there at the head of the conference room table in the plush, high-backed leader's chair, are you supposed to sit there and ask yourself the 12 questions offered by each triad? Is there really time for this? How long would this process even actually take? Ultimately, you are asking, is "*Moody's 720° Leadership Decision-Making Model* practical enough for me to use on a daily basis as I lead my organization?"

The answer to this question is a resounding "Yes!" My 720° Leadership Decision-Making Model is not only practical enough for you to engage on a daily basis when making critical decisions in your organization, but it will, in effect, ultimately speed up the way you have historically approached making final decisions in the past. You see, in the past, when it came time to make a decision, if you are like most other leaders, you took the time to make what you felt was the best decision to be made, but once it was made, you second-guessed yourself, because you were not sure that you had taken everything into consideration. "What if I make this critical decision but have missed something?" you've probably wondered to yourself. Not being sure that you made the right decision, you held off on communicating your final decision to your followers, because you were not sure that it was indeed your final decision, or you communicated your final decision but did not give the order to act upon the decision, because, once again, you were not sure if this was the decision that you ultimately wanted to go with.

Here is the reality: the only One that is able to make a fully-informed decision is God Himself; in His omniscience, He knows everything at all times, and no information is ever hidden from Him. As a result, when He makes a decision, there is never any danger of some new information or circumstance popping up that might cause Him to say, "Well, if I had known *that* was going to happen, I would have made a different decision!" No, His omniscience enables Him to make decisions that take into consideration everything that can possibly be considered. We, on the other hand, do not have the privilege of operating from such an advantage; all we can do is try to anticipate every potential factor that stands to impact the outcome of the decisions that we make, and then make the most "fully-informed" decision that our finite minds will allow us to make. Sometimes, our decisions result in the most wonderful, advantageous, and optimal benefits that we could have wished for;

> *Sometimes, our decisions result in dismal failures that make us want to crawl under a rock. It's the chance we take each time we make a decision. It's the price we pay for being human.*

other times, because of something that was beyond our ability to anticipate, our decisions result in dismal failures that make us want to crawl under a rock. It's the chance we take each time we make a decision. It's the price we pay for being human.

The good news is that even though we cannot make decisions that are literally "fully informed," because there will always be some aspects of knowledge that are unavailable for us to access, we can make decisions that are as close to being fully informed as possible using *Moody's 720° Leadership Decision-Making Model.* When you compare the prospect of making decisions based upon your gut feelings and a shallow, surface-level assessment of what is happening within your organization versus making decisions based upon a comprehensive roadmap – one that that systematically leads you in assessing all of the potential information that stands to impact the outcome of your decision – I would hope that you would choose the guided, systematic approach that can get you as close to fully-informed decision making as is humanly possible! It just makes better sense than your historical, random approach, and it promises to help you to realize better results by providing a compass for your decision making that points in the direction of the most effective outcomes for leadership success.

CHAPTER 20

THE 720° SNAPSHOT:

Developing a Clear Picture of the Organizational Dynamics at Play Using Moody's 720° 12-Minute Processing Snapshot Worksheet

The big question on the table is clear: how do I practically engage *Moody's 720° Leadership Decision-Making Model*? I like to refer to the employment of this model when making a decision as "taking a *720° Snapshot*" of as task or situation so that all of the dynamics that are at play in the organization can be considered when making a decision. When fully processed, the *720° Snapshot* will have combined elements from each one of the triads in order to form a clear picture of what you as a leader need to consider when making a decision about an organizational task or situation.

There are various stages to engaging the decision-making model in order to develop a *720° Snapshot* of the task or situation. In light of this, the way that you will engage and utilize the model when you first begin to employ it will be different from how you engage and utilize it a few months from now. In the first phases of use, you will engage it on a more deliberate and conscious level, and it will take a little more time to make decisions using the model. However, as you go on to master the use of the model, you will find yourself engaging it on a more intuitive and subconscious level, and it will take less time to arrive at a clear decision based upon your assessment.

> *Practicing decision making using Moody's 720° Leadership Decision-Making Model will never empower you to make "perfect" decisions, but it will at least empower you to make the best possible decisions for your organization.*

I have been using this model of decision making for years, and I can literally go through the entire assessment process, which includes consideration of each of the 12 assessment questions posed by the triad, in 30 seconds or less. Practicing decision making using *Moody's 720° Leadership Decision-Making Model* will never empower you to make "perfect" decisions, but it will at least empower you to make the best possible decisions for your organization.

Entering the Decision-Making Moment

Regardless of which method you utilize to take a *720° Snapshot* of a task or situation in order to make a decision, it all begins with entering the decision-making moment. This is the moment at which you, as a leader, are faced with making a critical decision about a particular task or situation that affects the organization. You can enter the decision-making moment at any point throughout your day, several times a day.

For example, you might be sitting in your office, and one of your followers will come in and inform you about a critical situation that has just emerged, and it needs your immediate attention – and for a decision to be made about how to address it. You might be in the middle of a meeting around the conference table and "accidentally" learn about a crisis that has been brewing in your organization, which no one has bothered to tell you about because they feared being reprimanded for their role in it. It has been going on so long that it has reached a critical point, and addressing it calls for immediate action on your part. You might even find yourself walking through the hallways of your organization when you overhear a "water cooler conversation" between a couple of your workers in the copy room that makes you aware of some critical information regarding another employee about which you previously had no knowledge. As you pass by and nod in their direction, though you maintain your poise and composure on the outside, on the inside, you find yourself in a state of near panic; something needs to be done immediately, or else the fallout from this particular employee's situation could have serious consequences for the organization! In other words, you can be thrust into a critical decision-making moment in a variety of ways; it might be handed to you, it can pop up out of nowhere, or you might stumble into it. In any case, once you enter into a critical decision-making moment, the decision is yours to make. The question is, what are you going to do about it? Time is no-doubt as critical as the decision you are faced with making, so you don't have a lot of time to waste in coming up with a game plan about how you will address the challenge. My advice: begin with taking a *720° Snapshot* of the task or situation so that you can base your ultimate decision on a clear and comprehensive picture of all of the dynamics at play!

The "12-Minute Processing Practice" of Developing a *720° Snapshot*

Today, we live in a world of digital photography; when we see something that is picture-worthy, we simply break out our mobile phone or tablet, snap the picture, and either carry the picture around on our device for our own private enjoyment or promptly upload it to our preferred social media site so that others may enjoy it as well. However, once upon a time, people enjoyed having hard copy photos in hand; once they took their pictures, they would take the film or digital snapshots to a company to have them processed, and after anywhere from one hour to a few days of processing time, the company would return a stack of colorful glossy photos for our viewing enjoyment.

While I enjoy the convenience and speed of being able to share photos digitally, I must admit that nothing beats the sound practicality of being able to carry around certain photos in my wallet or briefcase, particularly snapshots of my beautiful family. Even when my technology fails me by running out of battery power or succumbing to the perils of being repeatedly dropped on the floor, I can always whip out my sharp, crisp, hardcopy photos of the people I love and show them off to anyone willing to admire them. True, processing them takes a little more time than the instant results that digital photos have to offer, but in the end, the processing time is worth the clear, colorful snapshot that I have in hand.

As you first begin to learn how to take a *720° Snapshot* when approaching organizational decision making, you will utilize a method that I have found to work best for beginners in the first stage of making 720° assessments. It is called the "12-Minute Processing Practice." The use of this method is optimal if you are a leader who is new to this type of decision-making process because it allows you to step away from the pressure of the decision-making moment, isolate yourself, and process all of the information necessary to develop an accurate *720° Snapshot* of the organizational task or situation that you are facing. It takes a little more time to use this method to take a snapshot in the beginning, but in the end, the processing time is worth it because of the clear picture that results.

The 12-Minute Processing Practice is called such for good reason: it should realistically take a leader about 12 minutes to examine the dynamics of the organizational task or situation from every possible angle – from a 720° perspective – before using the information to make a sound decision. Mind you, the assessment process might take you longer than 12 minutes to complete when you first begin to use it. However, do not grow discouraged; the more you engage in the process, the faster and more adept you will become at completing the *720° Snapshot*. Rather than focus on the time that it takes you to take a snapshot using this model, focus on the fact that you are using a tool that is empowering you to factor in every possible consideration as you approach making a decision, and that this decision at which you arrive will yield the best possible results for your organization, allowing you to emerge as a more effective and productive leader. This is what really matters – not the processing time!

As you should recall, there are four triads (Task, Issue, Leader, and Follower), and each of the triads has three sides that pose one assessment question per side. All together, this represents 12 questions asked by the Tetra-triad (a term used to refer to all four triads taken into consideration as one). Ideally, in the 12-Minute Processing Practice, one minute is allotted for answering each of the questions associated with the four triads. This method of taking a *720° Snapshot* includes the use of a supplemental worksheet that will assist you in answering each of the 12 questions, compiling all of the considerations necessary for you to develop a clear snapshot that can guide you towards the best decision.

THE LEADERSHIP TETRA-TRIAD

343

As a leader who is new to taking a *720° Snapshot*, take the following steps.

Step 1:
Enter willingly into the critical decision-making moment.

When you realize that you are being faced with making a critical decision as a leader, do not fight it or try to push the responsibility off onto someone else; instead, embrace it. After all, you are the leader of the organization who must take ultimate responsibility for all decisions and outcomes, and now that you have been trained on how to make an assessment that will lead to making the best decisions possible for your organization, who better than you to take the bull by the horns and attack the challenge?

Step 2:
Evaluate those speaking – and yourself – as you listen to the particulars of the situation and collect data.

Once you realize that you are in the midst of a critical decision-making moment, your role should immediately shift to "data gatherer." Sit back and listen quietly to everything that is being said and any information that is being offered. Pay attention to both the verbal and non-verbal communication that is being shared by those who are offering up the information. As you listen to the informational details, consider the tone of those who are speaking, their background and history as employees or members of the organization, what their issues are, and whether you are aware of any hidden agendas that they might have. If you have any objective reason to believe that the

> *In high-pressure situations, one of the first indicators that you are succumbing to the pressure and stress of the critical decision-making moment is that, without realizing it, you stop breathing.*

information is being skewed by any of these factors, take this into consideration as you gather the data. For example, if you have reason to believe that certain data reported by some individuals is biased, you might want to sift through their issues that you believe are clouding the facts and try to listen between the lines – and between their issues – for the real story. If a particular person is prone to exaggeration, you might want to give less weight to data that is reported as extremes and listen between the lines to hear the real details of an account. Also, if a person is very emotional and prone to make assessments out of emotion rather than the facts, take this into consideration as you collect data by doing your best to filter out what you are hearing in order to get down to the gist of the matter.

While you are collecting data and paying attention to the people in the room, you should simultaneously be paying attention to yourself! Periodically evaluate your tone, your mood, your stress level, whether you are open and accepting or closed and defensive, and even whether or not you are breathing. In high-pressure situations like these, one of the first indicators that you are succumbing to the pressure and stress of the critical decision-making moment is that, without realizing it, you stop breathing. When I am in the midst of such situations, I have a mantra that I silently repeat to myself: "Air is your friend!" I do this to remind myself to breathe, because breathing ensures that I stay relaxed and calm so that I do not miss any vital details in the information that is being communicated to me.

Step 3:
Reflect back the details of the situation as you understand them.

Once those contributing to the conversation have had their say about the details of the situation, it is now time for you to do two things: 1) ask any clarifying questions and 2) explain your understanding of what was said. If you heard some information during the data-collection stage of the critical decision-making moment, now is the time to ask those in the room to clarify it for you. Perhaps they might have access to the information necessary to provide clarification, or perhaps they might need to get clarification from someone who is not currently present. In either case, ensure that you do whatever it takes to get clarification on the necessary details, because without a clear understanding of all of the significant details, you could end up using the wrong information to make an important decision.

Next, explain your understanding of what was said during the data-collection stage. If you took a few notes, feel free to refer to them as a guide to sharing your understanding of the matter. Otherwise, based upon what you remember, explain what you understand the situation, task, or challenge to be, and reflect back to them the details of the situation as you interpret them. When you are finished with your reflection, ask for their affirmation that you have a clear understanding of the challenge at hand. If everyone agrees that you do, it is time for you to excuse yourself and go process the information that you have learned.

Step 4:
Excuse yourself from the meeting to process the data with your 12-Minute Processing Practice worksheet.

While it is true that the 12-Minute Processing Practice might only take 12 minutes. If you need more time than this, feel free to revise the break time; you might even request to resume the meeting the following morning! Once you are in an isolated place in a location where you can focus your attention on making a comprehensive assessment of the matter at hand, take out your 12-Minute Processing Practice worksheet and complete it according to the instructions provided.

MOODY'S 720° 12-MINUTE PROCESSING SNAPSHOT WORKSHEET

Task Awareness | Process time: 3 min.

Organizational Resources: *What do I have to work with to execute my task?*

Tangible:

_____

_____

Intangible:

_____

_____

Human:

_____

_____

How do these results help to shape my decision?

```
┌─────────────────────────────────────────────┐
│                                             │
│                                             │
│                                             │
│                                             │
│                                             │
│                                             │
│                                             │
└─────────────────────────────────────────────┘
```

347

The 720° Snapshot

Appraisal: *Do we have the capacity to execute the task?*

Strengths:

_____

_____

Weaknesses:

_____

_____

Key Factors:

_____

_____

Level of Need:

_____

_____

Conclusion: ☐ Yes   ☐ Somewhat   ☐ No

How do these results help to shape my decision?

```
┌─────────────────────────────────────────────┐
│                                             │
│                                             │
│                                             │
│                                             │
│                                             │
│                                             │
└─────────────────────────────────────────────┘
```

Strategic Choices: *How can I gain an advantage over my competitors in the market or create a new market altogether?*

_____

_____

_____

_____

How do these results help to shape my decision?

Issue Awareness | Process time: 3 min.

Organizational Environment: *Are we internally positioned and prepared as an organization to do what we are seeking to do?*

People:

_____

_____

Design:

_____

_____

Rewards:

_____

_____

Strategy:

_____

_____

Processes:

_____

_____

The 720° Snapshot

Structure:

_____

_____

Conclusion: ☐ Yes   ☐ Somewhat   ☐ No

How do these results help to shape my decision?

_____

External Environment: *What forces or considerations outside of my organization affect my cost and ability to do what I do inside of my organization – and my ability to continue doing it in the future?*

Technology:

_____

_____

Market trends:

_____

_____

Demographics:

_____

_____

Porter's 5 Forces:

_____

_____

How do these results help to shape my decision?

Organizational Culture: *What is the structure and style of this organization's culture, and am I working with it or against it as I implement change?*

❏ Adhocracy (○ I'm working with / ○ I'm working against) OR
❏ Hierarchy (○ I'm working with / ○ I'm working against)

❏ Market   (○ I'm working with / ○ I'm working against) OR
❏ Clan   (○ I'm working with / ○ I'm working against)

How do these results help to shape my decision?

Leader's Self-Awareness | Process time: 3 min.

Personal Influences: *What known or hidden personal values, motivations, or feelings are present within me, and how do they affect* *my perceptions and interactions, skew my interpretation of the facts surrounding critical situations, and influence my decisions, actions, and reactions when dealing with others?*

C.O.R.E.:

_____

_____

S.H.O.E.S.:

_____

_____

P.O.R.K.:

_____

_____

S.T.A.R.C.H.:

_____

_____

How do these results help to shape my decision?

_____

Professional Expertise: *What are my professional capacities and limitations, and how can they be leveraged or compensated for, respectively, in order to increase my leadership effectiveness?*

Skills:

_____

_____

Training:

_____

_____

Experience:

_____

_____

How do these results help to shape my decision?

+---+
| |
| |
| |
| |
| |
| |
+---+

Adaptability: *How far am I willing to go to make shifts in my beliefs and behaviors in order to connect at a deeper level with others for the benefit of the organization?*

Emotional Intelligence:

_____

_____

Cultural Awareness:

_____

_____

Authenticity:

_____

_____

How do these results help to shape my decision?

```
┌─────────────────────────────────────────────┐
│                                             │
│                                             │
│                                             │
│                                             │
│                                             │
│                                             │
└─────────────────────────────────────────────┘
```

Follower Awareness | Process time: 3 min.

Personal Influences: *What known or hidden personal values, motivations, or feelings are present within me, and how do they affect my perceptions and interactions, skew my interpretation of the facts surrounding critical situations, and influence my decisions, actions, and reactions when dealing with others?*

C.O.R.E.:

_____

_____

S.H.O.E.S.:

_____

_____

P.O.R.K.:

_____

_____

S.T.A.R.C.H.:

_____

_____

How do these results help to shape my decision?

```



```

Followership Style: *What level of support does this follower offer to me as a leader, and how does it affect his or her propensity to challenge my directives when asked to execute an organizational task?*

Partner:

_____

_____

Implementer:

_____

_____

Individualist:

_____

_____

Resource:

_____

_____

How do these results help to shape my decision?

[ ]

Leader-Follower Relationship: *How close is the relationship that I share with this follower, and how should I order my interactions, communications, and expectations with him/her based upon this level of closeness?*

❒ Out Group / Stranger Phase:

_____

_____

❒ In Group / Acquaintance phase:

_____

_____

❒ In Group / Mature Partner Phase:

_____

_____

How do these results help to shape my decision?

[ ]

PART B: Using Assessments to Develop a Clear Snapshot of the Task or Situation

Which assessment results are most critical in influencing the development of the *720° Snapshot* from the following areas of awareness? Write the results inside of each corresponding box.

TASK	ISSUES
LEADER	FOLLOWER

PART C: Using the Snapshot to Develop Intermediate Decision Options

Based upon the snapshot that has been created, my top three options for an intermediate decision include:

Decision Option 1:

_____

_____

_____

_____

Decision Option 2:

_____

_____

_____

_____

Decision Option 3:

_____

_____

_____

_____

Step 5:
Examine the *720° Snapshot* before you, and determine three options that represent the best potential courses of action.

As you examine the *720° Snapshot* of the task or situation that was developed as a result of taking into account all of the various considerations that the 12-Minute Processing Practice brought to light, now it is time to make some decisions. Look at the snapshot sitting before you, and ask yourself the following questions:

- What is my primary gut reaction about how to proceed based on this *720° Snapshot* of the situation?
- What are two other alternative courses that I might want to consider based on this *720° Snapshot* of the situation?
- Is there anything about me that might be biasing me to lean towards making one of these potential decisions over another? If so, is my bias in this particular case strong enough to skew my perceptions to the point that one or more of the potential decisions on the table should not be deemed feasible? Note: If so, take the decision off of the table.
- Do I feel any level of discomfort with making either of the three decisions on the table because of the level of potential risk involved, the level of potential compromise involved, or because I have had to "reach too far" in my assessment of the situation in order to make this decision a viable alternative? Note: If so, take the decision off of the table.

Step 6:
Pray.

The Bible says in Psalm 37:23 that "The steps of a good man are ordered by the Lord." Whenever you are faced with making a critical leadership decision, as a spiritual leader, it is important to pray. After you have completed your *720° Snapshot*, arrived at three potential decisions, and questioned any potential biases that might be cause to dismiss either of them, it is now time to pray over those decisions that remain.

There are some critical decisions that are quite serious in nature and that will take significantly more than 12 minutes to process in order to arrive at a decision; these will also require more significant amounts of prayer. However, most of the critical decisions that we are faced with making in our organizations are those that can be made using a careful assessment of all of the dynamics at work in the situation from every potential angle – and neither this nor the prayer that is necessary to undergird it do not necessarily have to take significant amounts of time.

The Bible tells us in Matthew 6:7-8, *"And when you are praying, do not use meaningless repetition as the Gentiles do, for they suppose that they will be heard for their many words. So do not be like them; for your Father knows what you need before you ask Him...."* This tells us that when we are asking for God's guidance in making the right decision about a task or situation, in most cases, we do not have to have an hour-long prayer session! Instead, simply praise God for who He is, acknowledge His omniscience and His sovereignty, ask Him to order your steps as you lead the organization, and petition Him for the wisdom that you need to choose the right decision. All of this can be accomplished in a manner of seconds as you take a few moments to mentally evaluate and pray over each one of the decisions on the table.

Once you have become skilled at running your leadership decisions through the *720° Snapshot*, you might not even have to separate yourself from the group in order to process the snapshot. Instead, right there in the middle of a meeting, you can run through answering each of the 12 questions in the 12-Minute Processing Practice in your head, and in a matter of about 30 seconds, while the meeting is still proceeding, you can conduct a comprehensive assessment of the task or situation and produce a well thought-out decision. After years of using the decision making model, this is about the amount of time it takes for me to make a decision.

My followers marvel at how I can be right in the midst of a meeting, get quiet for a few seconds, and then confidently pronounce my decision about a matter, especially since my decision seems to have taken every possible contributing factor into consideration. It's not that I have any mysterious super powers, that I am an anomalous leadership guru, or that I have such superior intelligence that it places me heads and shoulders above all of the other leaders in the world. It's not even that I have a special relationship with God in which He gives me step-by-step directions on how to proceed in each and every matter throughout the day. No, it's simply that I have consistently practiced using my *720° Leadership Decision-Making Model* for so long that it is now second nature to me to make decisions utilizing it. What's more, the same can happen for you; the more you use it, the shorter the processing time will become, and the easier it will be to use. It will become second nature for you, too, and those within your organization will think that you are a leadership genius!

Step 7:
Announce or publish your "intermediate" decision and invite critiques of it.

Once you have reached an "intermediate" decision, announce it to the necessary parties (your assistant, a small executive staff, a leadership team, or whoever will play a key role in implementing the final decision), whether verbally or in written correspondence. It is best to announce the intermediate decision by saying things like, "I'm really leaning towards moving in this direction, and this is why," or "My first mind is to proceed by doing this..." Notice that I call this decision the "intermediate" decision rather than the "final" decision. This is because once you reveal your decision to your followers, the next step is to invite their critiques of it, and this critique process might call for some adjustments either in the details of the decision or the entire decision itself. Perhaps after they hear your decision, someone will "suddenly remember" to mention a key piece of information that was left out during the initial data gathering session – a significant piece of information that would have been critical to taking an accurate 720° *Snapshot* when making a decision about the task or situation. By the time you announce or publish your intermediate decision, some followers might have also mustered up the courage to reveal to you some vital history or staff dynamics, of which you were not previously aware because your followers kept them hidden. This new information might affect the outcomes that you had anticipated if you go with your current intermediate decision; thus, modifications of the intermediate decision become necessary.

Whatever you do, keep in mind that being faced with making adjustments to your intermediate decision is not a bad thing, and it does not suggest that you are a bad leader! As the leader of the organization, your goal should not be to have everyone simply fall in line like robots and accept your decision by saying, "Yes, sir! Whatever you like, sir!" or "Yes, ma'am! Anything you say ma'am!" Instead, your goal should be to make the best possible decision for the organization, and sometimes this means making an "intermediate" decision based upon the information to which you have access, announcing the decision, and then waiting to see if there are some critical-thinking followers in your organization that will toss it around, critique it, ask you to reconsider some parts of it, and work overall to make it better. Remember: this is about your effectiveness as a leader to make the best decision for the organization, not your ego!

> *Remember:*
> *This is about your*
> *effectiveness as a leader*
> *to make the best decision*
> *for your organization,*
> *not your ego!*

Once you announce your decision, your followers might also ask some really good questions about what will happen if the organization moves forward with your intermediate decision. Do not consider these questions to be challenges to you and your authority as a leader, and do not allow them to threaten you! Instead, embrace the opportunity to explain your rationale or your thought process behind making the decision, and provide a logical forecast of what you expect the outcomes to be if the organization moves ahead with your intermediate decision. After all, in order to make the decision, you already went through a comprehensive assessment of all of the data and dynamics at play surrounding the task or situation – at least, to those dynamics and data to which you had access at the time of assessment – so you can be confident in the decision at which you have arrived. People's questions should only make you verbally re-cap the 12-Minute Processing Practice that you underwent on your worksheet (or in your mind as you become more proficient with the decision-making method) and strengthen your confidence that you made the right intermediate choice! Therefore, invite question after question until all of your critical thinkers are "questioned out"! Then, based upon any new information that has come forward and any new considerations that need to be factored into the decision, make your final decision.

Step 8:
Announce or publish your "final" decision and provide any details or directives necessary for execution.

At last, it is time to reveal your final decision! Again, while I say "at last," this entire process could have taken place in under a few minutes, but for the sake of sequencing, after you have collected the data, performed the assessment, taken a *720° Snapshot*, arrived at an intermediate decision, vetted the decision through the critiques of your followers, and made any revisions necessary to your intermediate decision, it is now time to announce your final decision – at last!

The pronouncement of your final decision should not be a surprise to your followers, because you introduced them to the direction you were leaning towards when you announced your intermediate decision. Also, since some or all of them played a part in vetting your intermediate decision, they probably already have some inkling of what the final decision will look like; typically, it will essentially look like the intermediate decision with a few alternations, if any were necessary. Thus, through this process, your intended course of action surrounding the task or situation will have been gradually introduced to your followers, giving them an opportunity to mentally adjust to the impending final decision and to evaluate how your decision will ultimately affect them and the work that they do.

Announce or publish your decision to all necessary followers in the organization, and follow up your announcement with answers to the questions that people will immediately be asking upon hearing or reading about: "When does this decision take effect?" "Where do I go from here?" "What does this mean for me and my role in the organization?" "Will any extra time, energy, or resources be required from me?" "What does the leader/organization expect from me as a result of this decision?" Being proactive in answering these questions will allay any confusion or concerns that might crop up as a result of your final decision, and it will allow your followers to focus upon preparing to execute the decision rather than focus upon their anxiety surrounding how the decision will impact them and their roles in the organization.

CHAPTER 21

READY TO LAUNCH:

Committing Yourself to Leadership Effectiveness the 720° Decision-Making Model Way

Pairing Implementation with Your Information: Let the Good Leadership Decisions Roll!

Congratulations, leader! You are finally on your way to becoming a more effective and more successful leader, because you have been empowered with a higher level of awareness – something critical to your success as you lead an organization! Much like Madonna, Walmart, and all of the other trailblazers out there who always seem to make just the right kind of choices that help them to get on top and stay there, you have also learned how to engage in strategic decision making by using *Moody's 720° Leadership Decision-Making Model*. In learning the in's and out's of this proven and effective leadership decision-making model, you have increased your proficiency in how to tap into higher levels of awareness, absorb communication from the people, places, and things that surround you, process the body of data you gather, and use the results of your assessment as a platform to make the most excellent strategic choices that can possibly be made for your organization. Your continued use of the *720° Leadership Decision-Making Model* as you lead your organization will undoubtedly make you stand out as a "cream of the crop" leader, because you will become known for having a knack for always knowing what to do and for confidently acting upon your decisions with consistently effective results. In a manner of speaking, whether you realize it or not, your learning the *720° Leadership Decision-Making Model* has positioned you to be come a leadership rock star!

My prayer for you is that you will be able to utilize the years of research, experience, and professional training that have gone into the development of my *720° Leadership Decision-Making Model* to become the best leader that you can possibly be. It is my hope that, as you continue to use this model to guide and direct your decision making as a leader, that you become known for your savvy ability to make the right decisions at the right time, your ability to assess a situation, taking into account hidden dynamics that others fail to consider, and the depth of your wisdom that is evidenced through the successful outcomes of your leadership decisions.

I encourage you to make a commitment to yourself and to your organization to always listen – with both your natural and spiritual ears – to everything going on around you in the organization so that you can always maintain the high levels of awareness of the people, places, and things that are necessary to be an effective *720° Decision-Making Leader*. If you do, you will find that not only do you have access to everything you need to make the best decisions for your organization, but you will operate as a leader who is more in tune with and aware of your organization, your followers, and yourself! Godspeed and blessings on your journey to becoming an effective and successful leader!

REFERENCES

[1] http://www.psychologistanywhereanytime.com/emotional_problems_psychologist/pyschologist_frustration.htm

[2] http://en.wikipedia.org/wiki/Madonna_%28entertainer%29

[3] http://www.businessdictionary.com/definition/task.html

[4] http://www.businessdictionary.com/definition/key-success-factors.html

[5] http://www.businessdictionary.com/definition/strength.html

[6] http://www.businessdictionary.com/definition/weakness.html

[7] The Holy Bible. New King James Version. Numbers 13:17-20.

[8] http://www.businessdictionary.com/definition/competitive-advantage.html

[9] http://www.livescience.com/20727-internet-history.html

[10] Kim, W. C. and Mauborgne, R. (2005). Blue ocean strategy: How to create uncontested market space and make the competition irrelevant. Boston, Mass: Harvard Business School Press.

[11] Kim, W.C. and Mauborgne, R. (2005). Blue ocean strategy: From theory to practice. California Management Review. Vol. 47, No. 3, Spring 2005, p. 106.

[12] http://www.businessdictionary.com/definition/issue.html

[13] http://www.businessdictionary.com/definition/organizational-design.html

[14] Kluyver, C. and Pearce, J. (2009). Strategy: A view from the top. Third edition. Upper Saddle River, New Jersey: Pearson Education, Inc. p. 3.

[15] Galbraith, J. (2002). Designing organizations. An executive guide to strategy, structure, and process. San Francisco, CA: Jossey-Bass Publishers. p. 11.

[16] Grant, R. (2010). Contemporary strategy analysis. Seventh edition. West Sussex, United Kingdom: John Wiley & Sons Ltd. p. 9.

[17] http://www.businessdictionary.com/definition/reward.html

[18] The Holy Bible. New American Standard Bible Version. Ephesians 4:16.

[19] http://www.businessdictionary.com/definition/trend.html

[20] http://www.kng.com/blog/food-and-beverage-news/weather-impacts-restaurant-sales-and-traffic/

[21] http://www.bloomberg.com/bw/articles/2012-11-06/the-oddities-of-election-year-gasoline-prices

[22] http://www.businessdictionary.com/definition/technology.html

[23] Magretta, J. (2012). Understanding Michael Porter: The essential guide to competition and strategy. Boston, MA: Harvard Business Review Press., p. 39.

[24] http://en.wikipedia.org/wiki/Marvel_Comics

25 http://www.businessdictionary.com/definition/organizational-culture.html

26 Cameron, K. & Quinn, R. (2006). Diagnosing and changing organizational culture based on the competing values framework. San Francisco, CA: Jossey-Bass.

27 http://www.businessdictionary.com/definition/leader.html

28 http://www.businessdictionary.com/definition/skill.html

29 http://www.businessdictionary.com/definition/training.html

30 The Holy Bible. Proverbs 27:17

31 http://www.businessdictionary.com/definition/experience.html

32 The Holy Bible. Acts 17:22-23

33 http://www.statisticbrain.com/coffee-drinking-statistics/

34 http://www.slate.com/blogs/moneybox/2014/04/02/breakfast_wars_mcdonald_s_taco_bell_dunkin_donuts_and_fast_food_sellers.html

35 https://www.psychologytoday.com/basics/emotional-intelligence

36 http://www.culturosity.com/articles/whatisculturalawareness.htm

37 http://en.wikipedia.org/wiki/Etiquette_in_Asia

38 http://dictionary.reference.com/browse/empathy?s=t

39 http://en.wikipedia.org/wiki/Authentic_leadership

40 http://www.forbes.com/sites/kevinkruse/2013/05/12/what-is-authentic-leadership/

41 http://www.regent.edu/acad/global/publications/elj/vol6iss1/3elj_vol6iss1_emuwa.pdf

42 The Holy Bible. John 14:9

43 Chaleff, I. (2009). The courageous follower: Standing up to & for our leaders. 2nd ed. San Francisco: Berrett-Koehler Publishers, p. 40.

44 Ibid.

45 http://www.businessdictionary.com/definition/partner.html

46 Ibid.

47 Ibid. p. 41

48 Ibid. p. 41

49 Ibid. p. 42

50 The Holy Bible. Matthew 4:19

51 www.Changingminds.org. Leader Member Exchange (LMX) http://changingminds.org/explanations/theories/leader_member_exchange.htm. Retrieved July 17, 2012.

52 http://www.merriam-webster.com/dictionary/exchange

53 Northouse, P. (2010). Leadership: Theory and practice. Fifth Edition. Sage Publications. Thousand Oaks, CA. Pg. 152

54 http://www.armystudyguide.com/content/Prep_For_Basic_Training/Prep_for_basic_customs_and_courtesies/other-courtesies.shtml

55 http://jobs.aol.com/articles/2012/03/27/worlds-largest-employer-youll-never-guess/

[56] Northouse, P. (2010). Leadership: Theory and practice. Fifth Edition. Sage Publications. Thousand Oaks, CA. Pg. 152

[57] Ibid. p. 153

[58] https://hbr.org/2013/04/does-money-really-affect-motiv

[59] http://www.inc.com/jeff-haden/10-things-extraordinary-bosses-do-for-their-employees.html

[60] http://dictionary.reference.com/browse/objective

[61] http://dictionary.reference.com/browse/subjective

[62] The Holy Bible. Proverbs 11:14 and Proverbs 15:22

[63] Chaleff, I. (2009). The courageous follower: Standing up to & for our leaders. 2nd ed. San Francisco: Berrett-Koehler Publishers, p. 40.

[64] http://www.livestrong.com/article/76043-important-wear-good-walking-shoes/

[65] http://travel.state.gov/content/passports/english/passports/statistics.html

[66] http://livingbilingual.com/2013/05/28/exactly-how-many-people-are-bilingual/

[67] http://www.health.harvard.edu/blog/build-your-core-muscles-for-a-healthier-more-active-future-201212285698

[68] Ibid.

[69] Ibid.

[70] http://www.wisegeek.com/what-are-core-muscles.htm

[71] http://en.wikipedia.org/wiki/Abdomen

[72] The Holy Bible. Leviticus 11:1-47 and Deuteronomy 14:3-20

[73] https://www.psychologytoday.com/blog/perfect-health-diet/201202/is-pork-still-dangerous

[74] http://www.livestrong.com/article/522101-disadvantages-of-pork/

[75] Colbert, D. (2003). Deadly emotions. Understand the mind-body-spirit connection that can heal or destroy you. Nashville: Thomas Nelson Publishers, p. 30.

www.ingramcontent.com/pod-product-compliance
Lightning Source LLC
Chambersburg PA
CBHW061117220326
41599CB00024B/4073